D1192682

THE
ADOREMUS
HYMNAL

THE ADOREMUS HYMNAL

+

A CONGREGATIONAL
MISSAL / HYMNAL
FOR THE CELEBRATION OF
SUNG MASS IN THE ROMAN RITE

Produced by
Adoremus
in cooperation with the
Church Music Association of America

IGNATIUS PRESS   SAN FRANCISCO

CONTENTS

INDICES

PREFACE

It has now been more than thirty years since the promulgation of the Second Vatican Council's liturgical constitution, *Sacrosanctum concilium.* The section on sacred music, *De musica sacra,* was the culmination of over a century of theological reflection on liturgical music.[1] But the important insights and principles these studies produced have never been fully realized in the Church's liturgical music.

What sort of music is appropriate for celebration of the Holy Sacrifice of the Mass? According to the Second Vatican Council, sacred music, as a combination of sacred melody and words, "forms a necessary or integral part *(pars integrans)* of the solemn liturgy" and "is to be considered the more holy in proportion as it is connected to the liturgical action" *(SC* §112). So the first principle of sacred *music* is that it needs a sacred *text.* The Council intended that certain liturgical texts of the Mass — for example, the *Kyrie,* the *Gloria,* the *Sanctus,* and the *Agnus Dei* — were to be sung by the congregation. The active participation of the people in singing this essentially liturgical music was to be the norm for Catholic worship .

To assure that authentic liturgical music would be an integral part of the Mass, *Sacrosanctum concilium* emphasized that Gregorian chant is "specifically suited to the Roman liturgy", and "should be given pride of place in liturgical services" *(SC* §116). Sadly, this counsel has been honored only in the breach. Very recently recordings of this ancient Catholic music have become phenomenally popular in the secular world; but *few* Catholics have heard Gregorian chant in a Catholic Church. The loss of this historic Catholic music is more than a cultural deprivation; it is a diminishment of a sublime form of prayer.

Another form of sacred music is hymnody. The texts of hymns are sacred, but are not, strictly speaking, liturgical. Although they are not a substitute for the sung parts integral to the Mass, the Second Vatican Council encouraged the singing of hymns — the *cantus popularis religiosus* ("religious singing of the people" [*SC* §118]). However, in an authentic "sung Mass" *(Missa Cantata),* priority is given to the liturgical texts intended to be sung.

According to the 1967 Vatican Instruction *Musicam sacram* congregational singing of the acclamations and responses of the Order of Mass is the ideal minimum for celebration of Mass. *The Adoremus Hymnal's* musical settings for these parts of the Mass use the official liturgical texts approved by the Church. The

---

[1] This began in the 1830s with the work of Dom Guéranger, and continued with the formation of the Caecilian movement—most especially with the twentieth-century papal pronouncements on sacred music (Pius X's motu proprio *Tra le sollecitudini* [1903], Pius XI's apostolic constitution *Divini cultus sanctitatem* [1928], and Pius XII's encyclical *Musicae sacrae disciplina* [1955]).

Council fathers also envisioned that the vernacular languages would be used in Catholic worship to increase people's understanding of the sacred action; but they did not intend that the ancient language of the Church should vanish utterly from ordinary celebrations of Mass.

The Adoremus Hymnal consists of three major sections: (1) the Order of Mass, (2) musical settings for the Ordinaries, and (3) hymns. It begins with the text of the Mass in both Latin and English, incorporating the liturgical music integral to the Mass, the acclamations and responses.

The second section contains the musical settings for the Ordinaries for Mass. In addition to a sacred text, the music itself must possess three qualities: *holiness* (not simply popular music with a sacred text) and *artistry* (*Musicam sacram* §4a), and *universality* (*Tra le sollecitudini* §8). *Sacrosanctum concilium* stated that Gregorian chant is "proper to the Roman Rite" and urged that "steps should be taken so that the faithful may also be able to say or sing together in Latin those parts of the Ordinary of the Mass which pertain to them" (SC §54). Thus *The Adoremus Hymnal* includes several Gregorian chant settings of the liturgical texts of the Mass in Latin, as well as musical settings for the Mass in English.

The hymn section consists of a carefully made selection of the best of English and Latin hymnody ever composed, appropriate for every liturgical season. The hymns were selected by the Editorial Committee in cooperation with the Adoremus Executive Committee and with the consultation of many parish priests, Church musicians, and religious and lay Catholics. The hymns were chosen on the basis of holiness, beauty, Catholic tradition, theological orthodoxy, and, insofar as possible, familiarity and simplicity.

Many traditional Latin hymns are given in both Latin and English versions — chants such as the *Ave Maria,* and *Veni, veni, Emmanuel (O come, O come, Emmanuel)* set to ancient tunes, and others, such as *Concordi Laetitia,* in which the English translation, *Sounds of joy have put to flight,* has been set to a recent metrical version of the melody. There are also classic non-chant Latin hymns such as the *O Sanctissima,* and ancient Latin hymns, such as *Salve festa dies (Hail Thee Festival Day)* which were re-discovered, translated into English or set to music in the nineteenth and twentieth centuries.

The English-language hymns in the *Adoremus Hymnal* come from a variety of traditional sources. They include translated German hymns, such as *Now thank we all our God (Nun danket alle Gott),* and beloved English Catholic hymns *(Faith of our Fathers, Crown him with many crowns).* Also included are some English Catholic hymns little known in America, such as Cardinal Newman's *Help Lord the souls which thou hast made,* and other hymns more recently composed.

Adoremus has not tampered with the original English lyrics in this treasury of hymns. All the hymns appear exactly as in the traditional English texts. Standard English has been retained throughout. Words such as "thee", "thine", "hast", etc., are also unchanged, as are words like "righteousness", "beseech", and "blessed", which belong to the traditional Christian sacral vocabulary.

8

From its inception, Adoremus has been dedicated to authentic implementation of the liturgical reforms initiated by the Second Vatican Council. *The Adoremus Hymnal* is intended to contribute to this effort by providing an essential treasury of liturgical texts, chant and hymns drawn from the historic patrimony of the Church for ordinary parish celebrations of the Mass — *Ad Majorem Dei Gloriam.*

Christus vincit, Christus regnat, Christus imperat!
Adoremus — Society for the Renewal of the Sacred Liturgy
Feast of the Assumption of the Blessed Virgin Mary,
August 15, 1997

Hymnal Editorial Committee
Kurt Poterack, chairman
Calvert Shenk
Susan Treacy

Adoremus Executive Committee
Father Joseph Fessio, S.J.
Helen Hull Hitchcock
Father Jerry Pokorsky

Grateful acknowledgment for their contribution to the production of *The Adoremus Hymnal* is extended to Monsignor Richard Schuler, Father Robert Skeris and members of the Church Music Association of America who were consultants for the selection of hymns; to Theodore Marier, Kurt Poterack and Calvert Shenk for their Mass settings; to Richard Hough of Adoremus; to the editorial staff of Ignatius Press; and to the many Catholics in the United States and abroad who have inspired, supported and encouraged this project, and sustained this undertaking with their prayers.

ORDER OF MASS

ORDO MISSAE CUM POPULO
RITUS INITIALES

INTROITUS

Populo congregato, sacerdos cum ministris ad altare accedit, dum cantus ad introitum peragitur.

Cum ad altare pervenerit, facta cum ministris debita reverentia, osculo altare veneratur et, pro opportunitate, illud incensat. Postea cum ministris sedem petit.

SALUTATIO

Cantu ad introitum absoluto, sacerdos et fideles, stantes, signant se, dum sacerdos, ad populum conversus, dicit:

In nómine Patris, et Fí-li - i,   et Spí- ri- tus Sanc-ti.

Populus respondet:

Amen.

Deinde sacerdos, manus extendens, populum salutat, dicens:*

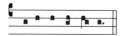   

(Episcopus)

Dómi-nus vo-bís-cum.   *Pax vo-bis.*

Populus respondet:

Et cum spí- ri-tu tu-o.

---

*Vel:

V. *Grátia Dómini nostri Iesu Christi, et cáritas Dei, et communicátio Sancti Spíritus sit cum ómnibus vobis.* **R. Et cum spíritu tuo**

*Vel:

V. *Grátia vobis et pax a Deo Pater nostro et Dómino Iesu Christo.*

R. Benedíctus Deus et Pater Dómini nostri Iesu Christi. (Vel: **Et cum spíritu tuo.**)

ORDER OF MASS WITH A CONGREGATION
INTRODUCTORY RITES

ENTRANCE SONG

After the people have assembled, the priest and the ministers go to the altar while the entrance song is being sung.

When the priest comes to the altar, he makes the customary reverence with the ministers, kisses the altar, and (if incense is used) incenses it. Then, with the ministers, he goes to the chair.

GREETING

After the entrance song, the priest and the faithful remain standing and make the sign of the cross, as the priest says:

In the name of the Fa-ther, and of the Son,   and of the Ho-ly Spir - it.

The people answer:

Amen.

Then the priest, facing the people, extends his hands and greets all present with ...*

The Lord be with you.

(Bishop)

Peace be with you.

The people answer:

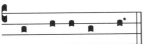

And al-so with you.

---

*or:
V. *The grace of our Lord Jesus Christ and the love of God and the fellowship of the Holy Spirit be with you all*. **R. And also with you.**

*or
V. *The grace and peace of God our Father and the Lord Jesus Christ be with you.*
R. Blessed be God, the Father of our Lord Jesus Christ. (or: **And also with you.**)

Sacerdos, vel diaconus vel alius minister idoneus, potest brevissimis verbis introducere fideles in Missam illius diei.

ACTUS PÆNITENTIALIS

Deinde sequitur actus pænitentialis. Sacerdos fideles invitat ad pænitentiam:

Fra-tres, agnoscámus peccáta nostra, ut ap-ti simus ad sacra mystéri-a celebránda.

(Pausa)*

A.   Confíteor Deo omnipoténti et vobis, fratres, quia peccávi nimis cogitatióne, verbo, ópere et omissióne:
et, percutientes sibi pectus, dicunt:
mea culpa, mea culpa, mea máxima culpa.
Deinde prosequuntur:
Ideo precor beátam Maríam semper Vírginem, omnes Angelos et Sanctos, et vos, fratres, oráre pro me ad Dóminum Deum nostrum.

---

* Loco formulae actus pænitentialis quae supra, no. 4, indicatur, adhiberi potest una ex sequentibus:

Postea sacerdos dicit:

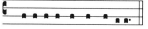

Mi-se-ré-re nostri, Dómine.

Populus respondet:

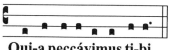

Qui-a peccávimus ti-bi.

Sacerdos:

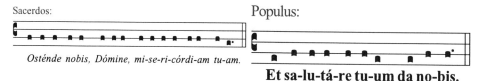

Osténde nobis, Dómine, mi-se-ri-córdi-am tu-am.

Populus:

Et sa-lu-tá-re tu-um da no-bis.

B. Deinde sacerdos, vel alius minister idoneus, sequentes, vel alias, invocationes cum "Kýrie, eléison" profert:

Qui missus es sanáre contrítos corde: Kýrie, eléison. Populus respondet: **Kýrie, eléison.**
Sacerdos: Qui peccatóres vocáre venísti:Christe, eléison.   Populus: **Christe, eléison.**
Sacerdos: Qui ad déxteram Patris sedes, ad interpellándum   Populus: **Kýrie, eléison.**
pro nobis: Kýrie, eléison.

14

The priest, or deacon, or other suitable minister may very briefly introduce the Mass of the day. [If the Mass is preceded by some part of the liturgy of the hours, the penitential rite is omitted, and the *Kyrie* may be omitted. (See General Instruction of the Liturgy of the Hours, nos. 94-96.)]

PENITENTIAL RITE

After the introduction to the day's Mass, the priest invites the people to recall their sins and to repent of them in silence:

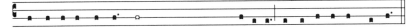

My brothers and sis-ters, to prepare ourselves
to celebrate the sacred mysteries, let us call to mind our sins.

A pause for silent reflection follows. After the silence, one of the following three forms is chosen.*

*A.   I confess to almighty God,
and to you, my brothers and sisters,
that I have sinned through my own fault

(They strike their breast)

in my thoughts and in my words,
in what I have done,
and in what I have failed to do;
and I ask blessed Mary, ever virgin,
all the angels and saints,
and you, my brothers and sisters,
to pray for me to the Lord our God.

*B.

After a brief silence, the priest says:

The people answer:

Lord, we have sinned a- gainst you; Lord, have mer-cy.

Lord, have mer-cy.

Priest:

The people answer:

Lord, show us your mer-cy   and love.

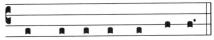

And grant us your sal - va-tion.

*C. The priest (or other suitable minister) makes the following or other invocations, with "Lord, have mercy."

Priest: *You were sent to heal the contrite: Lord have mercy.* People: **Lord, have mercy.**
Priest: *You came to call sinners:Christ, have mercy.* People: **Christ, have mercy.**
Priest: *You plead for us at the the right hand of the Father: Lord have mercy.* People: **Lord, have mercy.**

Sequitur absolutio sacerdotis:

Mi-se-re-á-tur nostri om-ni-po-tens De-us   et, di-mís-sis pec-cá-tis nostris, perdúcat

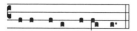

nos ad vi-tam æ-tér-nam.

Populus respondet:

Amen.

KYRIE ELEISON

(For musical settings of the Kyrie see # 200, 205, 210, 214, 218, 221.)

Sequuntur invocationes Kýrie, eléison, nisi iam praecesserint in aliqua formula actus paenitentialis.

V. Kýrie, eléison.   **R. Kýrie, eléison.**
V. Christe, eléison.   **R. Christe, eléison.**
V. Kýrie, eléison.   **R. Kýrie, eléison.**

GLORIA

(For musical settings of the Gloria see # 201, 206, 211, 215.)

Deinde, quando præscribitur, cantatur vel dicitur hymnus:

Glória in excélsis Deo
et in terra pax homínibus bonæ voluntátis.
Laudámus te,
benedícimus te,
adorámus te,
glorificámus te,
grátias ágimus tibi propter magnam glóriam tuam,
Dómine Deus, Rex cæléstis,

16

The priest says the absolution :

May al-might-y God have mer-cy on us, forgive us our sins, and bring us to

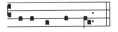

ev-er-last-ing life.

The people answer:

Amen.

KYRIE

(For musical settings of the Kyrie see # 250, 255, 260, 265, 269.)

The invocations, Lord, have mercy, or Kyrie eleison, follow, unless they have already been used in one of the forms of the act of penance.

V. Lord, have mercy.   **R. Lord, have mercy.**
V. Christ, have mercy.   **R. Christ, have mercy.**
V. Lord, have mercy.   **R. Lord, have mercy.**

GLORIA

(For musical settings of the Gloria see # 251, 256, 261, 266, 270.)

Then (when it is prescribed) this hymn is said or sung:

**Glory to God in the highest,
    and peace to his people on earth.**

**Lord God, heavenly King,
almighty God and Father,
    we worship you, we give you thanks,
    we praise you for your glory.**

**Lord Jesus Christ, only Son of the Father,
Lord God, Lamb of God,**

Deus Pater omnípotens.
Dómine Fili unigénite, Iesu Christe,
Dómine Deus, Agnus Dei, Fílius Patris,
qui tollis peccáta mundi, miserére nobis;
qui tollis peccáta mundi, súscipe deprecatiónem nostram.
Qui sedes ad déxteram Patris, miserére nobis.
Quóniam tu solus Sanctus,
tu solus Dóminus,
tu solus Altíssimus,
Iesu Christe, cum Sancto Spíritu: in glória Dei Patris.
Amen.

COLLECTA

Quo hymno finito, sacerdos, manibus iunctis, dicit:

O-ré-mus.

Et omnes una cum sacerdote per aliquod temporis spatium in silentio orant.
Tunc sacerdos, manibus extensis, dicit orationem; qua finita,

... per óm-ni - a sǽcu-la sæcu-ló-rum.

Populus acclamat:

Amen.

you take away the sin of the world:
    have mercy on us;
you are seated at the right hand of the Father:
    receive our prayer.

For you alone are the Holy One,
you alone are the Lord,
you alone are the Most High,
    Jesus Christ,
    with the Holy Spirit,
    in the glory of God the Father.
    Amen.

OPENING PRAYER

Afterwards the priest, with hands joined, sings or says:

Let us pray.

Priest and people pray silently for a while. Then the priest extends his hands and sings or says the opening prayer. At the end:

...for ev-er and ev-er.

The people respond:

Amen.

19

LITURGIA VERBI

PRIMA LECTIO

Deinde lector ad ambonem pergit, et legit primam lectionem, quam omnes sedentes auscultant. Ad finem lectionis significandam, lector subdit:

Verbum Dómi-ni.

Omnes acclamant:

De - o grá-ti- as.

PSALMUS RESPONSORIUS

Psalmista, seu cantor, psalmum dicit, populo responsum proferente.

SECUNDA LECTIO

Postea, si habenda sit secunda lectio, lector eam in ambone legit, ut supra. Ad finem lectionis significandam, lector subdit:

Verbum Dómi-ni.

Omnes acclamant:

De- o grá-ti-as.

EVANGELIUM

Sequitur Allelúia (cum verso), vel alter cantus.*

Al-le-lú-ia, al-le-lú-ia,   al-le-lu-ia.

---

*Tempore quo alleluia non est dicendum.

La-us tíbi,   Chrí-ste,   Rex æ-tér-næ gló-ri-æ!
La-us et hónor tí-bi,   Dó - mi -   ne   Ié-   su!
Gló-ri - a et laus tí-bi,   Chrí - ste!
Gló-ri - a tíbi, Chrí-ste,   Vér -   bó De -   i!

20

LITURGY OF THE WORD

FIRST READING

The reader goes to the lectern for the first reading. All sit and listen. To indicate the end, the reader adds:

The Word of the Lord.

All respond:

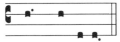

Thanks be to God.

RESPONSORIAL PSALM

The cantor sings or recites the psalm, and the people respond.

SECOND READING

When there is a second reading, it is read at the lectern as before. To indicate the end, the reader adds:

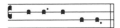

The Word of the Lord.

All respond:

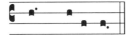

Thanks be to God.

GOSPEL

The alleluia or other chant follows.*

Al-le-lu-ia, al-le-lu-ia, al-le-lu-ia.

---

*Lenten acclamation: Any of the following lines may be used.

Praise to you, Lord Jesus Christ, king of endless glory!

Praise and honor to you, Lord Jesus Christ!

Glory and praise to you, Lord Jesus Christ!

Glory to you, Word of God, Lord Jesus Christ!

21

Si vero non adest diaconus,* sacerdos ante altare inclinatus secreto dicit: *Munda cor meum ac lábia mea, omnípotens Deus, ut sanctum Evangélium tuum digne váleam nuntiáre.*

Postea diaconus, vel sacerdos, ad ambonem pergit, ministris pro opportunitate cum incenso et cereis eum comitantibus, et dicit:

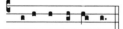

Dómi-nus vo-bís-cum.

Populus respondet:

Et cum spí-ri- tu tu-o.

Diaconus, vel sacerdos: (et interim signat librum et seipsum in fronte, ore et pectore.)

Léc-ti- o sancti Evangé- li -i   se-cúndum N.

Populus acclamat:

Gló-ri - a ti-bi, Dómi-ne.

Deinde diaconus, vel sacerdos, librum, si incensum adhibetur, thurificat, et Evangelium proclamat. Finito Evangelio, diaconus, vel sacerdos dicit:

Ver-bum Dómi- ni.

Omnibus acclamantibus:

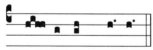

Laus ti- bi, Chri-ste.

Deinde librum•osculatur dicens secreto: *Per evangélica dicta deleántur nostra delicta.*

---

* Interim sacerdos incensum, si adhibetur, imponit. Postea diaconus, Evangelium prolaturus, ante sacerdotem inclinatus, benedictionem petit, submissa voce dicens: *Iube, domne, benedícere.* Sacerdos submissa voce dicit: *Dóminus sit in corde tuo et in lábiis tuis: ut digne competénter annúnties Evangélium suum: in nómine Patris, et Filii,✠ et Spíritus Sancti.* Diaconus respondet: *Amen.*

If there is no deacon,* the priest bows before the altar and says inaudibly: *Almighty God, cleanse my heart and my lips that I may worthily proclaim your gospel*

Then the deacon (or the priest) goes to the lectern. He may be accompanied by ministers with incense and candles. He sings or says:

The Lord be with you.

The people answer:

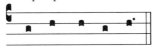

And al - so with you.

The deacon (or priest) sings or says: (He makes the sign of the cross on the book, and then on his forehead, lips, and breast.)

A read-ing from the ho-ly gos-pel   ac - cord-ing to N.

The people respond:

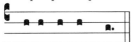

Glo-ry to you, Lord.

Then, if incense is used, the deacon (or priest) incenses the book, and proclaims the gospel. At the end of the gospel, the deacon (or priest) adds:

The gos - pel of the Lord.

All respond:

Praise to you, Lord Jesus Christ.

Then he kisses the book, saying inaudibly: *May the words of the gospel wipe away our sins.*

---

*Meanwhile, if incense is used, the priest puts some in the censer. Then the deacon who is to proclaim the gospel bows to the priest and in a low voice asks his blessing: *Father, give me your blessing.* The priest says in a low voice: *The Lord be in your heart and on your lips that you may worthily proclaim his gospel. In the name of the Father, and of the Son,✠ and of the Holy Spirit.* The deacon answers: *Amen.*

HOMILIA

Deinde fit homilia, quæ habenda est omnibus diebus dominicis et festis de præcepto; aliis diebus commendatur.

CREDO

(For musical settings of the Credo see # 202, 207.)

Homilia expleta, fit, quando præscribitur, professio fidei:

Credo in unum Deum,
Patrem omnipoténtem,
factórem cæli et terræ,
visibílium ómnium et invisibílium.
Et in unum Dóminum Iesum Christum,
Fílium Dei unigénitum,
et ex Patre natum, ante ómnia sæcula.
Deum de Deo, lumen de lúmine,
Deum verum de Deo vero,
génitum, non factum, consubstantiálem Patri:
per quem ómnia facta sunt.
Qui propter nos hómines et propter nostram salútem
descéndit de caelis.

Ad verba quæ sequuntur, usque ad factus est, omnes se inclinant.

Et incarnátus est de Spíritu Sancto
ex María Virgine, et homo factus est.
Crucifíxus étiam pro nobis sub Póntio Piláto;
passus et sepúltus est,
et resurréxit tértia die, secúndum Scriptúras,
et ascéndit in cælum, sedet ad déxteram Patris.
Et íterum ventúrus est cum glória,
iudicáre vivos et mórtuos,
cuius regni non erit finis.
Et in Spíritum Sanctum, Dóminum et vivificántem:
qui ex Patre Filióque procédit.
Qui cum Patre et Filio simul adorátur et conglorificátur:
qui locútus est per prophétas.
Et unam, sanctam, cathólicam et apostólicam Ecclésiam.

24

HOMILY

A homily shall be given on all Sundays and holy days of obligation; it is recommended for other days.

PROFESSION OF FAITH

(For musical settings of the Credo see # 252, 257, 262)

After the homily, the profession of faith is said on Sundays and solemnities. It may also be said in solemn local celebrations.

We believe in one God,
the Father, the Almighty,
maker of heaven and earth,
of all that is seen and unseen.

We believe in one Lord, Jesus Christ,
the only Son of God,
eternally begotten of the Father,
God from God, Light from Light,
true God from true God,
begotten, not made, one in Being with the Father.
Through him all things were made.
For us men and for our salvation
he came down from heaven:

All bow during these two lines:

by the power of the Holy Spirit
he was born of the Virgin Mary, and became man.

For our sake he was crucified under Pontius Pilate;
he suffered, died, and was buried.
On the third day he rose again
in fulfillment of the Scriptures;
he ascended into heaven
and is seated at the right hand of the Father.
He will come again in glory to judge the living and the dead,
and his kingdom will have no end.

We believe in the Holy Spirit, the Lord, the giver of life,
who proceeds from the Father and the Son.
With the Father and the Son he is worshipped and glorified.
He has spoken through the Prophets.
We believe in one holy catholic and apostolic Church.

25

**Confíteor unum baptísma in remissiónem peccatórum.
Et exspécto resurrectiónem mortuórum,
et vitam ventúri sǽculi. Amen.**

ORATIO UNIVERSALIS

Deinde fit oratio universalis, seu oratio fidelium.

Petitiones orationis universalis a diacono (vel cantore) dicuntur,

A.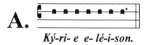

Ký-ri- e e- lé-i-son.

quibus respondeant:

Ký-ri-e,   elé-i-son.

Diaconus vel cantor:

B.

...exaudí-re digné-ris.

quibus respondeant:

Te rogámus aúdi nos.

**We acknowledge one baptism for the forgiveness of sins.
We look for the resurrection of the dead,
and the life of the world to come. Amen.**

GENERAL INTERCESSIONS

Then follow the general intercessions (prayer of the faithful). The priest presides at the prayer.
With a brief introduction, he invites the people to pray; after the intentions he says the concluding
prayer. It is desirable that the intentions be announced by the deacon, cantor, or other person.
(See General Instruction. no. 47.)

Deacon or cantor:

A.

Let us pray to the Lord.

they respond:

Lord have mer-cy.

Deacon or cantor:

B.

Let us pray to the Lord.

they respond:

Lord hear our prayer.

LITURGIA EUCHARISTICA

PRÆPARATIO DONORUM

Cantus offertorium

His absolutis, incipit cantus ad offertorium. Interim ministri corporale, purificatorium, calicem et missale in altari collocant.

Expedit ut fideles participationem suam oblatione manifestent, afferendo sive panem et vinum ad Eucharistiæ celebrationem, sive alia dona, quibus necessitatibus Ecclesiæ et pauperum subveniatur.

Sacerdos, stans ad altare, accipit patenam cum pane, eamque aliquantulum elevatam super altare tenet, secreto dicens:

Benedíctus es, Dómine, Deus univérsi,
quia de tua largitáte accépimus panem,
quem tibi offérimus,
fructum terrae et óperis mánuum hóminum:
ex quo nobis fiet panis vitæ.

Deinde deponit patenam cum pane super corporale.
Si vero cantus ad offertorium non peragitur,
sacerdoti licet hæc verba elata voce proferre; in fine populus acclamare potest:

Benedíctus Deus in sǽcula.

Diaconus, vel sacerdos, infundit vinum et parum aquæ in calicem, dicens secreto:

Per huius aquæ et vini mystérium
eius efficiámur divinitátis consórtes,
qui humanitátis nostræ fieri dignátus est párticeps.

Postea sacerdos accipit calicem, eumque aliquantulum elevatum super altare tenet, secreto dicens:

Benedíctus es, Dómine, Deus univérsi,
quia de tua largitáte accépimus vinum,
quod tibi offérimus,
fructum vitis et óperis mánuum hóminum,
ex quo nobis fiet potus spiritális.

LITURGY OF THE EUCHARIST

PREPARATION OF THE ALTAR AND THE GIFTS

Offertory Chant *(An Offertory Hymn may be sung instead.)*
After the liturgy of the word, the offertory song is begun. Meanwhile the ministers place the corporal, the purificator, the chalice, and the missal on the altar.

Sufficient hosts (and wine) for the communion of the faithful are to be prepared. It is most important that the faithful should receive the body of the Lord in hosts consecrated at the same Mass and should share the cup when it is permitted. Communion is thus a clearer sign of sharing in the sacrifice which is actually taking place.

It is desirable that the participation of the faithful be expressed by members of the congregation bringing up the bread and wine for the celebration of the eucharist or other gifts for the needs of the Church and the poor.

The priest, standing at the altar, takes the paten with the bread and, holding it slightly raised above the altar, says inaudibly:

Blessed are you, Lord, God of all creation.
Through your goodness we have this bread to offer,
which earth has given and human hands have made.
It will become for us the bread of life.

Then he places the paten with the bread on the corporal. If no offertory song is sung, the priest may say the preceding words in an audible voice; then the people may respond:

Blessed be God for ever.

The deacon (or the priest) pours wine and a little water into the chalice, saying inaudibly:

By the mystery of this water and wine
may we come to share in the divinity of Christ,
who humbled himself to share in our humanity.

Then the priest takes the chalice and, holding it slightly raised above the altar, says inaudibly:

Blessed are you, Lord, God of all creation.
Through your goodness we have this wine to offer,
fruit of the vine and work of human hands.
It will become our spiritual drink.

29

Deinde calicem super corporale deponit. Si vero cantus ad offertorium non peragitur, sacerdoti licet hæc verba elata voce proferre; in fine populus acclamare potest:

Benedíctus Deus in sǽcula.

Postea sacerdos, inclinatus, dicit secreto:

In spíritu humilitátis et in ánimo contríto
suscipiámur a te, Dómine;
et sic fiat sacrifícium nostrum in conspéctu tuo hódie,
ut pláceat tibi, Dómine Deus.

Et, pro opportunitate, incensat oblata et altare. Postea vero diaconus vel minister incensat sacerdotem et populum.

Deinde sacerdos, stans ad latus altaris, lavat manus, dicens secreto:

Lava me, Dómine, ab iniquitáte mea, et a peccáto meo munda me.

Stans postea in medio altaris, versus ad populum, extendens et iungens manus, dicit:

Oráte, fratres:
ut meum ac vestrum sacrifícium
acceptábile fiat apud Deum Patrem omnipoténtem.

Populus respondet:

Suscípiat Dóminus sacrifícium de mánibus tuis ad laudem et glóriam nóminis sui, ad utilitátem quoque nostram totiúsque Ecclésiæ suæ sanctæ.

ORATIO SUPER OBLATA

Deinde, manibus extensis, sacerdos dicit orationem super oblata; qua finita, populus acclamat:

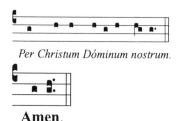

Per Christum Dóminum nostrum.

Amen.

Then he places the chalice on the corporal. If no offertory song is sung, the priest may say the preceding words in an audible voice; then the people may respond:

Blessed be God for ever.

The priest bows and says inaudibly:

Lord God, we ask you to receive us
and be pleased with the sacrifice we offer you
with humble and contrite hearts.

He may now incense the offerings and the altar. Afterwards the deacon or a minister incenses the priest and the people.

Next the priest stands at the side of the altar and washes his hands, saying inaudibly:

Lord, wash away my iniquity; cleanse me from my sin.

Standing at the center of the altar, facing the people, he extends and then joins his hands, saying:

Pray, brethren, that our sacrifice
may be acceptable to God, the almighty Father.

The people respond:

May the Lord accept the sacrifice at your hands
for the praise and glory of his name,
for our good, and the good of all his Church.

PRAYER OVER THE GIFTS

With hands extended, the priest sings or says the prayer over the gifts at the end of which the people respond:

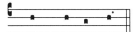

Through Christ our Lord.

Amen.

PREX EUCHARISTICA

Tunc sacerdos incipit Precem eucharisticam. Manus extendens, dicit:

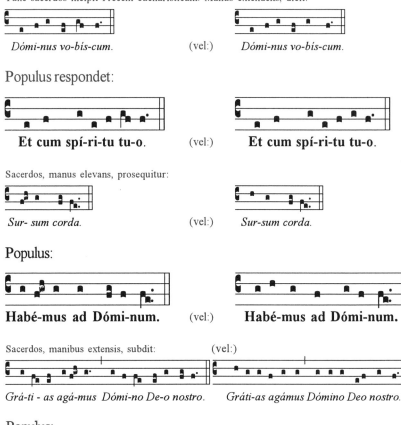

Dómi-nus vo-bís-cum.   (vel:)   *Dómi-nus vo-bís-cum.*

Populus respondet:

Et cum spí-ri-tu tu-o.   (vel:)   **Et cum spí-ri-tu tu-o.**

Sacerdos, manus elevans, prosequitur:

Sur- sum corda.   (vel:)   *Sur-sum corda.*

Populus:

Habé-mus ad Dómi-num.   (vel:)   **Habé-mus ad Dómi-num.**

Sacerdos, manibus extensis, subdit: (vel:)

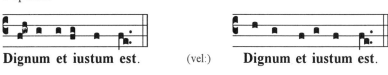

Grá-ti - as agá-mus Dómi-no De-o nostro.   *Gráti-as agámus Dómino Deo nostro.*

Populus:

Dignum et iustum est.   (vel:)   **Dignum et iustum est.**

PRÆFATIO

Sacerdos prosequitur præfationem manibus extensis.

EUCHARISTIC PRAYER

The priest begins the eucharistic prayer. With hands extended he sings or says:

The Lord be with you.

The people answer:

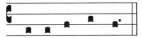

And al-so with you.

He lifts up his hands and continues:

Lift up your hearts.

The people:

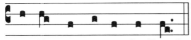

We lift them up to the Lord.

With hands extended, he continues:

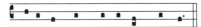

Let us give thanks to the Lord our God.

The people:

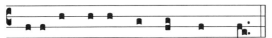

It is right to give him thanks and praise.

PREFACE

The priest continues the preface with hands extended.

33

In fine autem præfationis iungit manus et, una cum populo, ipsam præfationem concludit, cantans vel clara voce dicens:

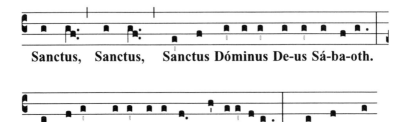

Sanctus, Sanctus, Sanctus Dóminus De-us Sá-ba-oth.

Ple - ni sunt cæli et terra gló-ri-a tu-a.   Ho-sán - na

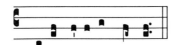

in ex-cél-sis. Be-ne-díc-tus qui venit in nómine Dómi-ni.

Hosánna in ex-cél-sis.

(For musical settings see # 203, 208, 212, 216, 219, 222.)

In omnibus Missis licet sacerdoti celebranti illas partes Precis eucharisticæ cantare, quæ in Missis concelebratis cantari possunt.

In Prece eucharistica prima, seu Canone Romano, ea quæ inter parentheses includuntur omitti possunt.

ACCLAMATION

At the end of the preface, he joins his hands and, together with the people, concludes it by singing or saying aloud:

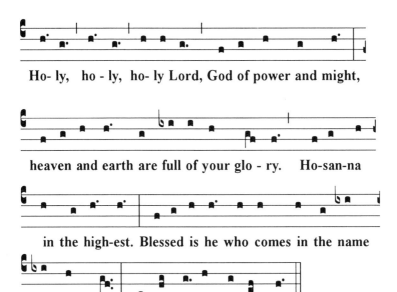

Ho- ly,   ho - ly,   ho- ly Lord, God of power and might,

heaven and earth are full of your glo - ry.   Ho-san-na

in the high-est. Blessed is he who comes in the name

of the Lord. Ho-san-na in the high- est.

(For musical settings of the Sanctus see # 253, 258, 263, 267, 271)

In all Masses the priest may say the eucharistic prayer in an audible voice. In sung Masses he may sing those parts of the eucharistic prayer which may be sung in a concelebrated Mass.

In the first eucharistic prayer (the Roman Canon) the words in brackets may be omitted.

PREX EUCHARISTICA I
SEU CANON ROMANUS

Sacerdos, manibus extensis, dicit:

Te ígitur, clementíssime Pater,
per Iesum Christum, Fílium tuum, Dóminum nostrum,
súpplices rogámus ac pétimus,

iungit manus et dicit:

uti accépta hábeas

signat semel super panem et calicem simul, dicens:

et benedícas ✠ hæc dona, hæc múnera,
hæc sancta sacrifícia illibáta,

extensis manibus prosequitur:

in primis, quæ tibi offérimus
pro Ecclésia tua sancta cathólica:
quam pacificáre, custodíre, adunáre
et régere dignéris toto orbe terrárum:
una cum fámulo tuo Papa nostro N.
et Antístite nostro N.*
et ómnibus orthodóxis atque cathólicæ
et apostólicæ fidei cultóribus.

Commemoratio pro vivis.

Meménto, Dómine, famulórum famularúmque
tuárum N. et N.

Iungit manus et orat aliquantulum pro quibus orare intendit.

Deinde, manibus extensis, prosequitur:

et ómnium circumstántium.
quorum tibi fides cógnita est et nota devótio,
pro quibus tibi offérimus:
vel qui tibi ófferunt hoc sacrificium laudis,
pro se suísque ómnibus:

---

* Hic fieri potest mentio de Episcopis Coadiutoribus vel Auxiliariis, ut in *Institutione generali Missalis Romani (1975)*, n. 109, (2000), n. 149, notatur.

EUCHARISTIC PRAYER I
ROMAN CANON

The priest, with hands extended, says:

We come to you, Father,
with praise and thanksgiving,
through Jesus Christ your Son.

He joins his hands and,
making the sign of the cross
once over both bread and chalice, says:

Through him we ask you to accept and bless ✠
these gifts we offer you in sacrifice.

With hands extended, he continues:

We offer them for your holy catholic Church,
watch over it, Lord, and guide it;
grant it peace and unity throughout the world.
We offer them for N. our Pope,
for N. our bishop,*
and for all who hold and teach the catholic faith
that comes to us from the apostles.

Commemoration of the living.

Remember, Lord, your people,
especially those for whom we now pray, N. and N.

He prays for them briefly with hands joined.

Then, with hands extended, he continues:

Remember all of us gathered here before you.
You know how firmly we believe in you
and dedicate ourselves to you.
We offer you this sacrifice of praise

---

* When several are to be named, a general form is used: for N. our bishop and his assistant bishops (General Instruction, no. 172).

pro redemptióne animárum suárum,
pro spe salútis et incolumitátis suæ:
tibíque reddunt vota sua
ætérno Deo, vivo et vero.

Infra Actionem

Communicántes,
et memóriam venerántes,
in primis gloriósæ semper Vírginis Maríæ,
Genetrícis Dei et Dómini nostri Iesu Christi:
† sed et beáti Ioseph, eiúsdem Vírginis Sponsi,
et beatórum Apostolórum ac Mártyrum
  tuórum,
Petri et Pauli, Andréæ,
(Iacóbi, Ioánnis,
Thomæ, Iacóbi, Philíppi,
Bartholomǽi, Matthǽi,
Simónis et Thaddǽi:
Lini, Cleti, Cleméntis, Xysti,
Cornélii, Cypriáni,
Lauréntii, Chrysógoni,
Ioánnis et Pauli,
Cosmæ et Damiáni)
et ómnium Sanctórum tuórum; quorum méritis precibúsque concédas,
ut in ómnibus protectiónis tuæ muniámur auxílio.
(Per Christum Dóminum nostrum. Amen)

COMMUNICANTES PROPRIA

In Nativitate Domini et per octavam

Communicántes,
et (noctem sacratíssimam) diem sacratíssimum celebrántes,
(qua) quo beátæ Maríæ intemeráta virgínitas
huic mundo édidit Salvatórem:
sed et memóriam venerántes,
in primis eiúsdem gloriósæ semper Vírginis Maríæ,
Genetrícis eiúsdem Dei et Dómini nostri Iesu Christi: †

for ourselves and those who are dear to us.
We pray to you, our living and true God,
for our well-being and redemption.
In union with the whole Church we honor Mary,
the ever-virgin mother of Jesus Christ our Lord and
 God.
† We honor Joseph, her husband,
the apostles and martyrs
Peter and Paul, Andrew,

> [James, John, Thomas, James, Philip,
> Bartholomew, Matthew, Simon and Jude;
> we honor Linus, Cletus, Clement, Sixtus,
> Cornelius, Cyprian, Lawrence, Chrysogonus,
> John and Paul, Cosmas and Damian]

and all the saints.
May their merits and prayers
gain us your constant help and protection.

> [Through Christ our Lord. Amen.]

SPECIAL FORM of "In union with the whole Church"

Christmas and during the octave
In union with the whole Church
we celebrate that day (night)
when Mary without loss of her virginity
gave the world its Savior.
We honor Mary,
the ever-virgin mother of Jesus Christ our Lord and God. †

In Epiphania Domini
Communicántes,
et diem sacratíssimum celebrántes,
quo Unigénitus tuus, in tua tecum glória coætérnus,
in veritáte carnis nostræ visibíliter corporális
appáruit: sed et memóriam venerántes,
in primis gloriósæ semper Vírginis Maríæ,
Genetrícis eiúsdem Dei et Dómini nostri Iesu Christi: †

In Cena Domini
Communicántes,
et diem sacratíssimum celebrántes,
quo Dóminus noster Iesus Christus
pro nobis est tráditus,
sed et memóriam venerántes,
in primis gloriósæ semper Virginis Mariæ,
Genetrícis eiúsdem Dei et Dómini nostri Iesu Christi: †

A Missa Vigiliæ paschalis usque ad dominicam II Paschæ
Communicántes,
et (noctem sacratíssimam) diem sacratíssimum
celebrántes Resurrectiónis Dómini nostri Iesu Christi
secúndum carnem: sed et memóriam venerántes,
in primis gloriósæ semper Vírginis Maríæ,
Genetrícis eiúsdem Dei et Dómini nostri Iesu Christi: †

In Ascensione Domini
Communicántes,
et diem sacratíssimum celebrántes,
quo Dóminus noster, unigénitus Fílius tuus,
unítam sibi fragilitátis nostræ substántiam
in glóriæ tuæ déxtera collocávit: sed et memóriam venerántes,
in primis gloriósæ semper Vírginis Maríæ,
Genetrícis eiúsdem Dei et Dómini nostri Iesu Christi: †

In dominica Pentecostes
Communicántes,
et diem sacratíssimum Pentecóstes celebrántes,
quo Spíritus Sanctus
Apóstolis in ígneis linguis appáruit:
sed et memóriam venerántes,
in primis gloriósæ semper Vírginis Maríæ,
Genetrícis Dei et Dómini nostri Iesu Christi: †

Eucharistic Prayer 1

Epiphany
In union with the whole Church
we celebrate that day
when your only Son,
sharing your eternal glory,
showed himself in a human body.
We honor Mary,
the ever-virgin mother of Jesus Christ our Lord and God. †

Holy Thursday
In union with the whole Church
we celebrate that day
when Jesus Christ, our Lord,
was betrayed for us.
We honor Mary,
the ever-virgin mother of Jesus Christ our Lord and God. †

From the Easter Vigil to the Second Sunday of Easter inclusive
In union with the whole Church
we celebrate that day (night)
when Jesus Christ, our Lord,
rose from the dead in his human body.
We honor Mary,
the ever-virgin mother of Jesus Christ our Lord and God. †

Ascension
In union with the whole Church
we celebrate that day
when your only Son, our Lord,
took his place with you
and raised our frail human nature to glory.
We honor Mary,
the ever-virgin mother of Jesus Christ our Lord and God. †

Pentecost
In union with the whole Church
we celebrate the day of Pentecost
when the Holy Spirit appeared to the apostles
in the form of countless tongues.
We honor Mary,
the ever-virgin mother of Jesus Christ our Lord and God. †

Manibus extensis, prosequitur

Hanc ígitur oblatiónem servitútis nostræ,
sed et cunctæ famíliæ tuæ,
quæsumus, Dómine, ut placátus accípias:
diésque nostros in tua pace dispónas,
atque ab ætérna damnatióne nos éripi
et in electórum tuórum iúbeas grege numerári.

Iungit manus.

(Per Christum Dóminum nostrum. Amen.)

In Cena Domini

Hanc ígitur oblatiónem servitútis nostræ,
sed et cunctæ famíliæ tuæ,
quam tibi offérimus ob diem,
in qua Dóminus noster Iesus Christus
trádidit discípulis suis
Córporis et Sánguinis sui mystéria celebránda,
quæsumus, Dómine, ut placátus accípias:
diésque nostros in tua pace dispónas,
atque ab ætérna damnatióne nos éripi
et in electórum tuórum iúbeas grege numerári.
Iungit manus.
(Per Christum Dóminum nostrum. Amen.)

**A Missa Vigiliæ paschalis usque
ad dominicam II Paschæ**

Hanc ígitur oblatiónem servitútis nostræ,
sed et cunctæ famíliæ tuæ,
quam tibi offérimus
pro his quoque, quos regeneráre dignátus es ex aqua et
Spíritu Sancto,
tríbuens eis remissiónem ómnium peccatórum,
quæsumus, Dómine, ut placátus accípias:
diésque nostros in tua pace dispónas,
atque ab ætérna damnatióne nos éripi
et in electórum tuórum iúbeas grege numerári.
Iungit manus.
(Per Christum Dóminum nostrum. Amen.)

Tenens manus expansas, super oblata, dicit:

Quam oblatiónem tu, Deus, in ómnibus, quæsumus,
benedíctam, adscríptam, ratam,
rationábilem, acceptabilémque fácere dignéris:
ut nobis Corpus et Sanguis fiat dilectíssimi Fílii tui,
Dómini nostri Iesu Christi.

Iungit manus.

Eucharistic Prayer I

With hands extended, he continues:

Father, accept this offering
from your whole family.
Grant us your peace in this life,
save us from final damnation,
and count us among those you have chosen.

He joins his hands.

[Through Christ our Lord. Amen.]

Holy Thursday

Father, accept this offering
from your whole family
in memory of the day when Jesus Christ, our Lord,
gave the mysteries of his body and blood
for his disciples to celebrate.
Grant us your peace in this life,
save us from final damnation,
and count us among those you have chosen.

He joins his hands.

[Through Christ our Lord. Amen.]

**From the Easter Vigil to the
Second Sunday of Easter inclusive**

Father, accept this offering
from your whole family
and from those born into the new life
of water and the Holy spirit,
with all their sins forgiven.
Grant us your peace in this life,
save us from final damnation,
and count us among those you have chosen.

He joins his hands.

[Through Christ our Lord. Amen.]

With hands outstretched over the offerings, he says:

Bless and approve our offering;
make it acceptable to you,
an offering in spirit and in truth.
Let it become for us
the body and blood of Jesus Christ,
your only Son, our Lord.

He joins his hands.

[Through Christ our Lord. Amen.]

43

The Order of Mass

In formulis quæ sequuntur, verba Domini proferantur distincte et aperte, prouti natura eorundem verborum requirit.

Qui, prídie quam paterétur,

accipit panem,
eumque parum elevatum super altare tenens,
prosequitur:

accépit panem in sanctas ac venerábiles manus suas,

elevat oculos,

et elevátis óculis in cælum ad te Deum Patrem suum omnipoténtem, tibi grátias agens benedíxit, fregit, dedítque discípulis suis, dicens:

parum se inclinat

ACCÍPITE ET MANDUCÁTE EX HOC OMNES:

HOC EST ENIM CORPUS MEUM,

QUOD PRO VOBIS TRADÉTUR.

Hostiam consecratam ostendit populo, reponit super patenam, et genuflexus adorat.

Postea prosequitur:

Símili modo, postquam cenátum est,

accipit calicem,
eumque parum elevatum super altare tenens,
prosequitur:

The words of the Lord in the following formulas should be spoken clearly and distinctly, as their meaning demands.

The day before he suffered

He takes the bread and,
raising it a little above the altar,
continues:

he took bread in his sacred hands

He looks upward.

and looking up to heaven, to you, his almighty Father, he gave you thanks and praise. He broke the bread, gave it to his disciples, and said:

He bows slightly.

TAKE THIS, ALL OF YOU, AND EAT IT:

THIS IS MY BODY

WHICH WILL BE GIVEN UP FOR YOU.

He shows the consecrated host to the people, places it on the paten, and genuflects in adoration.

Then he continues:

When supper was ended,

He takes the chalice and,
raising it a little above the altar,
continues:

accípiens et hunc præclárum cálicem
in sanctas ac venerábiles manus suas,
item tibi grátias agens benedíxit
dedítque discípulis suis, dicens:

parum se inclinat:

ACCIPÍTE ET BÍBITE EX EO OMNES:

HIC EST ENIM CALIX SÁNGUINIS MEI

NOVI ET ÆTÉRNI TESTAMÉNTI,

QUI PRO VOBIS ET PRO MULTIS EFFUNDÉTUR

IN REMISSIÓNEM PECCATÓRUM.

HOC FÁCITE IN MEAM COMMEMORATIÓNEM.

Calicem ostendit populo, deponit super corporale, et genuflexus adorat.
Deinde dicit:

Mystérium fi-de- i.   (vel:)   Mystérium fi - de- i.

Et populus prosequitur, acclamans:*

Mortem tu- am annunti-ámus, Dó-mi-ne, et tu-am re-sur-

recti-ó-nem confi-témur, do-nec vé-ni-as.

---

*Vel:

Salvátor mundi, salva nos, qui per crucem et resurrectiónem tuam liberásti nos.

Vel:

Quotiescúmque manducámus panem hunc et cálicem bíbimus,
mortem tuam annuntiámus, Dómine, donec vénias.

46

he took the cup.
Again he gave you thanks and praise,
gave the cup to his disciples, and said:

He bows slightly.

TAKE THIS, ALL OF YOU, AND DRINK FROM IT:

THIS IS THE CUP OF MY BLOOD,

THE BLOOD OF THE NEW AND EVERLASTING COVENANT.

IT WILL BE SHED FOR YOU AND FOR ALL

SO THAT SINS MAY BE FORGIVEN.

DO THIS IN MEMORY OF ME.

He shows the chalice to the people, places it on the corporal, and genuflects in adoration. Then he sings or says:

Let us pro-claim the mys-te-ry of faith:

People with celebrant and concelebrants:

Christ has died, Christ is ri-sen, Christ will come a-gain.

---

or:
Lord, by your cross and resurrection you have set us free. You are the Savior of the world.
or:
Dying you destroyed our death, rising you restored our life. Lord Jesus, come in glory.
or:
When we eat this bread and drink this cup, we proclaim your death, Lord Jesus, until you come in glory.

Unde et mémores, Dómine,
nos servi tui,
sed et plebs tua sancta,
eiúsdem Christi, Fílii tui, Dómini nostri,
tam beátæ passiónis,
necnon et ab ínferis resurrectiónis,
sed et in cælos gloriósæ ascensiónis:
offérimus praecláræ maiestáti tuæ
de tuis donis ac datis
hóstiam puram,
hóstiam sanctam,
hóstiam immaculátam,
Panem sanctum vitæ ætérnæ
et Cálicem salútis perpétuæ.

Supra quæ propítio ac seréno vultu
respícere dignéris:
et accépta habére,
sícuti accépta habére dignátus es
múnera púeri tui iusti Abel,
et sacrifícium Patriárchæ nostri Abrahæ,
et quod tibi óbtulit
summus sacérdos tuus Melchísedech,
sanctum sacrificium, immaculátam hóstiam.

Súpplices te rogámus, omnípotens Deus:
iube hæc perférri per manus sancti Angeli tui
in sublíme altáre tuum,
in conspéctu divínæ maiestátis tuæ;
ut, quotquot ex hac altáris participatióne
sacrosánctum Fílii tui Corpus et Sánguinem
  sumpsérimus,

Eucharistic Prayer I

Then, with hands extended, the priest says:

Father, we celebrate the memory of Christ, your Son.
We, your people and your ministers,
recall his passion,
his resurrection from the dead,
and his ascension into glory;
and from the many gifts you have given us
we offer to you, God of glory and majesty,
this holy and perfect sacrifice:
the bread of life
and the cup of eternal salvation.

Look with favor on these offerings
and accept them as once you accepted
the gifts of your servant Abel,
the sacrifice of Abraham, our father in faith,
and the bread and wine offered by your priest
          Melchisedech.

Bowing, with hands joined, he continues:

Almighty God,
we pray that your angel may take this sacrifice
to your altar in heaven.
Then, as we receive from this altar
the sacred body and blood of your Son,

erigit se atque seipsum signat, dicens:

omni benedictióne cælésti et grátia repleámur.

Iungit manus.

(Per Christum Dóminum nostrum. Amen.)

Commemoratio pro defunctis.

Manibus extensis, dicit:

Meménto étiam, Dómine,
famulórum famularúmque tuárum N. et N.,
qui nos præcessérunt cum signo fídei,
et dórmiunt in somno pacis.

Iungit manus et orat aliquantulum pro iis defunctis, pro quibis orare intendit.

Deinde, extensis manibus, prosequitur:

Ipsis, Dómine, et ómnibus in Christo quiescéntibus,
locum refrigérii, lucis et pacis,
ut indúlgeas, deprecámur.

Iungit manus.

(Per Christum Dóminum nostrum. Amen.)

Manu dextera percutit sibi pectus, dicens:

Nobis quoque peccatóribus fámulis tuis,

et extensis manibus prosequitur:

de multitúdine miseratiónum tuárum sperántibus,
partem áliquam et societátem donáre dignéris
cum tuis sanctis Apóstolis et Martýribus:
cum Ioánne, Stéphano,

50

He stands up straight and makes the sign of the cross, saying:

let us be filled with every grace and blessing.

He joins his hands.

[Through Christ our Lord. Amen.]

Commemoration of the dead.
With hands extended, he says:

Remember, Lord, those who have died
and have gone before us marked with the sign of faith,
especially those for whom we now pray, N. and N.

The priest prays for them briefly with joined hands.
Then, with hands extended, he continues:

May these, and all who sleep in Christ,
find in your presence
light, happiness, and peace.

He joins his hands.

[Through Christ our Lord. Amen.]

With hands extended, he continues:

For ourselves, too, we ask
some share in the fellowship
of your apostles and martyrs,
with John the Baptist, Stephen,

Matthía, Bárnaba,
(Ignátio, Alexándro,
Marcellíno, Petro,
Felicitáte, Perpétua,
Agatha, Lúcia,
Agnéte, Cæcília, Anastásia)
et ómnibus Sanctis tuis:
intra quorum nos consórtium,
non æstimátor mériti, sed véniæ,
quǽsumus, largítor admítte.

Iungit manus.

Per Christum Dóminum nostrum.

Et prosequitur:

Per quem hæc ómnia, Dómine,
semper bona creas, sanctíficas, vivíficas, benedícis, et
præstas nobis.

Accipit patenam cum hostia et calicem, et utrumque elevans, dicit:

Per ip-sum, et cum ip-so, et in ip-so, est ti-bi De-o Pa-tri om-ni-po-tén-ti,

in u-ni-tá-te Spí-ri-tus Sanc-ti, om-nis ho-nor et gló-ri-a per ómni-a sæcu-

la sæcu-ló-rum.

Populus acclamat:

Amen.

Deinde sequitur ritus communionis, p. 84.

Matthias, Barnabas,
[Ignatius, Alexander, Marcellinus, Peter,
Felicity, Perpetua, Agatha, Lucy,
Agnes, Cecilia, Anastasia]
and all the saints.

The priest strikes his breast with the right hand, saying:

Though we are sinners,
we trust in your mercy and love.

With hands extended as before, he continues:

Do not consider what we truly deserve,
but grant us your forgiveness.

He joins his hands.

Through Christ our Lord.

He continues:

Through him you give us all these gifts.
You fill them with life and goodness,
you bless them and make them holy.

He takes the chalice and the paten with the host and, lifting them up, sings or says:

Through him, with him, in him, in the u-ni-ty of the Ho-ly Spir-it,

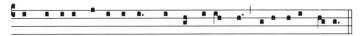

all glo-ry and hon-or is yours, al-might-y Fa-ther, for ev-er and ev-er.

The people respond:

Amen.

The Rite of Communion follows, p. 85.

53

PREX EUCHARISTICA II

V.   Dóminus vobíscum.
R.   **Et cum spíritu tuo.**

V.   Sursum corda.
R.   **Habémus ad Dóminum.**

V.   Grátias agámus Dómino Deo nostro.
R.   **Dignum et iustum est.**

Vere dignum et iustum est, æquum et salutáre,
nos tibi, sancte Pater, semper et ubíque
grátias ágere
per Fílium dilectiónis tuæ Iesum Christum.
Verbum tuum per quod cuncta fecísti:
quem misísti nobis Salvatórem et Redemptórem,
incarnátum de Spíritu Sancto et ex Vírgine natum.

Qui voluntátem tuam adímplens
et pópulum tibi sanctum acquírens
exténdit manus cum paterétur,
ut mortem sólveret et resurrectiónem manifestáret.

Et ídeo cum Angelis et ómnibus Sanctis
glóriam tuam prædicámus, una voce dicéntes:

Sanctus, Sanctus, Sanctus Dóminus Deus Sábaoth.
Pleni sunt cæli et terra glória tua.
Hosánna in excélsis.
Benedíctus qui venit in nómine Dómini.
Hosánna in excélsis.

(For musical settings of the Sanctus see # 203, 208, 212, 216, 219, 222.)

EUCHARISTIC PRAYER II

(This may be replaced by another preface.)

V. The Lord be with you
R. And also with you.

V. Lift up your hearts.
R. We lift them up to the Lord.

V. Let us give thanks to the Lord our God.
R. It is right to give him thanks and praise.

Father, it is our duty and our salvation,
always and everywhere
to give you thanks
through your beloved Son, Jesus Christ.

He is the Word through whom you made the universe,
the Savior you sent to redeem us.
By the power of the Holy Spirit
he took flesh and was born of the Virgin Mary.

For our sake he opened his arms on the cross;
he put an end to death
and revealed the resurrection.
In this he fulfilled your will
and won for you a holy people.

And so we join the angels and the saints
in proclaiming your glory
as we sing (say):

**Holy, holy, holy Lord, God of power and might,
heaven and earth are full of your glory.**
       Hosanna in the highest.
Blessed is he who comes in the name of the Lord.
       Hosanna in the highest.

(For musical settings of the Sanctus see # 253, 258, 263, 267, 271.)

55

Sacerdos, manibus extensis, dicit:

Vere Sanctus es, Dómine,
fons omnis sanctitátis.

Iungit manus, easque expansas super oblata tenens, dicit:

Hæc ergo dona, quǽsumus,
Spíritus tui rore sanctífica,

iungit manus

et signat semel super panem et calicem simul, dicens:

ut nobis Corpus et ✠ Sanguis fiant
Dómini nostri Iesu Christi.

Iungit manus.

In formulis quæ sequuntur, verba Domini proferantur distincte et aperte, prouti natura

eorundem verborum requirit.

Qui cum Passióni voluntárie traderétur,

accipit panem,

eumque parum elevatum super altare tenens, prosequitur:

accépit panem et grátias agens fregit,
dedítque discípulis suis, dicens:

parum se inclinat

ACCÍPITE ET MANDUCÁTE EX HOC OMNES:
HOC EST ENIM CORPUS MEUM,
QUOD PRO VOBIS TRADÉTUR.

Hostiam consecratam ostendit populo, reponit super patenam, et genuflexus adorat.

Postea prosequitur:

Símili modo, postquam cenátum est,

accipit cálicem,

eumque parum elevatum super altare tenens,

prosequitur:

The priest, with hands extended, says:

Lord, you are holy indeed,
the fountain of all holiness.

He joins his hands and holding them outstretched over the offerings, says:

Let your Spirit come upon these gifts to make them
 holy,
so that they may become for us

He joins his hands and, making the sign of the cross once over both bread and chalice, says:

the body ✠ and blood of our Lord, Jesus Christ.

He joins his hands.

The words of the Lord in the following formulas should be spoken clearly and distinctly, as their meaning demands.

Before he was given up to death,
a death he freely accepted,

He takes the bread and, raising it a little above the altar, continues:

he took bread and gave you thanks.
He broke the bread,
gave it to his disciples, and said:

He bows slightly.

TAKE THIS, ALL OF YOU, AND EAT IT:
THIS IS MY BODY
WHICH WILL BE GIVEN UP FOR YOU.

He shows the consecrated host to the people, places it on the paten, and genuflects in adoration.

Then he continues:

When supper was ended, he took the cup.

He takes the chalice and,

raising it a little above the altar,

continues:

accípiens et cálicem
íterum grátias agens dedit discípulis suis, dicens:

parum se inclinat:

ACCIPÍTE ET BÍBITE EX EO OMNES:

HIC EST ENIM CALIX SÁNGUINIS MEI

NOVI ET ÆTÉRNI TESTAMÉNTI,

QUI PRO VOBIS ET PRO MULTIS EFFUNDÉTUR

IN REMISSIÓNEM PECCATÓRUM.

HOC FÁCITE IN MEAM COMMEMORATIÓNEM.

Calicem ostendit populo, deponit super corporale, et genuflexus adorat.
Deinde dicit:

Mysté-ri-um fi-de- i.   (vel:)   *Mysté-ri-um fi - de- i.*

Et populus prosequitur, acclamans:*

Mórtem tu- am annunti-ámus, Dó-mi-ne,   et tu-am re-sur-

recti-ó-nem confi-témur, do-nec vé-ni-as.

*Vel:
Salvátor mundi, salva nos, qui per crucem et resurrectiónem tuam liberásti nos.

Vel:
Quotiescúmque manducámus panem hunc et cálicem bíbimus,
mortem tuam annuntiámus, Dómine, donec vénias.

Again he gave you thanks and praise,
gave the cup to his disciples, and said:

He bows slightly.

TAKE THIS, ALL OF YOU, AND DRINK FROM IT:

THIS IS THE CUP OF MY BLOOD,

THE BLOOD OF THE NEW AND EVERLASTING COVENANT.

IT WILL BE SHED FOR YOU AND FOR ALL

SO THAT SINS MAY BE FORGIVEN.

DO THIS IN MEMORY OF ME.

He shows the chalice to the people, places it on the corporal, and genuflects in adoration.
Then he sings or says:

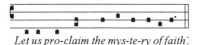

Let us pro-claim the mys-te-ry of faith:

People with celebrant and concelebrants

Christ has died, Christ is ri-sen, Christ will come a-gain.

---

or:
Lord, by your cross and resurrection you have set us free. You are the Savior of the world.
or:
Dying you destroyed our death, rising you restored our life. Lord Jesus, come in glory.
or:
When we eat this bread and drink this cup, we proclaim your death, Lord Jesus, until you come in glory.

Deinde sacerdos, extensis manibus, dicit:

Mémores ígitur mortis et resurrectiónis eius,
tibi, Dómine, panem vitæ
et cálicem salútis offérimus,
grátias agéntes quia nos dignos habuísti
astáre coram te et tibi ministráre.

Et súpplices deprecámur
ut Córporis et Sánguinis Christi partícipes
a Spíritu Sancto congregémur in unum.

Recordáre, Dómine, Ecclésiæ tuæ toto orbe diffúsæ,
ut eam in caritáte perfícias
una cum Papa nostro N. et Epíscopo nostro N.*
et univérso clero.

In Missis pro defunctis addi potest:

Meménto fámuli tui (fámulæ tuæ) N.
quem (quam) (hódie) ad te ex hoc mundo vocásti.
Concéde, ut, qui (quæ) complantátus (complantáta)
fuit similitúdini mortis Fílii tui,
simul fiat et resurrectiónis ipsíus.

Meménto étiam fratrum nostrórum,
qui in spe resurrectiónis dormiérunt,
omniúmque in tua miseratióne defunctórum,
et eos in lumen vultus tui admítte.

---

* Hic fieri potest mentio de Episcopis Coadiutoribus vel Auxiliarlis, ut in *Institutione generali Missalis Romani (1975)*, n. 109, (2000), n. 149, notatur.

Then, with hands extended, the priest says:

In memory of his death and resurrection,
we offer you, Father, this life-giving bread,
this saving cup.
We thank you for counting us worthy
to stand in your presence and serve you.
May all of us who share in the body and blood of Christ
be brought together in unity by the Holy Spirit.

Lord, remember your Church throughout the world;
make us grow in love,
together with N. our Pope,
N. our bishop, * and all the clergy.

In Masses for the dead the following may be added:

Remember N., whom you have called from this life.
In baptism he (she) died with Christ:
may he (she) also share his resurrection.

Remember our brothers and sisters
who have gone to their rest
in the hope of rising again;
bring them and all the departed
into the light of your presence.

---

* When several are to be named, a general form is used: for N. our bishop and his assistant bishops
(General Instruction, no. 172).

Omnium nostrum, quǽsumus, miserére,
ut cum beáta Dei Genetríce Vírgine María,
beátis Apóstolis et ómnibus Sanctis,
qui tibi a sǽculo placuérunt,
ætérnæ vitæ mereámur esse consórtes,
et te laudémus et glorificémus

iungit manus

per Fílium tuum Iesum Christum.

Accipit patenam cum hostia et calicem, et utrumque elevans, dicit:

Per ip-sum, et cum ip-so, et in ip-so,   est ti-bi De-o Pa-tri om-ni-po-tén-ti,

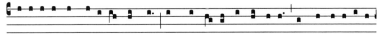

in u-ni-tá-te Spí-ri-tus Sanc-ti,   om-nis ho-nor et gló-ri-a   per ómni-a sǽcu-

la sæcu-ló-rum.

Populus acclamat:

Amen.

Deinde sequitur ritus communionis, p. 84.

Have mercy on us all;
make us worthy to share eternal life
with Mary, the virgin mother of God,
with the apostles, and with all the saints
who have done your will throughout the ages.
May we praise you in union with them,
and give you glory

He joins his hands.

through your Son, Jesus Christ.

He takes the chalice and the paten with the host and, lifting them up, sings or says:

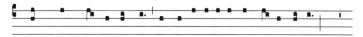

Through him, with him, in him,   in the u-ni-ty of the Ho-ly Spir-it,

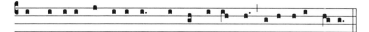

all glo-ry and hon-or is yours, al-might-y Fa-ther, for ev-er and ev-er.

The people respond:

Amen.

The Rite of Communion follows, p. 85.

PREX EUCHARISTICA III

Sacerdos, manibus extensis, dicit:

Vere Sanctus es, Dómine,
et mérito te laudat omnis a te cóndita creatúra,
quia per Fílium tuum,
Dóminum nostrum Iesum Christum,
Spíritus Sancti operánte virtúte,
vivíficas et santíficas univérsa,
et pópulum tibi congregáre non désinis,
ut a solis ortu usque ad occásum
oblátio munda offerátur nómini tuo.

Iungit manus, easque expansas super oblata tenens, dicit:

Súpplices ergo te, Dómine, deprecámur,
ut hæc múnera, quæ tibi sacránda detúlimus,
eódem Spíritu sanctificáre dignéris,

iungit manus

et signat semel super panem et calicem simul, dicens;

ut Corpus et ✠ Sanguis fiant
Fílii tui Dómini nostri Iesu Christi,

Iungit manus.

cuius mandáto hæc mystéria celebrámus.

In formulis quæ sequuntur, verba Domini proferantur distincte et aperte, prouti natura
eorundem verborum requirit:

Ipse enim in qua nocte tradebátur

accipit panem

eumque parum elevatum super altare tenens,

prosequitur:

accépit panem
et tibi grátias agens benedíxit,
fregit, dedítque discípulis suis, dicens:

parum se inclinat

EUCHARISTIC PRAYER III

The priest, with hands extended, says:

Father, you are holy indeed,
and all creation rightly gives you praise.
All life, all holiness comes from you
through your Son, Jesus Christ our Lord,
by the working of the Holy Spirit.
From age to age you gather a people to yourself,
so that from east to west
a perfect offering may be made
to the glory of your name.

He joins his hands and, holding them outstretched over the offerings, says:

And so, Father, we bring you these gifts.
We ask you to make them holy by the power of your Spirit,

He joins his hands and, making the sign of the cross once over both bread and chalice, says:

that they may become the body ✠ and blood
of your Son, our Lord Jesus Christ,

He joins his hands.

at whose command we celebrate this eucharist.

The words of the Lord in the following formulas should be spoken clearly and distinctly, as their meaning demands.

On the night he was betrayed,

He takes the bread and, raising it a little above the altar, continues:

He took bread and gave you thanks and praise.
He broke the bread, gave it to his disciples, and said:

He bows slightly.

ACCÍPITE ET MANDUCÁTE EX HOC OMNES:
HOC EST ENIM CORPUS MEUM,
QUOD PRO VOBIS TRADÉTUR.

Hostiam consecratam ostendit populo, deponit super patenam, et genuflexus adorat.

Postea prosequitur:

Símili modo, postquam cenátum est,

accipit cálicem, eumque parum elevatum super altare tenens, prosequitur:

accípiens cálicem,
et tibi grátias agens benedíxit,
dedítque discípulis suis, dicens:

parum se inclinat

ACCÍPITE ET BÍBITE EX EO OMNES:
HIC EST ENIM CALIX SÁNGUINIS MEI
NOVI ET AETÉRNI TESTAMÉNTI,
QUI PRO VOBIS ET PRO MULTIS EFFUNDÉTUR
IN REMISSIÓNEM PECCATÓRUM.
HOC FÁCITE IN MEAM COMMEMORATIÓNEM.

Calicem ostendit populo, deponit super corporale, et genuflexus adorat.

Diende dicit:

Mysté-ri-um fí-de- i.　　(vel:)　　*Mysté-ri-um fí - de- i.*

Et populus prosequitur, acclamans:*

Mortem tu- am annunti-ámus, Dó-mi-ne, et tu-am re-sur-

recti-ó-nem confi-témur, do-nec vé-ni-as.

---

*Vel:

Salvátor mundi, salva nos, qui per crucem et resurrectiónem tuam liberásti nos.

Vel:

Quotiescúmque manducámus panem hunc et cálicem bíbimus,

mortem tuam annuntiámus, Dómine, donec vénias.

TAKE THIS, ALL OF YOU, AND EAT IT:
THIS IS MY BODY
WHICH WILL BE GIVEN UP FOR YOU.

> He shows the consecrated host to the people, places it on the paten, and genuflects in adoration.

> Then he continues:

When supper was ended, he took the cup.

> He takes the chalice and, raising it a little above the altar, continues:

Again he gave you thanks and praise,
gave the cup to his disciples, and said:

> He bows slightly.

TAKE THIS, ALL OF YOU, AND DRINK FROM IT:
THIS IS THE CUP OF MY BLOOD,
THE BLOOD OF THE NEW AND EVERLASTING COVENANT.
IT WILL BE SHED FOR YOU AND FOR ALL
SO THAT SINS MAY BE FORGIVEN.
DO THIS IN MEMORY OF ME.

> He shows the chalice to the people, places it on the corporal, and genuflects in adoration.

> Then he sings or says:

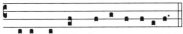

Let us pro-claim the mys-te-ry of faith:

People with celebrant and concelebrants

Christ has died, Christ is ri-sen, Christ will come a-gain.

> or:

Lord, by your cross and resurrection you have set us free. You are the Savior of the world.

> or:

Dying you destroyed our death, rising you restored our life. Lord Jesus, come in glory.

> or:

When we eat this bread and drink this cup, we proclaim your death, Lord Jesus, until you come in glory.

Mémores ígitur, Dómine,
eiusdem Fílii tui salutíferæ passiónis
necnon mirábilis resurrectiónis
et ascensiónis in cælum,
sed et præstolántes álterum eius advéntum,
offérimus tibi, grátias reteréntes,
hoc sacrifícium vivum et sanctum.

Réspice, quǽsumus, in oblatiónem Ecclésiæ tuæ
et, agnóscens Hóstiam,
cuius voluísti immolatióne placári,
concéde, ut qui Córpore et Sánguine Fílii tui refícimur,
Spíritu eius Sancto repléti,
unum corpus et unus spíritus inveniámur in Christo.

Ipse nos tibi perfíciat munus ætérnum,
ut cum eléctis tuis hereditátem cónsequi valeámus,
in primis cum beatíssima Vírgine, Dei Genetríce María,
cum beátis Apóstolis tuis et gloriósis Martýribus
(cum Sancto N.: Sancto diei vel patrono)
et ómnibus Sanctis,
quorum intercessióne
perpétuo apud te confídimus adiuvári.

Hæc Hóstia nostræ reconciliatiónis profíciat,
quæsumus, Dómine,
ad totíus mundi pacem atque salútem.
Ecclésiam tuam, peregrinántem in terra,
in fide et caritáte firmáre dignéris
cum fámulo tuo Papa nostro N. et Epíscopo nostro N.*

---

* Hic fieri potest mentio de Episcopis Coadiutoribus vel Auxiliariis, ut in *Institutione generali Missalis Romani (1975)*, n. 109, (2000), n. 149, notatur.

Eucharistic Prayer III

With hands extended, the priest says:

Father, calling to mind the death your Son endured
  for our salvation,
his glorious resurrection and ascension into heaven,
and ready to greet him when he comes again,
we offer you in thanksgiving this holy and living
  sacrifice.

Look with favor on your Church's offering,
and see the Victim whose death has reconciled us to
  yourself.
Grant that we, who are nourished by his body and blood,
may be filled with his Holy Spirit,
and become one body, one spirit in Christ.

May he make us an everlasting gift to you
and enable us to share in the inheritance of your saints,
with Mary, the virgin mother of God;
with the apostles, the martyrs,
(Saint N. — the saint of the day or the patron saint)
  and all your saints,
on whose constant intercession we rely for help.

Lord, may this sacrifice,
which has made our peace with you,
advance the peace and salvation of all the world.
Strengthen in faith and love your pilgrim
  Church on earth;
your servant, Pope N., our bishop N.,*

---

* When several are to be named, a general form is used: for N. our bishop and his assistant bishops
(General Instruction, no. 172).

cum episcopáli órdine et univérso clero
et omni pópulo acquisitiónis tuæ.
Votis huius famíliæ, quam tibi astáre voluísti,
adésto propítius.
Omnes filios tuos ubíque dispérsos
tibi, clemens Pater, miserátus coniúnge.
† Frates nostros defúnctos
et omnes qui, tibi placéntes, ex hoc sǽculo transiérunt,
in regnum tuum benígnus admítte,
ubi fore sperámus,
ut simul glória tua perénniter satiémur,

iungit manus

per Christum Dóminum nostrum,
per quem mundo bona cuncta largíris. †

Accipit patenam cum hostia et calicem, et utrumque elevans, dicit:

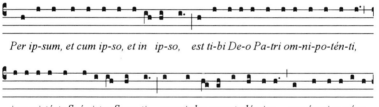

Per ip-sum, et cum ip-so, et in ip-so, est ti-bi De-o Pa-tri om-ni-po-tén-ti,

in u-ni-tá-te Spi-ri-tus Sanc-ti, om-nis ho-nor et gló-ri-a per ómni-a sǽcu-

la sæcu-ló-rum.

Populus acclamat:

Amen.

Deinde sequitur ritus communionis, p. 84.

and all the bishops,
with the clergy and the entire people your Son
 has gained for you.
Father, hear the prayers of the family you have
 gathered here before you.
In mercy and love unite all your children
wherever they may be.
Welcome into your kingdom our departed
 brothers and sisters,
and all who have left this world in your friendship.

He joins his hands.

We hope to enjoy for ever the vision of your glory, through Christ our Lord,
from whom all good things come.

He takes the chalice and the paten with the host and, lifting them up, sings or says:

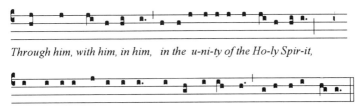

Through him, with him, in him, in the u-ni-ty of the Ho-ly Spir-it,

all glo-ry and hon-or is yours, al-might-y Fa-ther, for ev-er and ev-er.

The people respond:

Amen.

The Rite of Communion follows, p. 85.

PREX EUCHARISTICA IV

V.   Dóminus vobíscum.
R.   **Et cum spíritu tuo.**
V.   Sursum corda.
R.   **Habémus ad Dóminum.**
V.   Grátias agámus Dómino Deo nostro.
R.   **Dignum et iustum est.**

Vere dignum est tibi grátias ágere,
vere iustum est te glorificáre, Pater sancte,
quia unus es Deus vivus et verus,
qui es ante sæcula et pérmanes in ætérnum,
inaccessíbilem lucem inhábitans;
sed et qui unus bonus atque fons vitæ cuncta fecísti,
ut creatúras tuas benedictiónibus adimpléres
multásque lætificáres tui lúminis claritáte.
Et ídeo coram te innúmeræ astant turbæ angelórum,
qui die ac nocte sérviunt tibi
et, vultus tui glóriam contemplántes,
te incessánter gloríficant.
Cum quibus et nos et, per nostram vocem,
omnis quæ sub cælo est creatúra
nomen tuum in exsultatióne confitémur, canéntes:

Sanctus, Sanctus, Sanctus Dóminus Deus Sábaoth
Pleni sunt cæli et terra glória tua.
Hosánna in excélsis.
Benedíctus qui venit in nómine Dómini.
Hosánna in excélsis.

(For musical settings of the Sanctus see # 203, 208, 212, 216, 219, 222.)

Sacerdos, manibus extensis, dicit:

Confitémur tibi, Pater sancte,

EUCHARISTIC PRAYER IV

V.   The Lord be with you.
R.   **And also with you.**

V.   Lift up your hearts.
R.   **We lift them up to the Lord.**

V.   Let us give thanks to the Lord our God.
R.   **It is right to give him thanks and praise.**

Father in heaven,
it is right that we should give you thanks and glory:
you are the one God, living and true.
Through all eternity you live in unapproachable light.
Source of life and goodness, you have created all things,
to fill your creatures with every blessing
and lead all men to the joyful vision of your light.
Countless hosts of angels stand before you to do your will;
they look upon your splendor
and praise you, night and day.
United with them,
and in the name of every creature under heaven,
we too praise your glory as we say:

Holy, holy, holy Lord God of power and might,
heaven and earth are full of your glory.
  Hosanna in the highest.
Blessed is he who comes in the name of the Lord.
  Hosanna in the highest.

(For musical settings of the Sanctus see # 253, 258, 263, 267, 271.)

The priest, with hands extended, says:

Father, we acknowledge your greatness:

73

quia magnus es et ómnia ópera tua
in sapiéntia et caritáte fecísti.
Hóminem ad tuam imáginem condidísti,
eíque commisísti mundi curam univérsi,
ut, tibi soli Creatóri sérviens,
creatúris ómnibus imperáret.
Et cum amicítiam tuam, non obœdiens, amisísset,
non eum dereliquísti in mortis império.
Omnibus enim misericórditer subvenísti,
ut te quæréntes invenírent.
Sed et fœdera plúries homínibus obtulísti
eósque per prophétas erudísti in exspectatióne salútis.
Et sic, Pater sancte, mundum dilexísti,
ut, compléta plenitúdine témporum,
Unigénitum tuum nobis mítteres Salvatórem.
Qui, incarnátus de Spíritu Sancto
et natus ex María Vírgine,
in nostra condiciónis forma est conversátus
per ómnia absque peccáto;
salútem evangelizávit paupéribus,
redemptiónem captívis,
mæstis corde lætítiam.
Ut tuam vero dispensatiónem impléret,
in mortem trádidit semetípsum
ac, resúrgens a mórtuis,
mortem destrúxit vitámque renovávit.
Et, ut non ámplius nobismetípsis viverémus,
sed sibi qui pro nobis mórtuus est atque surréxit,
a te, Pater, misit Spíritum Sanctum
primítias credéntibus,
qui, opus suum in mundo perfíciens,
omnem sanctificatiónem compléret.

Iungit manus, easque expansas super oblata tenens, dicit:

Quǽsumus ígitur, Dómine,

all your actions show your wisdom and love.
You formed man in your own likeness
and set him over the whole world
to serve you, his creator,
and to rule over all creatures.
Even when he disobeyed you and lost your friendship
you did not abandon him to the power of death,
but helped all men to seek and find you.
Again and again you offered a covenant to man,
and through the prophets taught him to hope for
 salvation.
Father, you so loved the world
that in the fullness of time you sent your only Son to be
 our Savior
He was conceived through the power of the Holy Spirit,
and born of the Virgin Mary,
a man like us in all things but sin.
To the poor he proclaimed the good news of salvation,
to prisoners, freedom,
and to those in sorrow, joy.
In fulfillment of your will
he gave himself up to death;
but by rising from the dead,
he destroyed death and restored life.
And that we might live no longer for ourselves but
 for him,
he sent the Holy Spirit from you, Father,
as his first gift to those who believe,
to complete his work on earth
and bring us the fullness of grace.

He joins his hands and, holding them outstretched over the offerings, says:

Father, may the Holy Spirit sanctify these offerings.

ut idem Spíritus Sanctus
hæc múnera sanctificáre dignétur,

iungit manus

et signat semel super panem et calicem simul, dicens:

ut Corpus et ✠ Sanguis fiant
Dómini nostri Iesu Christi

iungit manus

ad hoc magnum mystérium celebrándum,
quod ipse nobis relíquit in fœdus ætérnum.

In formulis quæ sequuntur, verba Domini proferantur distincte et aperte, prouti natura

eorundem verborum requirit.

Ipse enim, cum hora venísset
ut glorificarétur a te, Pater sancte,
ac dilexísset suos qui erant in mundo,
in finem diléxit eos:
et cenántibus illis

accipit panem,

eumque parum elevatum super altare tenens,

prosequitur:

accépit panem, benedíxit ac fregit,
dedítque discípulis suis, dicens:

parum se inclinat

ACCÍPITE ET MANDUCÁTE EX HOC OMNES:
HOC EST ENIM CORPUS MEUM,
QUOD PRO VOBIS TRADÉTUR.

Hostiam consecratam ostendit populo, deponit super patenam, et genuflexus adorat.

Postea prosequitur:

Símili modo

accipit calicem,

eumque parum elevatum super altare tenens,

prosequitur:

He joins his hands and,

making the sign of the cross once over both bread and chalice, says:

Let them become the body ✠ and blood of Jesus Christ
our Lord

He joins his hands.

as we celebrate the great mystery
which he left us an everlasting covenant.

The words of the Lord in the following formulas should be spoken clearly and distinctly, as
their meaning demands.

He always loved those who were his own in the world.
When the time came for him to be glorified by you, his heavenly Father,
he showed the depth of his love.

He takes the bread and, raising it a little above the altar, continues:

While they were at supper,
he took bread, said the blessing, broke the bread
and gave it to his disciples, saying:

He bows slightly.

TAKE THIS, ALL OF YOU, AND EAT IT:
THIS IS MY BODY
WHICH WILL BE GIVEN UP FOR YOU.

He shows the consecrated host to the people, places it on the paten, and genuflects in adoration.

Then he continues.

In the same way, he took the cup, filled with wine.

He takes the chalice and, raising it a little above the altar, continues:

accípiens cálicem, ex genímine vitis replétum,
grátias egit, dedítque discípulis suis, dicens:

parum se inclinat

ACCIPÍTE ET BÍBITE EX EO OMNES:
HIC EST ENIM CALIX SÁNGUINIS MEI
NOVI ET ÆTÉRNI TESTAMÉNTI,
QUI PRO VOBIS ET PRO MULTIS EFFUNDÉTUR
IN REMISSIÓNEM PECCATÓRUM.
HOC FÁCITE IN MEAM COMMEMORATIÓNEM.

Calicem ostendit populo, deponit super corporale, et genuflexus adorat.

Deinde dicit:

(vel:)

Et populus prosequitur, acclamans:*

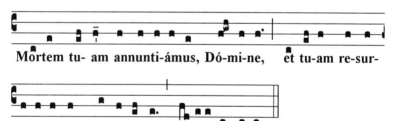

*Vel:
Salvátor mundi, salva nos, qui per crucem et resurrectiónem tuam liberásti nos.

Vel:
Quotiescúmque manducámus panem hunc et cálicem bíbimus,
mortem tuam annuntiámus, Domine, donec vénias.

He gave you thanks, and giving the cup to his disciples,
and said:

He bows slightly.

TAKE THIS, ALL OF YOU, AND DRINK FROM IT:
THIS IS THE CUP OF MY BLOOD,
THE BLOOD OF THE NEW AND EVERLASTING COVENANT.
IT WILL BE SHED FOR YOU AND FOR ALL
SO THAT SINS MAY BE FORGIVEN.
DO THIS IN MEMORY OF ME.

He shows the chalice to the people, places it on the corporal, and genuflects in adoration.

Then he sings or says:

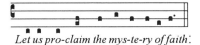

Let us pro-claim the mys-te-ry of faith:

People with celebrant and concelebrants

Christ has died, Christ is ri-sen, Christ will come a-gain.

---

or:
Lord, by your cross and resurrection you have set us free. You are the Savior of the world.
or:
Dying you destroyed our death, rising you restored our life. Lord Jesus, come in glory.
or:
When we eat this bread and drink this cup, we proclaim your death, Lord Jesus, until you come in glory.

Unde et nos, Dómine, redemptiónis nostræ memoriále
nunc celebrántes,
mortem Christi
eiúsque descénsum ad ínferos recólimus,
eius resurrectiónem
et ascensiónem ad tuam déxteram profitémur,
et, exspectántes ipsíus advéntum in glória,
offérimus tibi eius Corpus et Sánguinem,
sacrifícium tibi acceptábile et toti mundo salutáre.

Réspice, Dómine, in Hóstiam,
quam Ecclésiæ tuæ ipse parásti,
et concéde benígnus ómnibus
qui ex hoc uno pane participábunt et cálice,
ut, in unum corpus a Sancto Spíritu congregáti,
in Christo hóstia viva perficiántur,
ad laudem glóriæ tuæ.

Nunc ergo, Dómine, ómnium recordáre,
pro quibus tibi hanc oblatiónem offérimus:
in primis fámuli tui, Papæ nostri N.,
Epíscopi nostri N.*, et Episcopórum órdinis univérsi,
sed et totíus cleri, et offeréntium,
et circumstántium,
et cuncti pópuli tui,
et ómnium, qui te quærunt corde sincéro.

Meménto étiam illórum,
qui obiérunt in pace Christi tui,
et ómnium defunctórum,
quorum fidem tu solus cognovísti.

---

* Hic fieri potest mentio de Episcopis Coadiutoribus vel Auxiliariis, ut in *Institutione generali Missalis Romani (1975)*, n. 109, (2000), n. 149, notatur.

With hands extended, the priest says:

Father, we now celebrate this memorial of our
 redemption.
We recall Christ's death, his descent among the dead,
his resurrection, and his ascension to your right hand;
and, looking forward to his coming in glory,
we offer you his body and blood,
the acceptable sacrifice
which brings salvation to the whole world.

Lord, look upon this sacrifice which you have given
 to your Church;
and by your Holy Spirit, gather all who share this one
 bread and one cup
into the one body of Christ, a living sacrifice of praise.

Lord, remember those for whom we offer this sacrifice,
especially N. our Pope,
N. our bishop, * and bishops and clergy everywhere.
Remember those who take part in this offering,
those here present and all your people,
and all who seek you with a sincere heart.

Remember those who have died in the peace of Christ
and all the dead whose faith is known to you alone.

---

* When several are to be named, a general form is used: for N. our bishop and his assistant bishops
(General Instruction, no. 172).

Nobis ómnibus, filiis tuis,
clemens Pater, concéde,
ut cæléstem hereditátem cónsequi valeámus
cum beáta Vírgine, Dei Genetríce, María,
cum Apóstolis et Sanctis tuis
in regno tuo, ubi cum univérsa creatúra,
a corruptióne peccáti et mortis liberáta,
te glorificémus per Christum Dóminum nostrum,

iungit manus,

per quem mundo bona cuncta largíris.

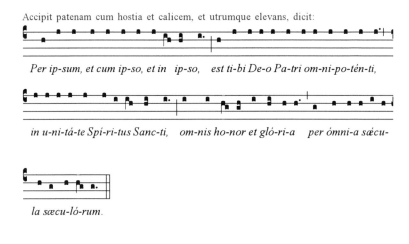

Accipit patenam cum hostia et calicem, et utrumque elevans, dicit:

Per ip-sum, et cum ip-so, et in ip-so, est ti-bi De-o Pa-tri om-ni-po-tén-ti,

in u-ni-tá-te Spí-ri-tus Sanc-ti, om-nis ho-nor et gló-ri-a per ómni-a sæcu-

la sæcu-ló-rum.

Populus acclamat:

Amen.

Deinde sequitur ritus communionis, p. 84.

Father, in your mercy grant also to us, your children,
to enter into our heavenly inheritance
in the company of the Virgin Mary, the Mother of God,
and your apostles and saints.
Then, in your kingdom, freed from the corruption of sin
  and death,
we shall sing your glory with every creature through
  Christ our Lord,

He joins his hands.

through whom you give us everything that is good.

He takes the chalice and the paten with the host and, lifting them up, sings or says:

Through him, with him, in him,   in the u-ni-ty of the Ho-ly Spir-it,

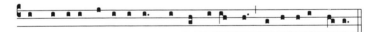

all glo-ry and hon-or is yours, al-might-y Fa-ther, for ev-er and ev-er.

The people respond:

Amen.

The Rite of Communion follows, p. 85.

83

RITUS COMMUNIONIS

PATER NOSTER

Calice et patena depositis, sacerdos, iunctis manibus, dicit:

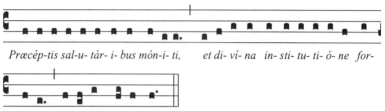

Præcép-tis sal-u- tár- i- bus món-i- ti,   et di- ví- na in- sti- tu- ti- ó- ne for-

má- ti,   au-dé-mus dí- ce- re: *

Extendit manus et, una cum populo, pergit:

Pa-ter noster, qui es in cæ-lis: sancti-fi-cé-tur nomen tu-um;

advé-ni-at regnum tu-um; fi-at vo-lúntas tu-a,   sic-ut in cæ-

lo,   et in terra.   Panem nostrum co-ti-di-á-num da no-bis

hó-di - e;   et dimítte no-bis dé-bi-ta nostra, sic-ut et nos

dimít-timus de-bi-tó-ri-bus nostris;   et ne nos indú-cas in ten-

ta-ti- ó- nem; sed lí-be-ra nos a ma-lo.

*Vel:

Et nunc orátionem, quam Chrístus Dóminus nos dócuit, ómnes símul dicámus:
      Vel:
Précem nóstram pergámus, advéntum régni Déi quaeréndo:

COMMUNION RITE

LORD'S PRAYER

The priest sets down the chalice and paten and with hands joined, sings or says:*

Let us pray with con-fi-dence to the Fa - ther in the words our Savior gave us:

He extends his hands and continues, with the people:

Our Fa-ther, who art in heav-en, hal-lowed be Thy name;

Thy king-dom come; Thy will be done on earth as it is in

heav- en. Give us this day our dai-ly bread; and for-give us

our tres-pass-es as we for-give those who tres-pass a-gainst

us; and lead us not in-to temp-ta-tion, but de-liv-er us

from e- vil.

---

*or:
Jesus taught us to call God our Father, and so we have the courage to say:
      or:
Let us ask our Father to forgive our sins and to bring us to forgive those who sin against us.
      or:
Let us pray for the coming of the kingdom as Jesus taught us.

85

Manibus extensis, sacerdos solus prosequitur, dicens:

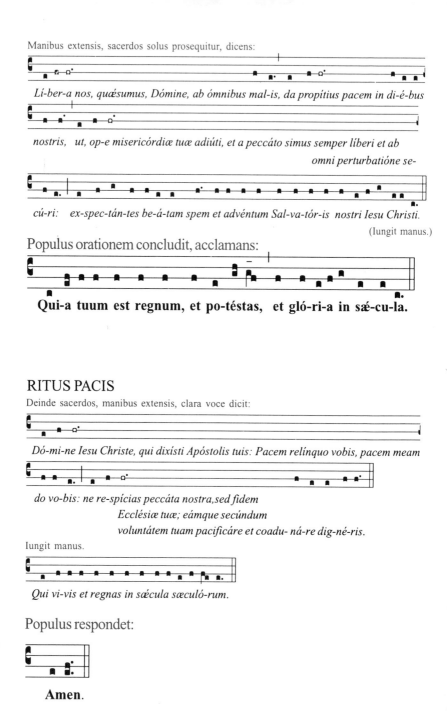

Lí-ber-a nos, quǽsumus, Dómine, ab ómnibus mal-is, da propítius pacem in di-é-bus

nostris,   ut, op-e misericórdiæ tuæ adiúti, et a peccáto simus semper líberi et ab

omni perturbatióne se-

cú-ri: ex-spec-tán-tes be-á-tam spem et advéntum Sal-va-tór-is nostri Iesu Christi.

(Iungit manus.)

Populus orationem concludit, acclamans:

Qui-a tuum est regnum, et po-téstas, et gló-ri-a in sǽ-cu-la.

RITUS PACIS

Deinde sacerdos, manibus extensis, clara voce dicit:

Dó-mi-ne Iesu Christe, qui dixísti Apóstolis tuis: Pacem relínquo vobis, pacem meam

do vo-bis: ne re-spícias peccáta nostra,sed fidem

Ecclésiæ tuæ; eámque secúndum

voluntátem tuam pacificáre et coadu- ná-re dig-né-ris.

Iungit manus.

Qui vi-vis et regnas in sǽcula sæculó-rum.

Populus respondet:

Amen.

Sacerdos, ad populum conversus, extendens et iungens manus, subdit:

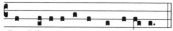

Pax Dómi-ni sit semper vobíscum.

With hands extended the priest continues alone:

Deliver us, Lord, from every evil, and grant us peace in our day. In your mercy keep

us free from sin and protect us from all anxi- e- ty as we wait in joyful hope for the

coming of our savior, Je-sus Christ. (He joins his hands.)

The people end the prayer with the acclamation:

For the king-dom, the power, and the glo-ry are yours, now

and for-ev-er.

SIGN OF PEACE

Then the priest, with hands extended, says aloud:

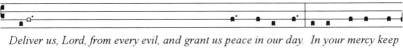

Lord Jesus Christ, you said to your a-pos-tles: I leave you peace, my peace I give

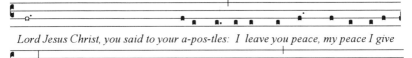

you. Look not on our sins, but on the faith of your Church, and grant us the peace

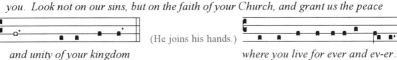

and unity of your kingdom (He joins his hands.) *where you live for ever and ev-er.*

The people answer:

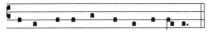

Amen.

The priest, extending and joining his hands, adds:

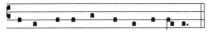

The peace of the Lord be with you al-ways.

Populus respondet:

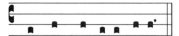

Et cum spí- ri-tu tu-o.

Deinde, pro opportunitate, diaconus, vel sacerdos, subiungit:
Offérte vobis pacem.

Et omnes, iuxta locorum consuetudines pacem et caritatem sibi invicem significant; sacerdos pacem dat diacono vel ministro.

FRACTIO PANIS

Deinde accipit hostiam eamque super patenam frangit, et particulam immittit in calicem, dicens secreto: *Hæc commíxtio Córporis et Sánguinis Dómini nostri Iesu Christi fiat accipiéntibus nobis in vitam ætérnam.*

Interim cantatur vel dicitur:

(For musical settings of the Agnus Dei see # 204, 209, 213, 217, 220, 223.)

**Agnus Dei, qui tollis peccáta mundi:
   miserére nobis.
Agnus Dei, qui tollis peccáta mundi:
   miserére nobis.
Agnus Dei, qui tollis peccáta mundi:
   dona nobis pacem.**

Quod etiam pluries repeti potest, si fractio panis protrahitur. Ultima tamen vice dicitur: **dona nobis pacem.**

COMMUNIO

Sacerdos deinde, manibus iunctis, dicit secreto:
Dómine Iesu Christe, Fili Dei vivi, qui ex voluntáte Patris, cooperánte Spíritu Sancto, per mortem tuam mundum vivificásti: líbera me per hoc sacrosánctum Corpus et Sánguinem tuum ab ómnibus iniquitátibus meis et univérsis malis: et fac me tuis semper inhærére mandátis, et a te numquam separári permittas.

Sacerdos genuflectit, accipit hostiam, eamque aliquantulum elevatam super patenam tenens, ad populum versus, clara voce dicit:
Ecce Agnus Dei, ecce qui tollit peccáta mundi. Beáti qui ad cenam Agni vocáti sunt.

Et una cum populo semel subdit:

**Dómine, non sum dignus ut intres sub tectum meum:
sed tantum dic verbo, et sanábitur ánima mea.**

The people answer:

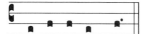

And al-so with you.

Then the deacon (or the priest) may add:

Let us offer each other the sign of peace.

All make an appropriate sign of peace, according to local custom. The priest gives the sign of peace to the deacon or the minister.

BREAKING OF THE BREAD

He then takes the host and breaks it over the paten. He places a small piece in the chalice, saying inaudibly: *May this mingling of the body and blood of our Lord Jesus Christ bring eternal life to us who receive it.*

Meanwhile the following is sung or said:

(For musical settings of the Agnus Dei see # 254, 259, 264, 268, 272.)

**Lamb of God, you take away the sins of the world:
      have mercy on us.
Lamb of God, you take away the sins of the world:
      have mercy on us.
Lamb of God, you take away the sins of the world:
      grant us peace.**

This may be repeated until the breaking of the bread is finished, but the last phrase is always **Grant us peace.**

COMMUNION

Then the priest joins his hands and says inaudibly:

Lord Jesus Christ, Son of the living God, by the will of the Father and the work of the Holy Spirit your death brought life to the world. By your holy body and blood free me from all my sins and from every evil. Keep me faithful to your teaching, and never let me be parted from you.

The priest genuflects. Taking the host, he raises it slightly over the paten and, facing the people, says aloud: *This is the Lamb of God who takes away the sins of the world. Happy are those who are called to his supper.*

He adds, once only, with the people:

**Lord, I am not worthy to receive you,
but only say the word and I shall be healed.**

Et sacerdos, ad altare versus, secreto dicit:
Corpus Christi custódiat me in vitam ætérnam.
Et reverenter sumit Corpus Christi.

Deinde accipit calicem et secreto dicit:
Sanguis Christi custódiat me in vitam ætérnam.
Et reverenter sumit Sanguinem Christi.

Postea accipit patenam vel pyxidem, accedit ad communicandos, et hostiam parum elevatam unicuique eorum ostendit, dicens: *Corpus Christi.*

Communicandus respondet: **Amen**.

Et communicatur. Eo modo agit et diaconus, si sacram Communionem distribuit.

ANTIPHONA AD COMMUNIONEM

Dum sacerdos sumit Corpus Christi, incipit cantus ad Communionem.

Distributione Communionis expleta, sacerdos vel diaconus vel acolythus purificat patenam super calicem et ipsum calicem. Dum purificationem peragit, sacerdos dicit secreto:
Quod ore súmpsimus, Dómine, pura mente capiámus, et de múnere temporáli fiat nobis remédium sempiternum.

SACRUM SILENTIUM

Tunc sacerdos ad sedem redire potest. Pro opportunitate sacrum silentium, per aliquod temporis spatium, servari, vel psalmus aut canticum laudis proferri potest.

ORATIO POST COMMUNIONEM

Deinde, stans ad sedem vel ad altare, sacerdos dicit:

O-ré-mus.

Et omnes una cum sacerdote per aliquod temporis spatium in silentio orant, nisi silentium iam præcesserit. Deindem sacerdos, manibus extensis, dicit orationem post Communionem.

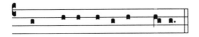

.. per Christum Domi-num nostrum.

Populus in fine acclamat:

Amen.

Facing the altar, the priest says inaudibly:
May the body of Christ bring me to everlasting life.
He reverently consumes the body of Christ.

Then he takes the chalice and says inaudibly:
May the blood of Christ bring me to everlasting life.
He reverently drinks the blood of Christ.

After this he takes the paten or other vessel and goes to the communicants. He takes a host for each one, raises it a little, and shows it, saying: *The body of Christ.*

The communicant answers: **Amen**.
and receives communion. When a deacon gives communion, he does the same.

COMMUNION SONG   *(A communion hymn may be sung instead.)*
While the priest receives the body of Christ, the communion song is begun.

The vessels are cleansed by the priest or deacon or acolyte after the communion or after Mass, if possible at the side table (General Instruction, no. 238). Meanwhile he says inaudibly:
Lord, may I receive these gifts in purity of heart.
May they bring me healing and strength, now and for ever.

PERIOD OF SILENCE
Then the priest may return to the chair. A period of silence may now be observed, or a psalm or song of praise may be sung.

PRAYER AFTER COMMUNION
Then, standing at the chair or at the altar, the priest sings or says:

Let us pray.
Priest and people pray in silence for a while, unless a period of silence has already been observed. Then the priest extends his hands and sings or says the prayer after communion.

...for ev - er and ev-er.

At the end of which the people respond:

Amen.

RITUS CONCLUSIONIS

Sequuntur, si habendæ sint, breves annuntiationes ad populum.

BENEDICTIO

Deinde fit dimissio. Sacerdos, versus ad populum, extendens manus, dicit:

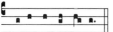

Dómi-nus vo-bís-cum.

Populus respondet:

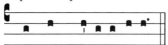

Et cum spí-ri-tu tu-o.

Sacerdos benedicit populum, dicens:

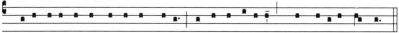

Bene-dí-cat vos omní-po-tens De-us, Pa-ter, et Fi- li- us, ✠ et Spí-ri-tus Sanctus.

Populus respondet:

Amen.

(Quibusdam diebus vel occasionibus, huic formulæ benedictionis præmittitur, iuxta rubricas, alia formula benedictionis sollemnior, vel oratio super populum.)

DIMISSIO

Deinde diaconus, vel ipse sacerdos,
manibus iunctis, ad populum versus dicit:

Populus respondet:

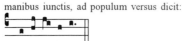

I-te mis-sa est.

De-o grá- ti-as.

Vel:

Sacerdos: *I - te missa est, al-le-lu-ia, alle -   lu - ia.*
Populus: De-o grá-ti - as al-le-lu-ia, alle -   lu - ia.

Deinde sacerdos altare osculo de more veneratur, ut initio. Facta denique debita reverentia cum ministris, recedit.

Si qua actio liturgica immediate sequatur, ritus dimissionis omittuntur.

CONCLUDING RITE

If there are any brief announcements, they are made at this time.

BLESSING

The dismissal follows. Facing the people, the priest extends his hands and sings or says:

The Lord be with you.

The people answer:

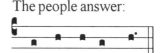

And al-so with you.

The priest blesses the people with these words:

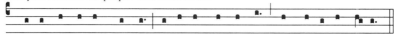

May al-might-y God bless you, the Fa-ther, and the Son, ✠ *and the Ho-ly Spir-it.*

The people answer:

Amen.

On certain days or occasions another more solemn form of blessing or prayer over the people may be used as the rubrics direct.

DISMISSAL

The deacon (or the priest),
with hands joined, sings or says:

The people answer:

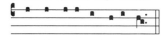

B. The Mass is ended, go in peace.

Thanks be to God.

A. Go in the peace of Christ.

C. Go in peace to love and serve the Lord.

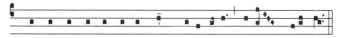

Priest: *The Mass is end - ed go in peace, al-le-lu-ia, al-le -   lu - ia.*

People: **Thanks be to God, al-le-lu-ia, al-le   lu - ia.**

The priest kisses the altar as at the beginning. Then he makes the customary reverence with the ministers and leaves.

If any liturgical service follows immediately, the rite of dismissal is omitted.

100

Asperges me, Domine

All:

A - spér - ges me, * Dó - mi - ne, hys- só - po,

et mun- dá - bor: la - vá - bis me, et su - per

Canto or Choir only:
Psalm (50) 51:7

ni - vem de - al - bá - bor. Mi - se - ré - re

me - i, De - us, se - cún - dum ma- gnam mi- se- ri -

cór - di- am tu - am. Gló - ri - a Pa- tri, et

Fí - li - o, et Spí - ri - tu - i San - cto.

Si - cut e - rat in prin- cí - pi - o, et nunc, et sem -

per, et in saé- cu- la sae- cu - ló- rum. A - men.

Repeat: *Asperges me*

TEXT: Psalm (50) 51: 7
MELODY: Plainchant, Mode VII, 13th century
HARMONIZATION: Jean-Hébert Desrocquettes, O.S.B., copyright by Ralph Jusko Publications

ASPERGES ME
Irregular

Sprinkle me, O Lord

101

All:

Sprin - kle me, ✳ O Lord, with hys - sop, and I shall be pu - ri - fied; wash me, and I shall be whi - ter than snow.

Cantor or Choir only:
Psalm 51:7

Have mercy on me, O God, according to thy stead - fast love;

TEXT: *Asperges me,* Psalm (50) 51: 7, translated by the International Committee on English in the Liturgy,
   copyright © by International Committee on English in the Liturgy,
   Psalm (50) 51:7 from the Revised Standard Version
MELODY: Plainchant, Mode III, by a Cistercian monk
HARMONIZATION: A Cistercian monk

ENGLISH ASPERGES
Irregular

102

Vidi aquam

All:

Vi - di a - quam * e - gre - di - én - tem de tem - plo, a lá - te - re dex - tro, al - le - lú - ia: et om - nes ad quos per - vé - nit a - qua i - sta, sal - vi fac - ti sunt, et di - cent, al - le - lú - ia, al - le - lú - ia.

Cantor or Choir only:
Psalm (117) 118:1

Con - fi - té - mi - ni Dó - mi - no quó - ni - am bo - nus: quó - ni - am in saé - cu - lum mi - se - ri - cór - di - a e - jus.

Gló - ri - a Pa - tri, et Fí - li - o, et Spí - ri - tu - i

San - cto. Si - cut e - rat in prin-cí - pi - o et nunc,

et sem - per, et in saé-cu-la sae-cu - ló - rum. A- men.

Repeat: *Vidi aquam*

TEXT: Ezekiel 47:1
MELODY: Plainchant, 10th century, Mode VIII
HARMONIZATION: Jean-Hébert Desrocquettes, O.S.B., copyright 1958 © by Ralph Jusko Publications

VIDI AQUAM
Irregular

SPRINKLING RITE (EASTER SEASON)

I saw water
103

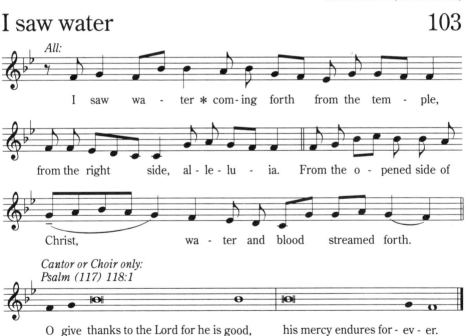

All:

I saw wa - ter * com- ing forth from the tem - ple,

from the right side, al - le - lu - ia. From the o - pened side of

Christ, wa - ter and blood streamed forth.

Cantor or Choir only:
Psalm (117) 118:1

O give thanks to the Lord for he is good, his mercy endures for - ev - er.

TEXT: *Vidi Aquam*, Ezekiel 47:1, translated by the International Committee on English in the Liturgy,
copyright © by International Committee on English in the Liturgy,
Psalm (117) 118:1 from the Revised Standard Version
MELODY: Plainchant, Mode VIII, A Cistercian monk
HARMONIZATION: A Cistercian monk

ENGLISH VIDI AQUAM

110   Memorial Acclamation

Christ has died, Christ is ris - en, Christ will come a - gain.

Mass of St. Theresa, Calvert Shenk (b. 1940). Copyright © 1997 by Calvert Shenk.

111   Amen

A - men. A - men. A - men.

Mass of St. Theresa, Calvert Shenk (b. 1940). Copyright © 1997 by Calvert Shenk.

112   Memorial Acclamation

Christ has died, Christ is ris- en, Christ will come a - gain.

A Community Mass, Richard Proulx (b. 1937). Copyright © 1970 by G.I.A. Publications, Inc.

113   Amen

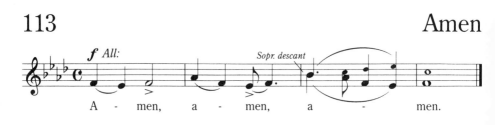

A - men, a - men, a - men.

A Community Mass, Richard Proulx (b. 1937). Copyright © 1970 by G.I.A. Publications, Inc.

ORDINARIES

MISSA
"JUBILATE DEO"

KYRIE *from Mass XVI* 200

XI-XIII. cent.

III.

Ky-ri- e   e - lé - i- son. *(bis)* Chri-ste e-lé- i- son. *(bis)* Ký - ri - e   e - lé - i - son.   Ký - ri - e   e - lé - i - son.

GLORIA *from Mass VIII* 201

XVI. cent.

v.

Ló - ri - a in ex - cél - sis De - o.   Et in ter - ra pax ho- mi-ni-bus bo-nae vo-lun - tá - tis.   Lau-dá -mus te.   Be-ne-dí - ci-mus te.   A - do- rá -mus te.   Glo - ri-fi-cá -mus te.   Grá - ti - as á -gi- mus ti - bi   prop-ter ma- gnam gló - ri- am tu - am.   Dó -mi-ne De- us, Rex cae- lés- tis, De- us Pa- ter om-ní - po-tens.

This is a composite of simple and familiar chants of the ordinary of the Mass included in the booklet *Jubilate Deo* which was issued on April 14, 1974, by Pope Paul VI for the purpose of promoting a "minimum repertoire of plain chant" among Catholics.

Dó- mi- ne Fi - li u - ni- gé- ni- te Ie- su Chri- ste. Dó- mi- ne

De- us, Ag-nus De - i, Fí - li - us Pa - tris. Qui tol-lis pec- cá -

ta mun -di, mi -se -ré - re no -bis. Qui tol - lis pec - cá - ta mun -

di, su- scí- pe de- pre- ca- ti- ó- nem nos- tram. Qui se- des ad

déx- te- ram Pa- tris, mi- se- ré- re no- bis. Quó- ni- am tu so- lus

sanc- tus. Tu so- lus Dó- mi- nus. Tu so- lus Al- tís- si- mus,

Ie- su Chri- ste. Cum Sanc- to Spí- ri- tu, in gló- ri- a De- i

Pa - tris. A - men.

XVII. cent.

Re-do in u-num De - um, Patrem om-ni-po-tén-tem,

fac-tó - rem cae-li et ter-rae, vi-si-bí-li-um óm - ni-um, et in-

vi-si-bí - li-um. Et in u-num Dó-mi-num Ie - sum Chri-stum,

Fí-li-um De-i u-ni-gé-ni-tum. Et ex Pa-tre na - tum an-te

óm-ni-a saé - cu-la. De-um de De-o, lú-men de lú-mi-ne,

De-um ve-rum de De-o ve-ro. Gé-ni-tum, non fa - ctum, con-

sub-stan-ti-á-lem Pa-tri : per quem óm-ni-a fa - cta sunt. Qui

prop-ter nos hó-mi-nes, et prop-ter nos-tram sa-lú-tem de-scén-

dit de cae-lis. Et in-car-ná-tus est de Spí-ri-tu San-cto ex

Ma-rí-a Vír-gi-ne : Et ho-mo fa-ctus est. Cru - ci - fi - xus

ét - i - am pro no-bis : sub Pón-ti-o Pi-lá-to pas-sus, et se-púl -

tus est. Et re - sur - ré - xit tér-ti - a di - e, se-cún-dum Scrip -

tú - ras. Et asc-én-dit in cae-lum : se-det ad déx-te-ram Pa -

tris. Et í-te-rum ven-tú-rus est cum gló-ri-a, iu-di-cá-re

vi-vos et mór-tu-os : cu-ius reg-ni non e-rit fi - nis. Et in

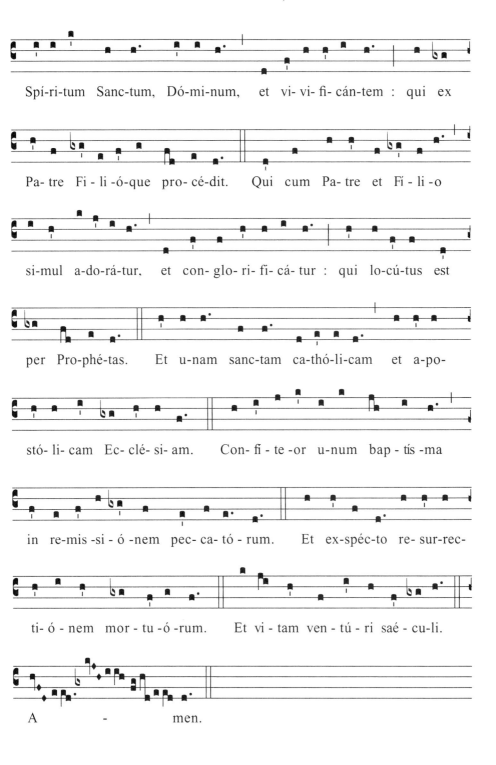

Spí-ri-tum Sanc-tum, Dó-mi-num, et vi- vi- fi- cán-tem : qui ex

Pa- tre Fi - li -ó-que pro- cé-dit. Qui cum Pa- tre et Fí - li -o

si-mul a-do-rá-tur, et con- glo- ri- fi- cá- tur : qui lo-cú-tus est

per Pro-phé-tas. Et u-nam sanc-tam ca-thó-li-cam et a-po-

stó- li- cam Ec- clé- si- am. Con- fí - te -or u-num bap - tís -ma

in re-mis -si - ó -nem pec- ca- tó - rum. Et ex-spéc-to re- sur-rec-

ti- ó - nem mor - tu -ó -rum. Et vi - tam ven - tú - ri saé - cu-li.

A - men.

203 SANCTUS *from Mass XVIII*

XIII. cent.

S Anc-tus, * Sanc-tus, Sanc-tus Dó-mi-nus De-us Sá -

ba-oth. Ple-ni sunt cae-li et ter-ra gló-ri-a tu-a. Ho-sán-na

in ex-cél-sis. Be-ne-díc-tus qui ve-nit in nó-mi-ne Dó-mi-ni.

Ho-sán-na in ex-cél-sis.

204 AGNUS DEI *from Mass XVIII*

XII. cent

A g - nus De - i, * qui tol-lis pec-cá-ta mun-di : mi-se-

ré-re no - bis. Ag-nus De - i, * qui tol-lis pec-cá-ta mun-di :

mi-se-ré-re no- bis. Ag-nus De -i, * qui tol-lis pec-cá-ta mun-

di : do-na no-bis pa-cem.

MISSA
"PRIMITIVA"

KYRIE *from Mass XVI* 205

XI-XIII. cent.

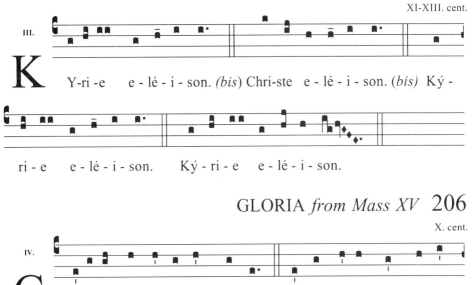

Ký-ri-e e-lé-i-son. *(bis)* Chri-ste e-lé-i-son. *(bis)* Ký-ri-e e-lé-i-son. Ký-ri-e e-lé-i-son.

GLORIA *from Mass XV* 206

X. cent.

Ló-ri-a in ex-cél-sis De-o. Et in ter-ra pax ho-mí-ni-bus bo-nae vo-lun-tá-tis. Lau-dá-mus te. Be-ne-dí-ci-mus te. A-do-rá-mus te. Glo-ri-fi-cá-mus te. Grá-ti-as á-gi-mus ti-bi-prop-ter mag-nam gló-ri-am tu-am. Dó-mi-ne De-us, Rex cae-lés-

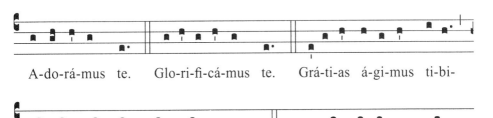

This is another composite Mass, somewhat different from the "Missa Jubilate Deo," which was recommended by Pope Pius XII in the document *Sacred Music and the Sacred Liturgy,* which was issued September 3, 1958. It was probably this Mass that the Fathers of the Second Vatican Council had in mind when they said, "steps should be taken to ensure that the faithful are able to say or sing together in Latin those parts of the ordinary of the Mass which pertain to them" (Constitution on the Sacred Liturgy, no. 54).

tis, De-us Pa-ter om-ní-po - tens. Dó-mi-ne Fi-li u-ni-gé-

ni-te Ie-su Chri-ste. Dó-mi-ne De - us, Ag-nus De-i, Fí-

li-us Pa-tris. Qui tol-lis pec-cá-ta mun-di, mi-se-ré-re no-bis.

Qui tol-lis pec-cá-ta mun-di, sú-sci-pe de-pre-ca-ti-ó-nem nos-

tram. Qui se-des ad déx-te-ram Pa-tris, mi-se-ré-re no-bis.

Quó-ni-am tu so-lus san-ctus. Tu so-lus Dó-mi-nus. Tu so-lus

Al-tís-si-mus, Ie-su Chri-ste. Cum Sanc-to Spí-ri-tu, in gló-

ri-a De-i Pa - tris. A - men.

XI. cent.

IV.

C Re-do in u-num De-um, Pa-trem om-ni-po-tén-tem, fac-

tó - rem cae-li et ter-rae, vi-si-bí-li-um óm - ni - um, et in-

vi-si-bí-li-um. Et in u-num Dó-mi-num Ie - sum Chri-stum,

Fí-li-um De-i u-ni-gé-ni-tum. Et ex Pa-tre na-tum an-te

óm-ni-a saé-cu -la. De-um de De-o, lu-men de lú-mi-ne,

De-um ve-rum de De-o ve-ro. Gé-ni-tum, non fac-tum, con-sub-

stan-ti-á-lem Pa-tri : per quem óm-ni-a fa - cta sunt. Qui prop-

ter nos hó-mi-nes, et prop-ter no-stram sa-lú-tem de-scén-dit de

cae-lis. Et in-car-ná-tus est de Spí-ri-tu San-cto ex Ma-rí-a

Vír-gi-ne : Et ho-mo fa-ctus est. Cru-ci-fi-xus ét - i - am pro

no-bis : sub Pón-ti-o Pi-lá-to pas-sus, et se-púl-tus est. Et

re-sur-ré-xit tér-ti-a di-e, se-cún-dum Scrip-tú-ras. Et asc-én-

dit in cae-lum : se-det ad déx-te-ram Pa-tris. Et í-te-rum ven-

tú-rus est cum gló-ri-a, iu-di-cá-re vi-vos et mór-tu-os :

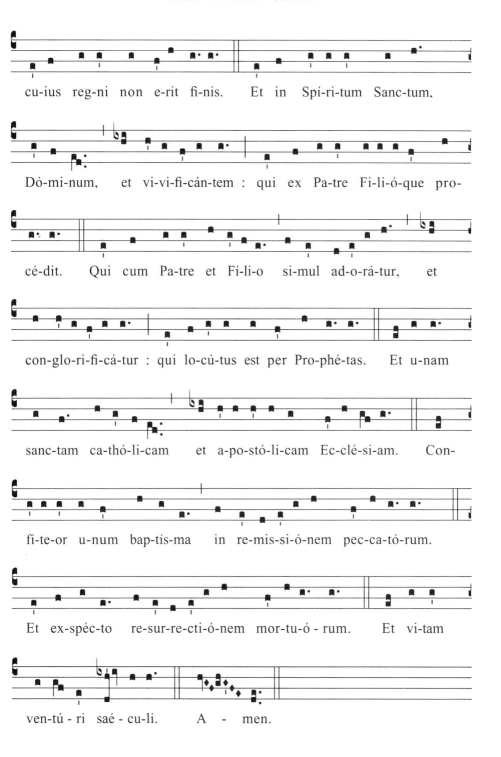

cu-ius reg-ni non e-rit fi-nis. Et in Spí-ri-tum Sanc-tum,

Dó-mi-num, et vi-vi-fi-cán-tem : qui ex Pa-tre Fi-li-ó-que pro-

cé-dit. Qui cum Pa-tre et Fí-li-o si-mul ad-o-rá-tur, et

con-glo-ri-fi-cá-tur : qui lo-cú-tus est per Pro-phé-tas. Et u-nam

sanc-tam ca-thó-li-cam et a-po-stó-li-cam Ec-clé-si-am. Con-

fí-te-or u-num bap-tís-ma in re-mis-si-ó-nem pec-ca-tó-rum.

Et ex-spéc-to re-sur-re-cti-ó-nem mor-tu-ó - rum. Et vi-tam

ven-tú - ri saé - cu-li. A - men.

208 SANCTUS *from Mass XVIII*

XIII. cent.

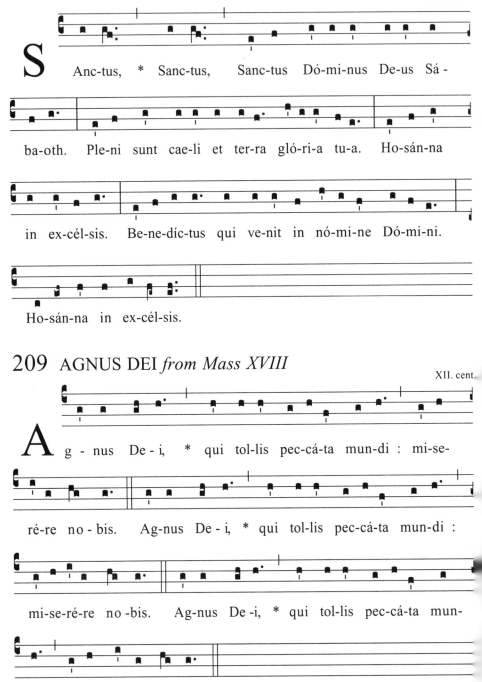

Sanc-tus, * Sanc-tus, Sanc-tus Dó-mi-nus De-us Sá-ba-oth. Ple-ni sunt cae-li et ter-ra gló-ri-a tu-a. Ho-sán-na in ex-cél-sis. Be-ne-díc-tus qui ve-nit in nó-mi-ne Dó-mi-ni. Ho-sán-na in ex-cél-sis.

209 AGNUS DEI *from Mass XVIII*

XII. cent.

Ag-nus De-i, * qui tol-lis pec-cá-ta mun-di : mi-se-ré-re no-bis. Ag-nus De-i, * qui tol-lis pec-cá-ta mun-di : mi-se-ré-re no-bis. Ag-nus De-i, * qui tol-lis pec-cá-ta mun-di : do-na no-bis pa-cem.

MISSA
DE ANGELIS
(Mass VIII)

XV-XVI. cent.

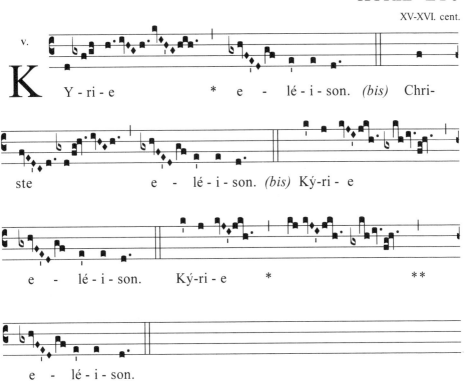

v.

K Y - ri - e   *   e - lé - i - son. *(bis)* Chri-

ste   e - lé - i - son. *(bis)* Ký-ri - e

e - lé - i - son.   Ký-ri - e   *   **

e - lé - i - son.

XVI. cent.

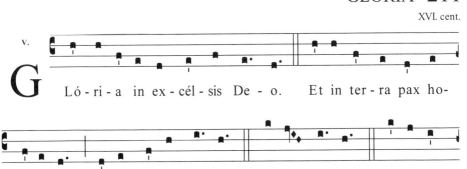

v.

G Ló - ri - a in ex - cél - sis De - o.   Et in ter - ra pax ho-

mi-ni-bus bo-nae vo-lun - tá - tis.   Lau-dá -mus te.   Be-ne-dí -

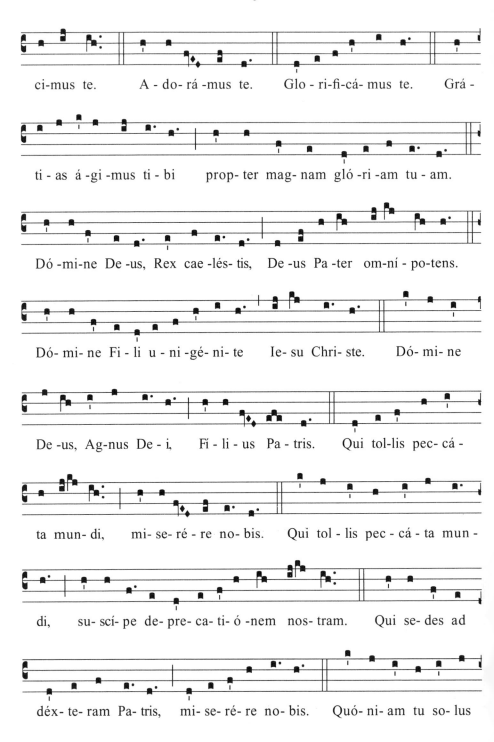

Missa de Angelis, Gloria

ci-mus te. A - do- rá -mus te. Glo - ri-fi-cá- mus te. Grá -

ti - as á -gi -mus ti - bi prop- ter mag- nam gló -ri -am tu - am.

Dó -mi-ne De -us, Rex cae -lés- tis, De -us Pa -ter om-ní - po-tens.

Dó- mi- ne Fi - li u - ni -gé- ni- te Ie- su Chri- ste. Dó- mi - ne

De -us, Ag-nus De - i, Fí - li - us Pa - tris. Qui tol-lis pec- cá -

ta mun- di, mi- se- ré - re no- bis. Qui tol - lis pec - cá - ta mun -

di, su- scí- pe de- pre- ca- ti- ó -nem nos- tram. Qui se- des ad

déx- te- ram Pa- tris, mi- se- ré- re no- bis. Quó- ni- am tu so- lus

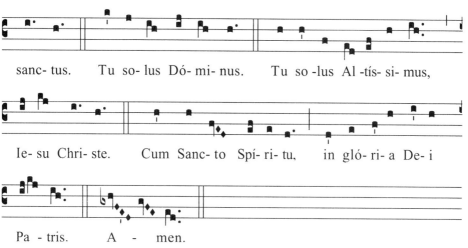

sanc- tus.   Tu so- lus Dó- mi- nus.   Tu so -lus Al -tís- si- mus,

Ie- su Chri- ste.   Cum Sanc- to Spí- ri- tu,   in gló- ri- a De- i

Pa - tris.   A - men.

SANCTUS 212

(XI) XII. cent.

VI.

S Anc - tus, * Sanc-tus, Sanc - tus Dó - mi - nus

De - us Sá - ba - oth.   Ple-ni sunt cae - li et

ter - ra gló - ri - a tu - a.   Ho-sán-na in ex-cél - sis

Be-ne-díc - tus qui ve - nit   in nó-mi-ne Dó -mi-ni.   Ho-

sán - na in ex-cél - sis.

213 AGNUS DEI

XV. cent.

VI.

Agnus Dei, * qui tol-lis pec-cá-ta mun-di : mi-se-ré-re no-bis. Ag-nus De - i, * qui tol - lis pec-cá-ta mun-di : mi-se-ré - re no - bis. Ag - nus De - i, * qui tol-lis pec-cá-ta mun-di : do-na no - bis pa-cem.

MISSA
CUM JUBILO
(Mass IX)

XII. cent.

XI. cent.

VII.

Ló - ri - a in ex - cél - sis De - o. Et in ter - ra pax ho-

mí-ni - bus bo-nae vo-lun-tá - tis. Lau-dá - mus te. Be-ne-

dí-cí-mus te. A-do - rá - mus te. Glo - rí - fi - cá - mus te.

Grá-ti-as á-gi-mus ti - bi prop-ter mag-nam gló - ri - am tu - am.

Dó-mi-ne De - us, Rex cae - lés-tis, De - us Pa - ter om - ní-

po - tens. Dó-mi-ne Fi-li u-ni-gé - ni-te Ie-su Chri - ste.

Dó - mi-ne Deus, Ag - nus De - i, Fí - li - us Pa - tris. Qui

tol-lis pec-cá-ta mun-dí, mi-se-ré - re no-bis. Qui tol-lis pec-

cá - ta mun - di, sú - sci-pe de-pre-ca - ti - ó - nem nos-tram.

Qui se-des ad déxteram Pa-tris, mi-se-ré-re no-bis. Quó-ni-am

tu so-lus sanc-tus. Tu so-lus Dó-mi-nus. Tu so-lus Al-tís-si-

mus, Ie-su Chri - ste. Cum San-cto Spí-ri-tu, in gló-ri-a

De - i Pa - tris. A - men.

SANCTUS 216

XIV. cent.

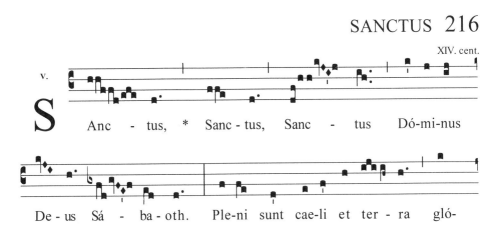

v.

S Anc - tus, * Sanc - tus, Sanc - tus Dó-mi-nus

De - us Sá - ba - oth. Ple-ni sunt cae-li et ter - ra gló-

ri - a tu - a. Ho-sán - na in ex-cél - sis. Be - ne - díc - tus

qui ve - nit in nó - mi - ne Dó - mi - ni. Ho -

sán - na in ex - cél - sis.

217 AGNUS DEI

(X) XIII. cent.

v.

A g - nus De - i, * qui tol - lis pec-cá-ta mun-

di : mi - se - ré - re no - bis. Ag-nus De - i, * qui tol-

lis pec-cá - ta mun-di : mi - se - ré - re no - bis. Ag-nus

De - i, * qui tol - lis pec-cá-ta mun - di : do - na

no - bis pa - cem.

MISSA
ORBIS FACTOR
(Mass XI)

KYRIE (B) 218

(X) XIV-XVI. cent.

K Y - ri - e * e - lé - i - son. *(bis)* Chri - ste
e - lé - i - son. *(bis)* Ký - ri - e e - lé - i - son.
Ký - ri - e e - lé - i - son.

SANCTUS 219

XI. cent.

S Anc - tus, * Sanc - tus, Sanc - tus Dó - mi - nus De - us
Sá - ba-oth. Ple - ni sunt cae - li et ter - ra gló - ri - a
tu - a. Ho-sán-na in ex - cél-sis. Be-ne-dí-ctus qui

ve - nit   in   nó - mi - ne   Dó - mi - ni.   Ho-sán-na

in   ex - cél-sis.

220 AGNUS DEI

XIV. cent.

I.

Ag - nus De - i, * qui tol-lis pec - cá - ta mun-di :   mi-

se-ré - re no - bis.   Ag-nus De - i, * qui tol - lis   pec-cá-ta

mun - di :   mi-se-ré-re no -bis.   Ag-nus De -i, * qui tol-lis

pec - cá - ta mun-di :   do-na no-bis pa-cem.

MISSA
PRO DEFUNCTIS
(Mass XVIII)

KYRIE (B) 221

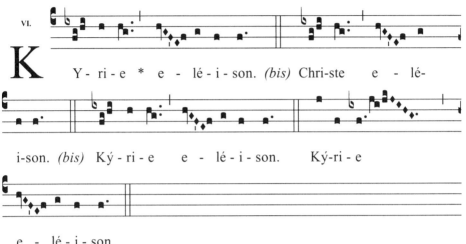

VI.

K Y - ri - e * e - lé - i - son. *(bis)* Chri-ste e - lé-

i-son. *(bis)* Ký - ri - e e - lé - i - son. Ký-ri - e

e - lé - i - son.

SANCTUS 222

XIII. cent.

S Anc-tus, * Sanc-tus, Sanc-tus Dó-mi-nus De-us Sá -

ba-oth. Ple-ni sunt cae-li et ter-ra gló-ri-a tu-a. Ho-sán-na

in ex-cél-sis. Be-ne-díc-tus qui ve-nit in nó-mi-ne Dó-mi-ni.

Ho-sán-na in ex-cél-sis.

223 AGNUS DEI

XII. cent.

Ag - nus De - i, * qui tol-lis pec-cá-ta mun-di : mi-se-

ré-re no - bis. Ag-nus De - i, * qui tol-lis pec-cá-ta mun-di :

mi-se-ré-re no -bis. Ag-nus De -i, * qui tol-lis pec-cá-ta mun-

di : do-na no-bis pa-cem.

ENGLISH CHANT MASS

by Theodore Marier

KYRIE **250**

Cel., Cantor or Choir:
Lord, have mer - cy.

All:
Lord, have mer - cy.

Cel., Cantor or Choir:
Christ, have mer - cy.

All:
Christ, have mer - cy.

Cel., Cantor or Choir:
Lord, have mer - cy.

All:
Lord, have mer - cy.

GLORIA **251**

Organ

Celebrant, Cantor or Choir:
Glo - ry to God in the high - est,

All:
and peace to his peo - ple on earth.

Lord, God, heav-en-ly King, al-might-y God and Fa - ther,

we wor - ship you, we give you thanks,

we praise you for your glo - ry. Lord Je - sus Christ,

on - ly Son of the Fa - ther, Lord God, Lamb of God,

you take a - way the sin of the world : have mer - cy on us;

you are seat - ed at the right hand of the Fa - ther :

re - ceive our prayer. For you a - lone are the Ho - ly One,

you a - lone are the Lord, you a - lone are the Most High, Je - sus Christ,

with the Ho - ly Spir - it, in the glo - ry of God the

Fa - ther. A - men, a - men.

252 CREDO

Organ

Cantor or Celebrant:

We be - lieve in one God,

All:

the Fa - ther, the Al - might - y, mak - er of

English Chant Mass, Credo

heav - en and earth, of all that is seen and un - seen.

We be-lieve in one Lord, Je - sus Christ, the on - ly Son of God, e - ter-nal - ly be-got-ten of the Fa - ther, God from God, Light from Light, true God from true God, be - got - ten, not made, one in Be - ing with the Fa - ther. Through him all things were made. For us men and for our sal - va - tion he came down from heav - en :

All bow during the following two lines

by the power of the Ho - ly Spir - it he was born of the Vir - gin Ma - ry, and be - came man.

English Chant Mass, Credo

For our sake he was cru-ci-fied un-der Pon-tius Pi-late; he suf-fered, died, and was bur-ied. On the third day he rose a-gain in ful-fil-ment of the Scrip-tures; he as-cend-ed in-to heav-en and is seat-ed at the right hand of the Fa-ther. He will come a-gain in glo-ry to judge the liv-ing and the dead, and his king-dom will have no end. We be-lieve in the Ho-ly Spir-it, the Lord, the giv-er of life, who pro-ceeds from the Fa-ther and the Son. With the Fa-ther and the Son he is

English Chant Mass, Credo

wor - shiped and glo - ri - fied. He has spo - ken through the

Proph - ets. We be - lieve in one ho - ly

ca - tho - lic and ap - os - tol - ic Church. We ac - knowl-edge one

bap - tism for the for - give - ness of sins.

We look for the res - ur - rec - tion of the dead,

and the life of the world to come.

A - men, a - men.

SANCTUS 253

All:

Ho - ly, ho - ly, ho - ly Lord, God of power and might,

heaven and earth are full of your glo - ry. Ho - san - na

in the high - est. Bless-ed is he who comes in the name

of the Lord. Ho - san - na in the high - est.

254 AGNUS DEI

Cantor: Lamb of God, *All:* you take

a - way the sins of the world: have mer - cy on us.

Cantor: Lamb of God, *All:* you take a - way the sins of the

world: have mer - cy on us. *Cantor:* Lamb of God, *All:* you take

a - way the sins of the world: grant us peace.

ENGLISH "MISSA PRIMITIVA"

by a Cistercian monk

KYRIE 255

Lord, have mer - cy. Lord, have mer - cy.

Christ, have mer - cy. Christ, have mer - cy.

Lord, have mer - cy. Lord, have mer - cy.

GLORIA 256

Glo-ry to God in the high-est, ∗ and peace to his peo-ple on earth.

Lord God, heav-en-ly King, al-might-y God and Fa - ther,

we wor-ship you, we give you thanks, we praise you for your glo - ry.

Lord Je - sus Christ, on - ly Son of the Fa - ther,

Lord God, Lamb of God, you take a - way the sin of the world:

have mer-cy on us; you are seat-ed at the right hand of the Fa - ther:

re - ceive our prayer. For you a - lone are the Ho - ly One,

you a-lone are the Lord, you a-lone are the Most High, Je-sus Christ,

with the Ho-ly Spir - it, in the glo-ry of God the Fa - ther. A - men.

257 CREDO

We be-lieve in one God, the Fa - ther, the Al-might-y,

mak-er of heav-en and earth, of all that is seen and un - seen.

We be-lieve in one Lord, Je - sus Christ, the on-ly Son of God,

e - ter - nal-ly be-got-ten of the Fa-ther, God from God, Light

from Light, true God from true God, be-got - ten, not

made, one in Be-ing with the Fa - ther. Through him all things were made.

English "Missa Primitiva", Credo

For us men and for our sal-va-tion he came down from heav-en:

by the pow-er of the Ho-ly Spir-it, he was born of the

Vir-gin Ma-ry, and be-came man. For our sake he was cru-ci-fied

un - der Pon-tius Pi - late; he suf-fered, died, and was bur - ied.

On the third day he rose a-gain in ful - fil - ment of the Scrip-tures;

he as-cend-ed in - to heav-en and is seat - ed at the right hand of the

Fa-ther. He will come a-gain in glo - ry to judge the liv-ing

and the dead, and his king-dom will have no end. We be-lieve in the

Ho - ly Spir - it, the Lord, the giv-er of life, who pro-ceeds

from the Fa-ther and the Son. With the Fa-ther and the Son he is wor-shiped and

glo-ri-fied. He has spo-ken through the Proph-ets. We be-lieve in one ho - ly

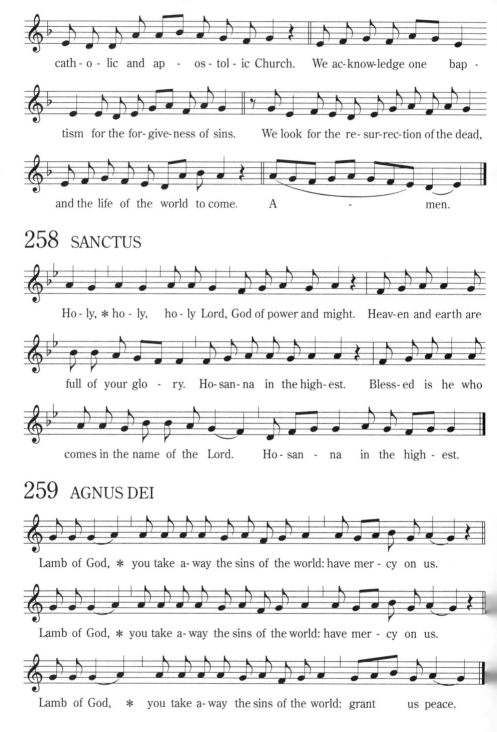

cath - o - lic and ap - os - tol - ic Church. We ac-know-ledge one bap -

tism for the for- give-ness of sins. We look for the re- sur-rec-tion of the dead,

and the life of the world to come. A - men.

258 SANCTUS

Ho - ly, * ho - ly, ho - ly Lord, God of power and might. Heav-en and earth are

full of your glo - ry. Ho-san-na in the high-est. Bless-ed is he who

comes in the name of the Lord. Ho - san - na in the high - est.

259 AGNUS DEI

Lamb of God, * you take a- way the sins of the world: have mer - cy on us.

Lamb of God, * you take a- way the sins of the world: have mer - cy on us.

Lamb of God, * you take a- way the sins of the world: grant us peace.

PSALM-TONE MASS

by Kurt Poterack

KYRIE 260

GLORIA 261

Based on Tone 1 (endings f and D²), copyright © 1997 by Kurt Poterack

262 CREDO

We be - lieve in one God, the Fa- ther, the Al - might- y,

maker of heaven and earth, of all that is seen and un - seen.

We be - lieve in one Lord, Jesus Christ, the only
Son of God, eternally begotten of the Fa- ther, God from God,

Light from Light, true God from true God,

begotten, not made, one in Being
with the Father. Through him all things were made.

For us men and for our salvation he came down from heav - en:

by the power of the Holy Spirit
he was born of the Virgin Mary, and be - came man.

For our sake he was crucified
under Pontius Pilate; he suffered, died, and was bur - ied.

Psalm-Tone Mass, Credo

On the third day he rose again in ful - fil - ment of the Scrip - tures;

he as - cended into heaven and is seated at the right hand of the Fa - ther.

He will come again in glory to judge the
living and the dead, and his kingdom will have no end.

We be - lieve in the Holy Spirit, the Lord, the
giver of life, who proceeds from the Fa - ther and the Son.

With the Father and the Son he is
worshiped and glorified. He has spo - ken through the Pro - phets.

We be - lieve in one holy catholic and apostolic Church.
We acknowledge one baptism for the for - give- ness of sins.

We look for the resurrection A - men.
of the dead, and the life of the world to come.

263 SANCTUS

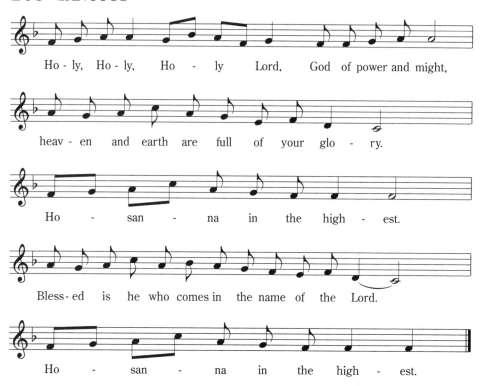

Ho - ly, Ho - ly, Ho - ly Lord, God of power and might,

heav - en and earth are full of your glo - ry.

Ho - san - na in the high - est.

Bless- ed is he who comes in the name of the Lord.

Ho - san - na in the high - est.

264 AGNUS DEI

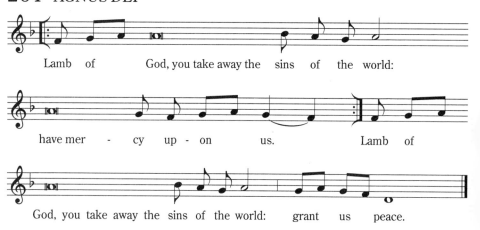

Lamb of God, you take away the sins of the world:

have mer - cy up - on us. Lamb of

God, you take away the sins of the world: grant us peace.

MASS OF ST. THERESA

by Calvert Shenk

KYRIE **265**

GLORIA **266**

Mass of St. Theresa, Gloria

praise you for your glo - ry. Lord Je - sus

Christ, on - ly Son of the Fa - ther, Lord God,

Lamb of God, you take a - way the

sin of the world: have mer - cy on us;

you are seat-ed at the right hand of the Fa -

ther: re - ceive our prayer.

For you a - lone are the Ho - ly One, you a -

lone are Lord, you a - lone are the

Most High, Je - sus Christ, with the

Ho - ly Spi - rit, in the glo - ry of God the

Fa - ther. A - men.

Maestoso

Ho - ly, ho - ly, ho - ly Lord, God of power and might, hea - ven and earth are full of your glo - ry. Ho - san - na in the high - est. Bless - ed is he who comes in the name of the Lord. Ho - san - na in the high - est.

AGNUS DEI 268

Andante

Lamb of God, you take a - way the sins of the world: have mer - cy on us. Lamb of God, you take a - way the sins of the world: have mer - cy on us. Lamb of God, you take a - way the sins of the world: grant us___ peace.

COMMUNITY MASS

269 KYRIE

by Richard Proulx

Cantor: *All:*

Lord, have mer - cy, Lord, have mer - cy.

Cantor: *All:*

Christ, have mer - cy, Christ, have mer - cy.

Cantor: *All:*

Lord, have mer - cy, Lord, have mer - cy.

270 GLORIA

Glo - ry to God in the high - est, and peace to his peo - ple on

earth. Lord God, heav-en - ly King, al - might - y God and

Fa - ther, we wor - ship you, we give you thanks, we

praise you for your glo - ry. Lord Je - sus

Christ, on - ly Son of the Fa - ther, Lord God,

Community Mass, Gloria

Lamb of God, you take a - way the sin of the
world: have mer - cy on us; you are
seat - ed at the right hand of the Fa - ther:
re - ceive our prayer, re - ceive, re -
ceive our prayer. For you a - lone are the
Ho - ly One, you a - lone are the Lord, you a -
lone are the Most High, Je - sus Christ, with the Ho - ly
Spir - it, in the glo - ry of God the Fa - ther.
(Sop. Descant)
A - men. A - men.

271 SANCTUS

With majesty

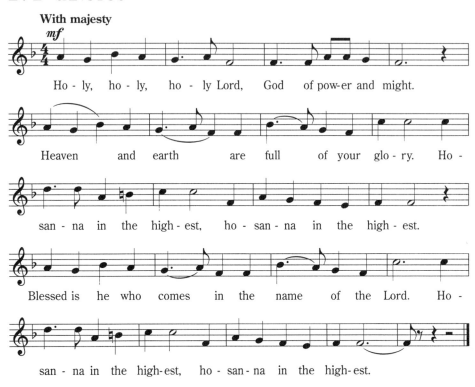

Ho - ly, ho - ly, ho - ly Lord, God of pow-er and might.

Heaven and earth are full of your glo - ry. Ho -

san - na in the high - est, ho - san - na in the high - est.

Blessed is he who comes in the name of the Lord. Ho -

san - na in the high-est, ho - san - na in the high-est.

272 AGNUS DEI

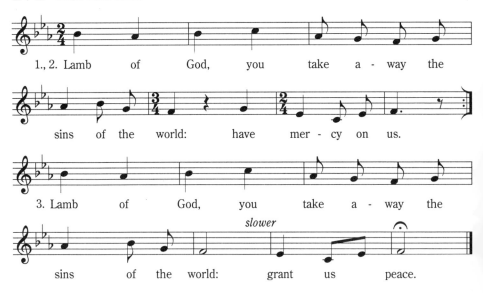

1., 2. Lamb of God, you take a - way the

sins of the world: have mer - cy on us.

3. Lamb of God, you take a - way the

slower

sins of the world: grant us peace.

HYMNS

300

Veni, veni, Emmanuel

1 Ve - ni, ve - ni, Em - má - nu - el; Cap - tí - vum sol - ve
2 Ve - ni, ve - ni, Rex gén - ti - um Ve - ni, Re - dém - ptor
3 Ve - ni, ve - ni, O O - ri - ens; So - lá - re nos ad -
4 Ve - ni, Cla - vis Da - vid - í - ca, Re - gna re - clú - de
5 Ve - ni, O Jes - se Vir - gu - la; Ex ho - stis tu - os

Ís - ra - el Qui ge - mit in e - xí - li - o,
óm - ni - um. Ut sal - vas tu - os fám - u - los
vé - ni - ens; No - ctis de - pél - le né - bu - las
cae - li - ca, Fac i - ter tu - tum su - per - num,
ún - gu - la, De spe - cu tu - os tár - ta - ri

Refrain

Pri - vá - tus De - i fí - li - o.
Pec - cá - ti si - bi cón - sci - os.
Di - rás - que no - ctis té - ne - bras. Gau - de! Gau - de!
Et clau - de vi - as ín - fer - um.
E - duc, et an - tro bá - ra - thri.

Em - má - nu - el Na - scé - tur pro te Ís - ra - el.

6 Veni, veni, Adónai,
 Qui pópulo in Sinai
 Legem dedísti vértice
 In majestáte glóriae.

7 Veni, O Sapientia,
 Quae hic dispónis ómnia;
 Veni, viam prudéntiae
 Ut docéas et glóriae.

TEXT: Latin 9th century
MELODY: adapted by Thomas Helmore, 1811-1890,
 from a responsory in a 15th century French processional, 1854
HARMONIZATION: Jean-Hébert Desrocquettes, O.S.B.

VENI, VENI, EMMANUEL
8 8 . 8 8 with Refrain

O come, O come, Emmanuel

301

(Dec. 23) 1 O come, O come, Em- man - u - el, And
(Dec. 22) 2 O come, of all the na - tions King, The
(Dec. 21) 3 O come, thou Day- spring, come and cheer Our
(Dec. 20) 4 O come, thou Key of Da - vid, come, And

ran - som cap - tive Is - ra - el, That mourns in lone - ly
world a - waits thy ran - som - ing; Re - move our hate and
spir - its by thine ad - vent here; Dis - perse the gloom - y
op - en wide our heav'n - ly home; Make safe the way that

ex - ile here Un - til the Son of God ap - pear.
faith - less- ness, U - nite us who thy Name con - fess.
clouds of night, And death's dark shad - ows put to flight.
leads on high, and close the path to mi - se - ry.

Refrain

Re - joice, re - joice! Em - man - u -

el Shall come to thee, O Is - ra - el.

(Dec. 19)   5   O come, thou Rod of Jesse, free
Thine own from Satan's tyranny;
From depths of hell thy people save
And give them vict'ry o'er the grave. *Refrain*

(Dec. 18)   6   O come, O come, thou Lord of Might,
Who to thy tribes, on Sinai's height,
In ancient times didst give the law
In cloud, and majesty, and awe. *Refrain*

(Dec. 17)   7   O come, thou Wisdom born in heaven's height,
Come peacefully, thy peoples set aright,
To us the path of knowledge show,
And help us in that way to go. *Refrain*

This hymn, "O Come, O Come Emmanuel," has verses based on the Great "O" Antiphons which are sung in conjunction with the Magnificat at Vespers on Dec. 17-23 – K.P.

TEXT: Latin 9th century, translated by John Mason Neale, 1818-1866, alt.
    Stanzas 1, 3, 4, 5 and 6
    Stanzas 2 and 7 copyright © 1966 by Benziger Editions, Inc.
MELODY: adapted by Thomas Helmore, 1811-1890, from a Responsory in a 15th cent. French processional
HARMONIZATION: Willie Aue, b.1889

VENI, VENI EMMANUEL
8 8 . 8 8 with Refrain

302   Savior of the nations, come

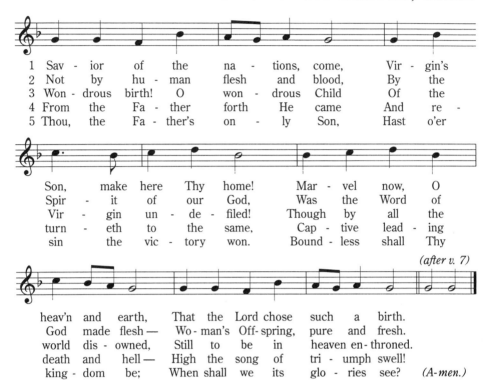

1 Sav -	ior	of	the	na -	tions,	come,	Vir -	gin's
2 Not	by	hu -	man	flesh	and	blood,	By	the
3 Won -	drous	birth!	O	won -	drous	Child	Of	the
4 From	the	Fa -	ther	forth	He	came	And	re -
5 Thou,	the	Fa -	ther's	on -	ly	Son,	Hast	o'er

Son,	make	here	Thy	home!	Mar -	vel	now,	O
Spir -	it	of	our	God,	Was	the	Word	of
Vir -	gin	un -	de -	filed!	Though	by	all	the
turn -	eth	to	the	same,	Cap -	tive	lead -	ing
sin	the	vic -	tory	won.	Bound -	less	shall	Thy

(after v. 7)

heav'n	and	earth,	That	the	Lord	chose	such	a	birth.
God	made	flesh —	Wo -	man's	Off-	spring,	pure	and	fresh.
world	dis -	owned,	Still	to	be	in	heaven	en-	throned.
death	and	hell —	High	the	song	of	tri -	umph	swell!
king -	dom	be;	When	shall	we	its	glo -	ries	see? *(A-men.)*

6 Brightly doth Thy manger shine,
  Glorious is its light divine.
  Let not sin o'er cloud this light;
  Ever be our faith thus bright.

7 Praise to God the Father sing,
  Praise to God the Son, our King,
  Praise to God the Spirit be
  Ever and eternally. Amen.

TEXT: *Veni, Redemptor gentium*, St. Ambrose, 340-397,
  translated by William M. Reynolds, 1812-1876, alt.
MELODY: from *Erfurt Enchiridion*, 1524
HARMONIZATION: Melchior Vulpius, 1560?-1616, from *Erfurt Enchiridion*, 1524

NUN KOMM, DER HEIDEN HEILAND
7 7 . 7 7

On Jordan's bank the Baptist's cry 303

1 On Jor - dan's bank the Bap - tist's cry An -
2 Then cleansed be ev - 'ry breast from sin; Make
3 For thou art our sal - va - tion, Lord, Our
4 To heal the sick stretch out thine hand, And
5 All praise, e - ter - nal Son, to thee Whose

noun - ces that the Lord is nigh; A - wake and hear - ken,
straight the way of God with - in; Pre - pare we in our
ref - uge and our great re - ward; With - out thy grace we
bid the fal - len sin - ner stand; Shine forth, and let thy
ad - vent doth thy peo - ple free, Whom with the Fath - er

for he brings Glad tid - ings of the King of kings.
hearts a home, Where such a might - y guest may come.
waste a - way, Like flow'rs that with - er and de - cay.
light re - store Earth's own true love - li - ness once more.
we a - dore And Ho - ly Ghost for ev - er - more. A - men.

TEXT: *Iordanis ora praevia*, Charles Coffin, 1676-1749, written for the *1736 Paris Breviary*,
   translated by John Chandler, 1808-1896, and compilers of *Hymns Ancient and Modern*
MELODY: adapted from a chorale in *Musikalisches Handbuch*, Hamburg, 1690
HARMONIZATION: William Henry Monk, 1823-1889, alt.

WINCHESTER NEW
88.88

304 Lo! he comes, with clouds descending

1 Lo! he comes, with clouds de - scend - ing, Once for our sal -
2 Ev - 'ry eye shall now be - hold him, Robed in dread - ful
3 Those dear tok - ens of his pas - sion Still his dazz - ling
4 Yea, A - men! let all a - dore thee, High on thine e -

va - tion slain; Thou - sand thou - sand saints at - tend - ing
ma - jes - ty; Those who set at naught and sold him,
bod - y bears, Cause of end - less ex - ul - ta - tion
ter - nal throne; Sav - ior, take the power and glo - ry;

Swell the tri - umph of his train: Al - le - lu - ia,
Pierced, and nailed him to the tree, Deep - ly wail - ing,
To his ran - somed wor - ship - pers: With what rap - ture,
Claim the king - dom for thine own: Al - le - lu - ia,

al - le - lu - ia! Christ the Lord re - turns to reign.
deep - ly wail - ing, Shall the true Mes - si - ah see.
with what rap - ture, Gaze we on those glo - rious scars!
al - le - lu - ia! Thou shalt reign, and thou a - lone.

TEXT: Charles Wesley, 1707-1788, alt.
MELODY: from *Cantus Diversi* by John Francis Wade, c.1711-1786
HARMONIZATION: attributed to Vincent Francis Novello, 1781-1861

ST. THOMAS
87.87.87

O Word, that goest forth on high

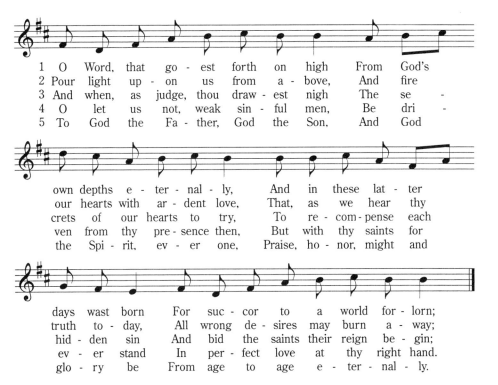

1 O Word, that go-est forth on high From God's
2 Pour light up-on us from a-bove, And fire
3 And when, as judge, thou draw-est nigh The se -
4 O let us not, weak sin-ful men, Be dri -
5 To God the Fa-ther, God the Son, And God

own depths e-ter-nal-ly, And in these lat-ter
our hearts with ar-dent love, That, as we hear thy
crets of our hearts to try, To re-com-pense each
ven from thy pre-sence then, But with thy saints for
the Spi-rit, ev-er one, Praise, ho-nor, might and

days wast born For suc-cor to a world for-lorn;
truth to-day, All wrong de-sires may burn a-way;
hid-den sin And bid the saints their reign be-gin;
ev-er stand In per-fect love at thy right hand.
glo-ry be From age to age e-ter-nal-ly.

TEXT: *Verbum Supernum*, 10th century, translation from *The Hymnal*, 1940
MELODY: Ambrosian hymn, Mode II, c.6th century
HARMONIZATION: from *The Hymnal*, 1940, alt.

EN CLARA VOX REDARGUIT
88.88

306 Wake, awake, for night is flying

1 Wake, a - wake, for night is fly - ing:
2 Si - on hears the watch - men sing - ing,
3 Lamb of God, the heav'ns a - dore thee,

The watch - men on the heights are cry -
Her heart with deep de - light is spring -
And men and an - gels sing be - fore

ing, A - wake, Je - ru - sa - lem, a - rise!
ing, She wakes, she rise - es from her gloom:
thee, With harp and cym - bal's clear - est tone.

Mid - night's sol - emn hour is toll - ing,
Forth her Bride - groom comes, all glo - rious,
By the pearl - y gates in won - der

His char - iot wheels are near - er roll -
In grace ar - rayed, by truth vic - to -
We stand, and swell the voice of thun -

ing, He comes; pre - pare, ye vir - gins wise.
rious; Her star is ris'n, her light is come!
der That ech - oes round thy dazz - ling throne.

Rise up, with will - ing feet Go
All hail, In - car - nate Lord, Our
No vi - sion ev - er brought, No

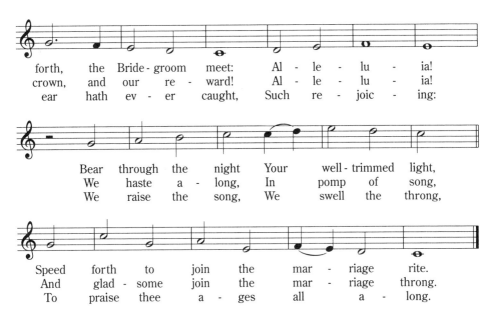

forth,	the	Bride - groom	meet:	Al -	le -	lu -	ia!
crown,	and	our	re - ward!	Al -	le -	lu -	ia!
ear	hath	ev - er	caught,	Such	re -	joic -	ing:

Bear	through	the	night	Your	well - trimmed	light,
We	haste	a - long,	In	pomp	of	song,
We	raise	the	song,	We	swell	the	throng,

Speed	forth	to	join	the	mar - riage	rite.
And	glad - some	join	the	mar - riage	throng.
To	praise	thee	a - ges	all	a - long.

TEXT: *Wachet auf, ruft uns die Stimme*, Philip Nicolai, 1556-1608,
    translated by Catherine Winkworth, 1827-1878, alt.
MELODY: Philip Nicolai, 1556-1608
HARMONIZATION: Johann Sebastian Bach, 1685-1750

SLEEPERS WAKE (WACHET AUF)
898.898.664.448

Rorate caeli

Response

Ro - rá - te cae - li dé - su - per et nu - bes plu - ant ju - stum.

Verses

1 Ne i - ra - scá - ris Dó - mi - ne, ne ul - tra me - mí - ne - ris in - i - qui - tá - tis:

ec - ce cí - vi-tas Sán - cti fa - cta est de - sér- ta: Si - on de - sér - ta fa - cta est:

Je - rú - sa- lem de - so- lá - ta est: do - mus san - cti - fi - ca - ti - ó - nis tu - ae

(to Response)

et gló - ri - ae tu - ae u - bi lau - da - vé - runt te pa - tres nos - tri.

2 Pec - cá - vi - mus, et fa - cti su-mus tam-quam im - mún - dus nos,

et ce - cí - di - mus qua - si fó - li - um u - ni - vér - si:

et in - i - qui - tá - tes nos-trae qua - si ven-tus ab - stu - lé - runt nos:

ab - scon - dí - sti fá - ci - em tu - am a no - bis, et

(to Response)

al - li - sí - sti nos in ma - nu in - i - qui - tá - tis nos - trae.

3 Vi - de Dó - mi - ne af - fli - cti - ó - nem pó - pu - li tu - i
et mít - te quem mi - sú - rus es: e - mít - te A - gnum
do - mi - na - tó - rem ter - rae de pe - tra de - sér - ti
ad mon - tem fí - li - ae Si - on: ut áu - fe - rat

(to Response)

ip - se ju - gum cap - ti - vi - tá - tis nos - trae.

4 Con - so - lá - mi - ni, con - so - lá - mi - ni, pó - pu - le me - us: ci - to
vé - ni - et sa - lus tu - a: qua - re moe - ró - re con - sú - me - ris,
qu - ia in - no - vá - vit te do - lor? Sal - vá - bo te,
no - li ti - mé - re, e - go e - nim sum Dó - mi - nus

(to Response)

De - us tu - us, San - ctus Is - ra - el, re - dém - ptor tu - us.

TEXT: Latin, translation copyright © 1939 by Burns & Oates, Ltd.
MELODY: Plainchant, Mode I
HARMONIZATION: A. Gregory Murray, O.S.B., b.1905, copyright © 1939 by Burns & Oates, Ltd.

RORATE CAELI
Irregular

308 Conditor alme siderum

1 Con - di - tor al - me sí - de - rum,
2 Qui cón - do - lens in - tér - i - tu
3 Ver - gén - te mun - di vés - pe - re,
4 Cu - ius for - ti po - tén - ti - ae
5 Te, Sanc - te, fi - de quaé - su - mus,
6 Sit, Chris - te, rex pi - ís - si - me,

ae - tér - na lux cre - dén - ti - um,
mor - tis per - í - re saé - cu - lum,
u - ti spon - sus de thá - la - mo,
ge - nu cur - ván - tur óm - ni - a;
ven - tú - re iu - dex saé - cu - li,
ti - bi Pa - trí - que gló - ri - a

Chris - te, re - démp - tor óm - ni - um,
sal - vás - ti mun - dum lán - gui - dum,
e - grés - sus ho - nes - tís - si - ma
cae - lés - ti - a, ter - rés - tri - a
con - sér - va nos in tém - po - re
cum Spí - ri - tu Pa - rá - cli - to,

ex - áu - di pre - ces súp - pli - cum.
do - nans re - is re - mé - di - um.
Vír - gi - nis ma - tris claú - su - la.
nu - tu fa - tén - tur súb - di - ta.
hos - tis a te - lo pér - fi - di.
in sem - pi - tér - na saé - cu - la. A - men.

TEXT: Latin 9th century, anonymous
MELODY: Plainchant, Mode III, 9th century
HARMONIZATION: Bruce Neswick, b.1956, copyright © 1984 by Bruce Neswick

CONDITOR ALME SIDERUM
88.88

Creator of the stars of night

309

1 Cre - a - tor of the stars of night,
2 Thou, griev - ing at the bit - ter cry,
3 Thou cam - est, Bride - groom of the bride,
4 At thy great name, ex - alt - ed now,
5 To thee, O Ho - ly One, we pray,
6 All praise, et - er - nal Son, to thee,

Thy peo - ple's ev - er - last - ing light,
Of all cre - a - tion doomed to die,
As drew the world to ev - 'ning tide,
All knees must bend, all hearts must bow,
Our judge in that tre - mend - ous day,
Whose ad - vent sets thy peo - ple free,

O Je - sus, Sa - viour of us all,
Didst come to save a ru - ined race
Pro - ceed - ing from a vir - gin shrine,
And things in heav'n and earth shall own
Pre - serve us, while we dwell be - low,
Whom with the Fa - ther we a - dore,

Re - gard thy ser - vants when they call.
With heal - ing gifts of heav'n - ly grace.
The Son of Man, yet Lord di - vine.
That thou art Lord and King a - lone.
From ev - 'ry on - slaught of the foe.
And Spir - it blest, for ev - er - more. A - men.

TEXT: Latin 9th century, anonymous, translated by John Mason Neale, 1818-1866, alt., translation copyright © 1986 by The Canterbury Press Norwich
MELODY: Plainchant, Mode III, 9th century
HARMONIZATION: Bruce Neswick, b. 1956, copyright © 1984 by Bruce Neswick, alt.

CONDITOR ALME SIDERUM
88.88

310   Come, thou long expected Jesus

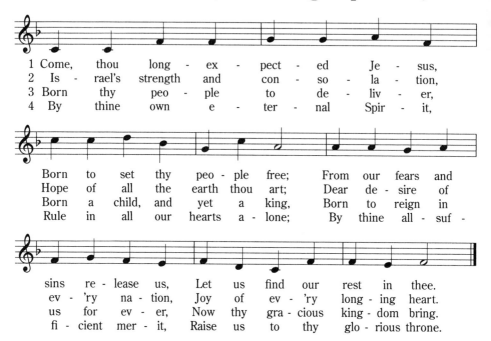

1 Come, thou long - ex - pect - ed Je - sus,
2 Is - rael's strength and con - so - la - tion,
3 Born thy peo - ple to de - liv - er,
4 By thine own e - ter - nal Spir - it,

Born to set thy peo - ple free; From our fears and
Hope of all the earth thou art; Dear de - sire of
Born a child, and yet a king, Born to reign in
Rule in all our hearts a - lone; By thine all - suf -

sins re - lease us, Let us find our rest in thee.
ev - 'ry na - tion, Joy of ev - 'ry long - ing heart.
us for ev - er, Now thy gra - cious king - dom bring.
fi - cient mer - it, Raise us to thy glo - rious throne.

TEXT: Charles Wesley, 1707-1788
MELODY: adapted from a melody by Christian Friedrich Witt, c.1660-1716, in *Psalmodia Sacra*, 1715
HARMONIZATION: from *Hymns Ancient and Modern*, 1861, alt.

STUTTGART
8 7 . 8 7

Joy to the world!

1 Joy to the world! the Lord is come: Let earth re - ceive her
2 Joy to the world! the Sa - viour reigns: Let men their songs em -
3 No more let sins and sor - rows grow, Nor thorns in - fest the
4 He rules the world! with truth and grace, And makes the na - tions

King; Let ev - 'ry heart pre - pare him
ploy, While fields and floods, rocks, hills, and
ground; He comes to make his bless - ings
prove the glo - ries of his righ - teous -

room, And heav'n and na - ture sing. And heav'n and na - ture
plains, Re - peat the sound-ing joy. Re - peat the sound-ing
flow Far as the curse is found. Far as the curse is
ness, And won-ders of his love. And won-ders of his

sing. And heav'n, and heav'n and na - ture sing.
joy. Re - peat, re - peat the sound - ing joy.
found. Far as, far as the curse is found.
love. And won-ders, and won - ders of his love.

TEXT: Isaac Watts, 1674-1748, based on Psalm 98
MELODY: from melodies in *Messiah,* by George Frideric Handel, 1685-1759,
  adapted and arranged by Lowell Mason, 1792-1872
HARMONIZATION: Lowell Mason, 1792-1872

ANTIOCH
8 6 . 8 6 with Repeat

321

Adeste, fideles

1 A - dé - ste, fi - dé - les, Lae - ti tri - um - phán - tes; Ve -
2 De - um de De - o, Lu - men de lú - mi - ne,
3 Can - tet nunc I - o! Cho- rus an - ge - ló - rum:
4 Er - go qui na - tus Di - e ho - di - ér - na,

ní - te, ve - ní - te in Béth - le - hem;
Ge - stant pu - él - lae ví - sce - ra;
Can - tet nunc au - la cae - lé - sti - um:
Je - su ti - bi sit gló - ri - a:

Na - tum vi - dé - te Re - gem an - ge - ló - rum:
De - um ve - rum, Gé - ni - tum, non fa - ctum:
Gló - ri - a, gló - ria, In ex - cél - sis De - o!
Pa - tris ae - tér - ni Ver - bum ca - ro fa - ctum!

Refrain

Ve - ní - te a - do - ré - mus, Ve - ní - te a - do - ré - mus,

Ve - ní - te a - do - ré - mus Dó - mi - num.

TEXT: John Francis Wade, c.1711-1786
MELODY: John Francis Wade, c.1711-1786
HARMONIZATION: Traditional

ADESTE FIDELES
Irregular with Refrain

O come, all ye faithful

322

1 O come, all ye faith - ful, Joy - ful and tri - umph - ant, O
2 God of God, Light of Light,
3 Sing, choirs of an - gels, Sing in ex - ul - ta - tion,
4 Yea, Lord we greet thee, Born this hap - py morn - ing;

come ye, O come ye to Beth - le - hem;
Lo! he ab - hors not the Vir - gin's womb:
Sing, all ye ci - ti - zens of heav'n a - bove;
Je - sus, to thee be glo - ry giv'n;

Come and be - hold him, Born the King of an - gels;
Ve - ry God, Be - got - ten, not cre - a - ted;
Glo - ry to God In the high - est;
Word of the Fa - ther, Now in flesh ap - pear - ing;

Refrain

O come, let us a - dore him, O come, let us a - dore him,

O come, let us a - dore him, Christ the Lord.

TEXT: John Francis Wade, c.1711-1786, translated by Frederick Oakley, 1802-1880, alt.
MELODY: John Francis Wade, c.1711-1786
HARMONIZATION: Traditional

ADESTE FIDELES
Irregular with Refrain

323 Angels we have heard on high

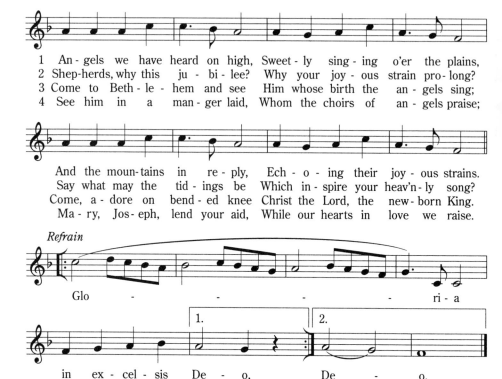

1 An-gels we have heard on high, Sweet-ly sing-ing o'er the plains,
2 Shep-herds, why this ju-bi-lee? Why your joy-ous strain pro-long?
3 Come to Beth-le-hem and see Him whose birth the an-gels sing;
4 See him in a man-ger laid, Whom the choirs of an-gels praise;

And the moun-tains in re-ply, Ech-o-ing their joy-ous strains.
Say what may the tid-ings be Which in-spire your heav'n-ly song?
Come, a-dore on bend-ed knee Christ the Lord, the new-born King.
Ma-ry, Jos-eph, lend your aid, While our hearts in love we raise.

Refrain

Glo - - - - ri - a

1. 2.

in ex-cel-sis De - o, De - o.

TEXT: French, anonymous, translated by James Chadwick, 1813-1882, alt.
MELODY: Traditional French carol
HARMONIZATION: Edward Shippen Barnes, 1887-1958, copyright © 1937 by the Fleming H. Revell Company, alt.

GLORIA
7 7 . 7 7, with Refrain

Puer natus in Bethlehem

324

1 Pu - er na - tus in Béth - le - hem, al - le - lú - ia:
2 Hic ja - cet in prae - sé - pi - o, al - le - lú - ia,
3 In hoc na - tá - li gaú - di - o, al - le - lú - ia,
4 Lau - dé - tur san - cta Tri - ni - tas, al - le - lú - ia;

Un - de gau - det Je - rú - sa - lem, al - le - lú - ia,
Qui re - gnat si - ne tér - mi - no, al - le - lú - ia,
Be - ne - di - cá - mus Dó - mi - no, al - le - lú - ia,
De - o di - cá - mus grá - ti - as, al - le - lú - ia,

Refrain

al - le - lú - ia.
al - le - lú - ia.   In cor - dis jú - bi - lo, Chri - stum
al - le - lú - ia.
al - le - lú - ia.

na - tum a - do - ré - mus Cum no - vo cán - ti - co.

English Translation

Refrain

With joy in our hearts,
let us adore the new-born Christ with a new song.

Verses

1 *The Child is born in Bethlehem, Alleluia.*
Therefore, does Jerusalem rejoice, Alleluia.

2 *Here lies in a manger, Alleluia,*
He who rules forever, Alleluia.

3 *In this joyful nativity, Alleluia,*
Let us bless the Lord, Alleluia.

4 *Praise be the Holy Trinity, Alleluia.*
Let us give thanks to God, Alleluia.

TEXT: from V. Babst's *Gesangbuch*, 1545, translation by Richard Divozzo, b.1955. Used with permission.
MELODY: Plainchant, Mode I, 14th century, Benedictine processional
HARMONIZATION: Jean-Hébert Desrocquettes, O.S.B., copyright © 1958 by Ralph Jusko Publications, Inc.

PUER NATUS
8 8 with Alleluias and Refrain

325 Hark! the herald angels sing

1 Hark! the her - ald an - gels sing Glo - ry to the new-born King!
2 Christ, by high - est heav'n a - dored; Christ, the ev - er - last - ing Lord;
3 Mild he lays his glo - ry by, Born that man no more may die,

Peace on earth and mer - cy mild, God and sin - ners re - con - ciled!
Late in time be - hold him come, Off-spring of the Vir - gin's womb.
Born to raise the sons of earth, Born to give them sec - ond birth.

Joy - ful, all ye na - tions, rise, Join the tri - umph of the skies;
Veiled in flesh the God-head see; Hail the in - car - nate De - i - ty,
Ris'n with heal - ing in his wings, Light and life to all he brings.

With the an - gel - ic host pro - claim Christ is born in Beth - le - hem!
Pleased as man with man to dwell; Je - sus our Em - man - u - el!
Hail, the Sun of Right-eous - ness! Hail, the heav'n-born Prince of Peace!

Refrain

Hark! the her - ald an - gels sing Glo - ry to the new-born King!

TEXT: Charles Wesley, 1707-1788, alt.
MELODY: Adapted by William H. Cummings, 1831-1915,
   from a chorus by Felix B. Mendelssohn, 1808-1847
HARMONIZATION: Adapted by William H. Cummings, 1831-1915,
   from a chorus by Felix B. Mendelssohn, 1808-1847

MENDELSSOHN
7 7 . 7 7 . D with Refrain

God rest you merry gentlemen 326

1 God rest you mer - ry gen- tle- men, Let noth - ing you dis - may,
2 From God our heav'n- ly Fa - ther A bless - ed an - gel came;
3 "Fear not, then," said the an - gel, "Let noth - ing you af - fright;
4 Now to the Lord sing prais - es, All you with - in this place,

Re - mem- ber Christ our Sav - ior was born on Christ- mas Day;
And un - to cer - tain shep - herds Brought tid - ings of the same;
This day is born a Sav - ior Of a pure vir - gin bright,
And with true love and bro- ther- hood Each oth - er now em - brace;

To save us all from Sa- tan's power When we were gone a - stray.
How that in Beth- le - hem was born The Son of God by name.
To free all those who trust in him From Sa- tan's power and might."
This ho - ly tide of Christ - mas Doth bring re- deem- ing grace.

Refrain

O tid - ings of com - fort and joy, com- fort and

joy; O tid - ings of com - fort and joy!

TEXT: London Carol, c.1770, alt.
MELODY: *Little Book of Carols*, c.1850
HARMONIZATION: Winfred Charles Douglas, 1867-1944, copyrighted by Church Publishing, Inc.

GOD REST YOU MERRY
8 6 . 8 6 . 8 6 with Refrain

327

The first Nowell

1 The first Now - ell the an - gel did say Was to
2 They look - èd up and saw a star Shin- ing
3 And by the light of that same star Three

cer - tain poor shep- herds in fields as they lay; In
in the east be - yond them far, And
wise men came from the coun - try far; To

fields as they lay keep - ing their sheep, On a
to the earth it gave great light. And
seek for a king was their in - tent, And to

cold win - ter's night that was so deep.
so it con - tin - ued both day and night.
fol - low the star where - ev - er it went.

Refrain

Now - ell, Now - ell, Now - ell, Now - ell,

Born is the King of Is - ra - el.

4 This star drew nigh to the northwest,
O'er Bethlehem it took its rest,
And there it did both stop and stay
Right over the place where Jesus lay.

5 Then entered in those wise men three
Full rev'rently upon their knee,
And offered there in his presence
Their gold, and myrrh, and frankincense.

6 Then let us all with one accord
Sing praises to our heav'nly Lord;
That hath made heav'n and earth of naught,
And with his blood mankind hath bought.

TEXT: English carol, 17th century, first published in *Christmas Carols, Ancient and Modern*, 1833
MELODY: English carol, 17th century
HARMONIZATION: Richard Runciman Terry, 1865-1938, copyright © by Burns and Oates, Ltd.

THE FIRST NOWELL
Irregular with Refrain

Once in royal David's city

328

1 Once in roy - al Da - vid's ci - ty Stood a low - ly cat - tle shed,
2 He came down to earth from hea - ven, Who is God and Lord of all,
3 And our eyes at last shall see him, Through his own re - deem - ing love;

Where a moth - er laid her ba - by In a man - ger for his bed;
And his shel - ter was a sta - ble, And his cra - dle was a stall;
For that child so dear and gen - tle Is our Lord in heav'n a - bove;

Ma - ry was that moth - er mild, Je - sus Christ her lit - tle child.
With the poor, and mean, and low - ly, Lived on earth our Sa - vior ho - ly.
And he leads his child - ren on To the place where he is gone.

TEXT: Cecil Frances Alexander, 1818-1895
MELODY: Henry J. Gauntlett, 1805-1876
HARMONIZATION: Henry J. Gauntlett, 1805-1876

IRBY
87.87.77

329   Lo, how a rose e'er blooming

1 Lo, how a rose e'er bloom-ing From ten-der stem hath sprung!
2 I - sa - iah 'twas fore-told it, The Rose I have in mind.
3 O Flow'r, whose fra-grance ten - der With sweet-ness fills the air.

Of Jes-se's lin-eage com - ing As pro-phets long have sung.
With Ma - ry we be - hold it, The vir - gin Moth-er kind.
Dis - pel in glo-rious splen-dor The dark-ness ev - 'ry-where:

It came, a flow - 'ret bright, A - mid the cold of
To show God's love a - right, She bore to us a
True man, yet ver - y God, From sin and death now

win - ter, When half - spent was the night.
Sav - ior, When half - spent was the night.
save us, And share our ev - 'ry load.

TEXT: Vv. 1-2, German 15th cent.; v. 3, Friedrich Layritz, 1808-1859,
   vv. 1-2 translated by Theodore Baker, 1851-1934;
   v. 3 translated by Harriet Reynolds Krauth Spaeth, 1845-1925,
   v. 3 copyright © 1985 by Church Publishing, Inc.
MELODY: German melody, 16th cent.
HARMONIZATION: Michael Praetorius, 1571-1621

EST IST EIN ROS' ENTSPRUNGEN
76.76.676

What child is this

1 What child is this, who laid to rest, On Ma-ry's lap is sleep-ing?
2 Why lies he in such mean es-tate Where ox and ass are feed-ing?
3 So bring him in-cense, gold, and myrrh, Come, peas-ant, king, to own him,

Whom an-gels greet with an-thems sweet, While shep-herds watch are keep-ing?
Good Chris-tian, fear: for sin-ners here The si-lent Word is plead-ing.
The King of kings sal-va-tion brings, Let lov-ing hearts en-throne him.

Refrain

This, this is Christ the King, Whom shep-herds guard and an-gels sing:

Haste, haste to bring him laud, The babe, the son of Ma-ry.

TEXT: William Chatterton Dix, 1837-1898
MELODY: Traditional English melody, first recorded reference–1580
HARMONIZATION: *Christmas Carols New and Old*, 1871

GREENSLEEVES
8 7 . 8 7 with Refrain

331 Of the Father's love begotten

1 Of the Fa-ther's love be - got - ten, Ere the worlds be - gan to be,
2 O that birth for ev - er bless - ed, When the Vir - gin, full of grace,
3 O ye heights of heav'n a - dore him; An - gel hosts, his prais - es sing;
4 Christ, to thee with God the Fa - ther, And, O Ho - ly Ghost, to thee,

He is Al - pha and O - me - ga, He the source, the end - ing he,
By the Ho - ly Ghost con - ceiv - ing, Bare the Sav - ior of our race;
Powers, do - min - ions, bow be - fore him, And ex - tol our God and King;
Hymn and chant and high thanks-giv - ing, And un - wear - ied prais - es be:

Of the things that are, that have been, And that future years shall see,
And the Babe, the world's Re-deem - er, First re-vealed his sa-cred face,
Let no tongue on earth be si - lent, Ev-ery voice in concert ring,
Hon-or, glo-ry, and do-min - ion, And e - ter-nal vic-to-ry,

Ev - er-more and ev - er - more!
Ev - er-more and ev - er - more!
Ev - er-more and ev - er - more!
Ev - er-more and ev - er - more! A - men.

TEXT: Aurelius Clemens Prudentius, 348-413,
    translated by John Mason Neale, 1818-1866, and Henry Williams Baker, 1821-1877
MELODY: Plainchant, Mode V, 13th century
HARMONIZATION: Winfred Charles Douglas, 1867-1944, copyrighted by Church Publishing, Inc.

DIVINUM MYSTERIUM
87.87.877

While shepherds watched their flocks 332

1 While shep-herds watch'd their flocks by night, All seat - ed on the ground,
2 "Fear not," said he, for might - y dread Had seized their troub-led mind;
3 "To you, in Da - vid's town, this day Is born of Da - vid's line
4 "The heav'n - ly Babe you there shall find To hu - man view dis- played,

The an - gel of the Lord came down, And glo - ry shone a - round.
"Glad tid - ings of great joy I bring To you and all man - kind."
The Sav - ior, who is Christ the Lord; And this shall be the sign:
All mean - ly wrapped in swath - ing bands, And in a man - ger laid."

5 Thus spake the seraph, and forthwith
Appeared a shining throng
Of angels praising God, who thus
Addressed their joyful song:

6 "All glory be to God on high
And on the earth be peace;
Good will henceforth from heav'n to men
Begin and never cease."

TEXT: Nahum Tate, 1652-1715
MELODY: from Thomas Est's *Whole Book of Psalms*, 1592
HARMONIZATION: Thomas Est, c.1540-c.1608

WINCHESTER OLD
86.86

333 O little town of Bethlehem

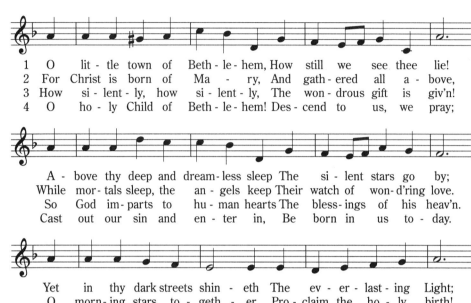

1 O lit - tle town of Beth - le - hem, How still we see thee lie!
2 For Christ is born of Ma - ry, And gath - ered all a - bove,
3 How si - lent - ly, how si - lent - ly, The won - drous gift is giv'n!
4 O ho - ly Child of Beth - le - hem! Des - cend to us, we pray;

A - bove thy deep and dream - less sleep The si - lent stars go by;
While mor - tals sleep, the an - gels keep Their watch of won - d'ring love.
So God im - parts to hu - man hearts The bless - ings of his heav'n.
Cast out our sin and en - ter in, Be born in us to - day.

Yet in thy dark streets shin - eth The ev - er - last - ing Light;
O morn - ing stars, to - geth - er Pro - claim the ho - ly birth!
No ear may hear his com - ing, But in this world of sin,
We hear the Christ - mas an - gels The great glad tid - ings tell;

The hopes and fears of all the years Are met in thee to - night.
And prais - es sing to God the King, And peace to men on earth.
Where meek souls will re - ceive him, still The dear Christ en - ters in.
O come to us, a - bide in us, Our Lord Em - man - u - el!

TEXT: Phillips Brooks, 1835-1893
MELODY: Lewis H. Redner, 1831-1908
HARMONIZATION: Lewis H. Redner, 1831-1908

ST. LOUIS
86.86.76.86

Good Christian men, rejoice

334

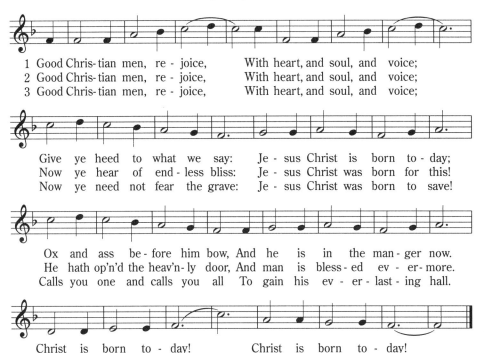

1 Good Chris-tian men, re - joice,   With heart, and soul, and voice;
2 Good Chris-tian men, re - joice,   With heart, and soul, and voice;
3 Good Chris-tian men, re - joice,   With heart, and soul, and voice;

Give ye heed to what we say: Je - sus Christ is born to - day;
Now ye hear of end - less bliss: Je - sus Christ was born for this!
Now ye need not fear the grave: Je - sus Christ was born to save!

Ox and ass be - fore him bow, And he is in the man - ger now.
He hath op'n'd the heav'n- ly door, And man is bless - ed ev - er- more.
Calls you one and calls you all To gain his ev - er - last - ing hall.

Christ is born to - day!   Christ is born to - day!
Christ was born for this!   Christ was born for this!
Christ was born to save!   Christ was born to save!

TEXT: 14th century German-Latin carol attributed to Bl. Henry Suso, d.1366, translated by John Mason Neale, 1818-1866   **IN DULCI JUBILO**
MELODY: German-Latin carol, 14th century   **66.77.78.55**
HARMONIZATION: Robert L. Pearsall, 1795-1856

335   It came upon the midnight clear

1 It came up-on the mid-night clear, That glo-rious song of old,
2 Still through the clo-ven skies they come With peace-ful wings un-furled,
3 Yet with the woes of sin and strife The world has suf-fered long:

From an-gels bend-ing near the earth To touch their harps of gold:
And still their heav'n-ly mu-sic floats O'er all the wear-y world;
Be-neath the heav'n-ly strain have rolled Two thou-sand years of wrong;

"Peace on the earth, good will to men, From heav'n all-glo-rious King."
A-bove its sad and low-ly plains They bend on hov-'ring wing.
And man, at war with man, hears not The tid-ings which they bring;

The world in sol-emn still-ness lay To hear the an-gels sing.
And ev-er o'er its Ba-bel-sounds The bless-ed an-gels sing.
O hush the noise, ye men of strife, And hear the an-gels sing!

TEXT: Edmund Hamilton Sears, 1810-1876
MELODY: Richard Storrs Willis, 1819-1900
HARMONIZATION: Traditional

CAROL
86.86.D

Away in a manger

336

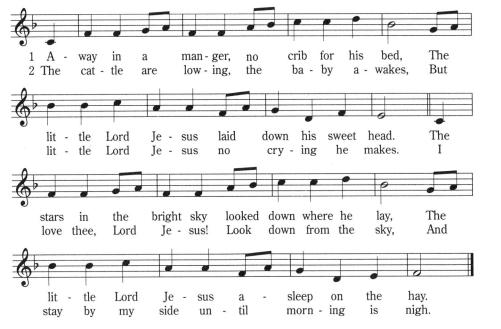

1 A - way in a man - ger, no crib for his bed, The
2 The cat - tle are low - ing, the ba - by a - wakes, But

lit - tle Lord Je - sus laid down his sweet head. The
lit - tle Lord Je - sus no cry - ing he makes. I

stars in the bright sky looked down where he lay, The
love thee, Lord Je - sus! Look down from the sky, And

lit - tle Lord Je - sus a - sleep on the hay.
stay by my side un - til morn - ing is nigh.

TEXT: Traditional carol
MELODY: William James Kirkpatrick, 1838-1921
HARMONIZATION: Ralph Vaughan Williams, 1872-1958, copyright © by Oxford University Press,
  from the *Revised Church Hymnary 1927* by permission of Oxford University Press.

CRADLE SONG
11.11.11.11

337

Sleep, holy Babe

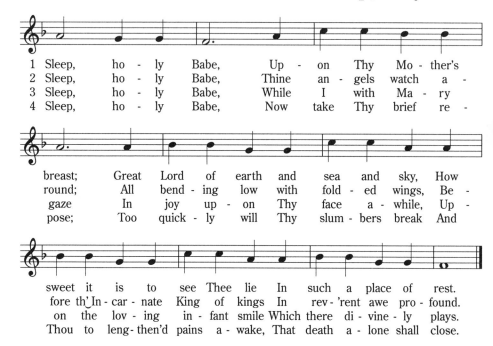

1 Sleep, ho - ly Babe, Up - on Thy Mo - ther's
2 Sleep, ho - ly Babe, Thine an - gels watch a -
3 Sleep, ho - ly Babe, While I with Ma - ry
4 Sleep, ho - ly Babe, Now take Thy brief re -

breast; Great Lord of earth and sea and sky, How
round; All bend - ing low with fold - ed wings, Be -
gaze In joy up - on Thy face a - while, Up -
pose; Too quick - ly will Thy slum - bers break And

sweet it is to see Thee lie In such a place of rest.
fore th' In - car - nate King of kings In rev - 'rent awe pro - found.
on the lov - ing in - fant smile Which there di - vine - ly plays.
Thou to leng - then'd pains a - wake, That death a - lone shall close.

TEXT: Edward Caswall, 1814-1878
MELODY: adapted from a melody by Louise Reichardt, 1779-1826
HARMONIZATION: Thomas B. Mailloux, C.S.B., copyright © 1958 by Ralph Jusko Publications, Inc.

SLEEP HOLY BABE
4.6.88.6

Silent night, holy night!

338

1 Si - lent night, ho - ly night! All is calm,
2 Si - lent night, ho - ly night! Shep - herds quake
3 Si - lent night, ho - ly night! Son of God,

all is bright, 'Round yon Vir - gin Moth - er and Child,
at the sight! Glo - ries stream from heav - en a - far,
love's pure light Ra - diant beams from Thy ho - ly face,

Ho - ly In - fant so ten - der and mild: Sleep in heav - en - ly
Heav'n - ly hosts sing Al - le - lu - ia: Christ, the Sav - ior is
With the dawn of re - deem - ing grace, Je - sus, Lord, at Thy

peace, Sleep in heav - en - ly peace!
born, Christ, the Sav - ior is born!
birth, Je - sus, Lord, at Thy birth!

TEXT: Joseph Mohr, 1792-1848, translated by John Freeman Young, 1820-1885
MELODY: Franz Gruber, 1787-1863
HARMONIZATION: Healey Willan, 1880-1968, copyright 1958 © by Ralph Jusko Publications, Inc.

STILLE NACHT
Irregular

350   We three kings of Orient are

1 We three kings of O - ri - ent are, Bear - ing
2 Born a King on Beth - le - hem's plain, Gold I
3 Frank - in - cense to of - fer have I, In - cense
4 Myrrh is mine; its bit - ter per - fume Breathes a
5 Glo - rious now be - hold him a - rise, King, and

gifts we trav - erse a - far, Field and foun - tain,
bring to crown him a - gain, King for ev - er,
owns a De - i - ty nigh, Prayer and prais - ing,
life of gath - er - ing gloom; Sor - rowing, sigh - ing,
God, and Sac - ri - fice, Heav'n sings Al - le -

Moor and moun - tain, Fol - low - ing yon - der star.
Ceas - ing nev - er O - ver us all to reign.
All men rais - ing, Wor - ship him, God on high.
Bleed - ing, dy - ing, Sealed in the stone - cold tomb.
lu - ia: Al - le - lu - ia the earth re - plies.

Refrain

O star of won - der, star of night, Star with

roy - al beau - ty bright; West - ward lead - ing, Still pro -

ceed - ing, Guide us to thy per - fect light!

TEXT: John Henry Hopkins, Jr., 1861-1945
MELODY: John Henry Hopkins, Jr., 1861-1945
HARMONIZATION: Traditional

THREE KINGS OF ORIENT
8 8 . 4 4 6 with Refrain

Songs of thankfulness and praise 351

1 Songs of thank-ful-ness and praise, Je-sus, Lord, to thee we raise,
2 Man-i-fest at Jor-dan's stream, Proph-et, Priest, and King su-preme;
3 Man-i-fest in mak-ing whole Pal-sied limbs and wea-ry soul;
4 Grant us grace to see thee, Lord, Mir-rored in thy ho-ly Word;

Man-i-fest-ed by the star To the sag-es from a-far;
And at Ca-na, wed-ding guest, In thy God-head man-i-fest
Man-i-fest in val-iant fight, Quell-ing all the dev-il's might;
May we im-i-tate thee now And be pure as pure art thou;

Branch of roy-al Da-vid's stem In thy birth at Beth-le-hem;
Man-i-fest in power di-vine, Chang-ing wa-ter in-to wine;
Man-i-fest in gra-cious will, Ev-er bring-ing good from ill;
That we like to thee may be At thy great E-pi-pha-ny;

An-thems be to thee ad-dressed, God in man made man-i-fest.
An-thems be to thee ad-dressed, God in man made man-i-fest.
An-thems be to thee ad-dressed, God in man made man-i-fest.
And may praise thee, ev-er blest, God in man made man-i-fest.

TEXT: Christopher Wordsworth, 1807-1885
MELODY: Jakob Hintze, 1622-1702
HARMONIZATION: Johann Sebastian Bach, 1685-1750

SALZBURG
77.77.D

352   Bethlehem, of noblest cities

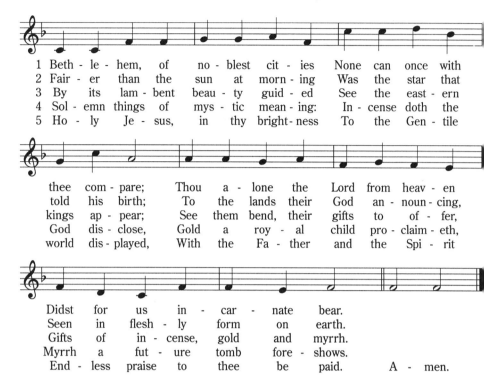

1 Beth - le - hem, of no - blest cit - ies None can once with
2 Fair - er than the sun at morn - ing Was the star that
3 By its lam - bent beau - ty guid - ed See the east - ern
4 Sol - emn things of mys - tic mean - ing: In - cense doth the
5 Ho - ly Je - sus, in thy bright- ness To the Gen - tile

thee com - pare; Thou a - lone the Lord from heav - en
told his birth; To the lands their God an - noun - cing,
kings ap - pear; See them bend, their gifts to of - fer,
God dis - close, Gold a roy - al child pro - claim - eth,
world dis - played, With the Fa - ther and the Spi - rit

Didst for us in - car - nate bear.
Seen in flesh - ly form on earth.
Gifts of in - cense, gold and myrrh.
Myrrh a fut - ure tomb fore - shows.
End - less praise to thee be paid.   A - men.

TEXT: *O sola magnarum urbium* by Aurelius Clemens Prudentius, 348-413, translated by Edward Caswall, 1814-1878
MELODY: adapted from a melody by Christian Friedrich Witt, 1600-1716, in *Psalmodia Sacra*, 1715
HARMONIZATION: from *Hymns Ancient and Modern*, 1861, alt.

STUTTGART
87.87

As with gladness men of old

353

1 As with glad-ness men of old Did the guid-ing star be-hold;
2 As with joy-ful steps they sped To that low-ly man-ger bed;
3 As they of-fer'd gifts most rare At that man-ger rude and bare;
4 Ho-ly Je-sus! ev-'ry day Keep us in the nar-row way;
5 In the heav'n-ly coun-try bright, Need they no cre-a-ted light;

As with joy they hailed its light, Lead-ing on-ward, beam-ing bright;
There to bend the knee be-fore Him whom heav'n and earth a-dore:
So may we with ho-ly joy, Pure and free from sin's al-loy
And, when earth-ly things are past, Bring our ran-somed souls at last
Thou its light, its joy, its crown, Thou its sun which goes not down:

So, most gra-cious Lord, may we Ev-er-more be led to thee.
So may we with will-ing feet Ev-er seek the mer-cy-seat.
All our cost-liest trea-sures bring, Christ, to Thee our heaven-ly King.
Where they need no star to guide, Where no clouds thy glo-ry hide.
There for-ev-er may we sing Al-le-lu-ias to our King.

TEXT: William Chatterton Dix, 1837-1898
MELODY: Conrad Kocher, 1786-1872
HARMONIZATION: from a chorale by Conrad Kocher, 1786-1872, abridged by William Henry Monk, 1823-1889

DIX
77.77.77

354 Hail to the Lord's Anointed!

1 Hail to the Lord's A - noint - ed! Great Da - vid's great - er Son;
2 He comes with suc - cor speed - y To those who suf - fer wrong;
3 By such shall He be fear - éd While sun and moon en - dure,
4 He shall come down like show - ers Up - on the fruit - ful earth,
5 Kings shall bow down be - fore Him And gold and in - cense bring;
6 O'er ev - 'ry foe vic - to - ri - ous, He on His throne shall rest;

Hail, in the time ap - point - ed, His reign on earth be - gun!
To help the poor and need - y, And bid the weak be strong;
Be - lov'd, o - beyed, re - ver - éd; For He shall judge the poor,
And love, joy, hope, like flow - ers Spring in His path to birth;
All na - tions shall a - dore Him, His praise all peo - ple sing;
From age to age more glo - ri - ous, All - bless - ing and all - blest;

He comes to break op - pres - sion, To set the cap - tive free;
To give them songs for sigh - ing, Their dark-ness turn to light,
Through chang - ing gen - er - a - tions, With jus - tice, mer - cy, truth.
Be - fore Him on the moun - tains Shall peace, the her - ald, go;
To Him shall pray'r un - ceas - ing And dai - ly vows as - cend;
The tide of time shall ne - ver His cov - e - nant re - move;

To take a - way trans - gres - sion, And rule in e - qui - ty.
Whose souls, con - demned and dy - ing, Were pre - cious in His sight.
While stars main - tain their sta - tions Or moons re - new their youth.
And right - eous - ness in foun - tains From hill to val - ley flow.
His king - dom still in - creas - ing, A king - dom with - out end.
His Name shall stand for - ev - er; His change-less Name of Love.

TEXT: James Montgomery, 1771-1854
MELODY: adapted from a melody in the *Würtemburg Gesangbuch*, 1784
HARMONIZATION: William Henry Monk, 1823-1889, alt.

ELLACOMBE
76.76.D

Lord, who throughout these forty days

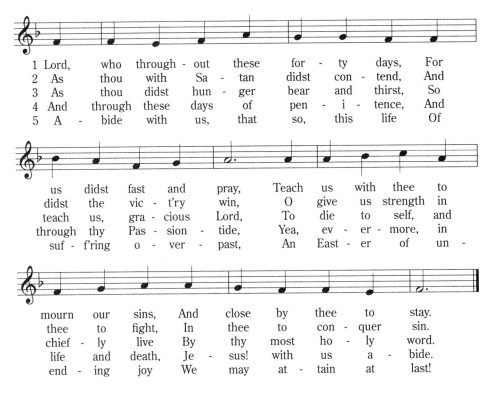

1 Lord, who through - out these for - ty days, For
2 As thou with Sa - tan didst con - tend, And
3 As thou didst hun - ger bear and thirst, So
4 And through these days of pen - i - tence, And
5 A - bide with us, that so, this life Of

us didst fast and pray, Teach us with thee to
didst the vic - t'ry win, O give us strength in
teach us, gra - cious Lord, To die to self, and
through thy Pas - sion - tide, Yea, ev - er - more, in
suf - f'ring o - ver - past, An East - er of un -

mourn our sins, And close by thee to stay.
thee to fight, In thee to con - quer sin.
chief - ly live By thy most ho - ly word.
life and death, Je - sus! with us a - bide.
end - ing joy We may at - tain at last!

TEXT: Claudia Frances Hernaman, 1838-1898
MELODY: from *John Day's Psalter*, 1562
HARMONIZATION: Richard Redhead, 1820-1901

ST. FLAVIAN
86.86

361   O Cross of Christ, immortal tree

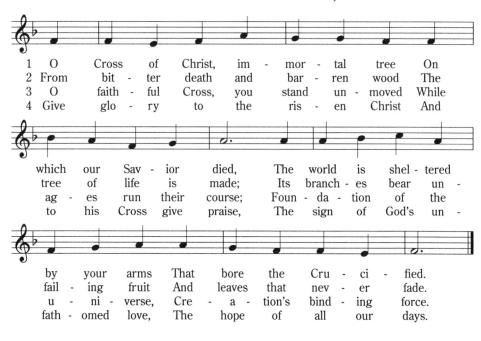

1 O Cross of Christ, im - mor - tal tree On
2 From bit - ter death and bar - ren wood The
3 O faith - ful Cross, you stand un - moved While
4 Give glo - ry to the ris - en Christ And

which our Sav - ior died, The world is shel - tered
tree of life is made; Its branch - es bear un -
ag - es run their course; Foun - da - tion of the
to his Cross give praise, The sign of God's un -

by your arms That bore the Cru - ci - fied.
fail - ing fruit And leaves that nev - er fade.
u - ni - verse, Cre - a - tion's bind - ing force.
fath - omed love, The hope of all our days.

TEXT: from the *Stanbrook Abbey Hymnal*, copyright © 1974 by Stanbrook Abbey
MELODY: from *John Day's Psalter*, 1562
HARMONIZATION: Richard Redhead, 1820-1901

ST. FLAVIAN
86.86

362   Forty days and forty nights

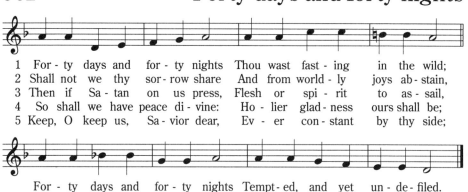

1 For - ty days and for - ty nights Thou wast fast - ing in the wild;
2 Shall not we thy sor - row share And from world - ly joys ab - stain,
3 Then if Sa - tan on us press, Flesh or spi - rit to as - sail,
4 So shall we have peace di - vine: Ho - lier glad - ness ours shall be;
5 Keep, O keep us, Sa - vior dear, Ev - er con - stant by thy side;

For - ty days and for - ty nights Tempt - ed, and yet un - de - filed.
Fast - ing with un - ceas - ing prayer, Strong with thee to suf - fer pain?
Vic - tor in the wil - der - ness, Grant we may not faint nor fail!
Round us, too, shall an - gels shine, Such as min - is - tered to thee.
That with thee we may ap - pear At the e - ter - nal Eas - ter - tide.

TEXT: George Hunt Smyttan, 1822-1870, alt.
MELODY: from *Nürnbergisches Gesangbuch*, 1676, attributed to Martin Herbst, 1654-1681
HARMONIZATION: William Henry Monk, 1823-1889

HEINLEIN
77.77

The glory of these forty days 363

1 The glo - ry of these for - ty days We
2 A - lone and fast - ing Mo - ses saw The
3 So Dan - iel trained his mys - tic sight, De -
4 Then grant us, Lord, like them to be Full
5 O Fa - ther, Son, and Spir - it blest, To

cel - e - brate with songs of praise; For Christ, by whom all
lov - ing God who gave the law; And to E - li - jah,
liv - er'd from the li - on's might; And John, the Bride - groom's
oft in fast and prayer with thee; Our spir - its strength - en
thee be ev - ery prayer ad - drest; Who art in three - fold

things were made, Him - self has fast - ed and has prayed.
fast - ing came The steeds and char - i - ots of flame.
friend, be - came The her - ald of Mes - si - ah's name.
with thy grace, And give us joy to see thy face.
Name a - dored, From age to age, the on - ly Lord. A - men.

TEXT: Ascribed to St. Gregory the Great, 540-604, translated by Maurice F. Bell, 1862-1947
MELODY: from Joseph Klug's *Geistliche Lieder*, 1543
HARMONIZATION: Johann Sebastian Bach, 1685-1750

ERHALT UNS HERR
88.88

364

Lord Jesus, think on me

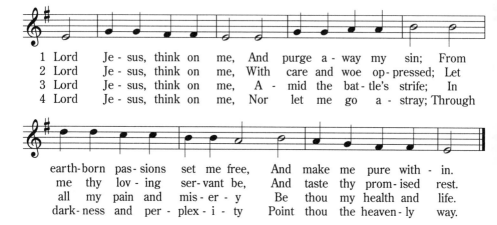

1 Lord Je-sus, think on me, And purge a-way my sin; From
2 Lord Je-sus, think on me, With care and woe op-pressed; Let
3 Lord Je-sus, think on me, A - mid the bat-tle's strife; In
4 Lord Je-sus, think on me, Nor let me go a - stray; Through

earth-born pas-sions set me free, And make me pure with - in.
me thy lov - ing ser-vant be, And taste thy prom-ised rest.
all my pain and mis-er - y Be thou my health and life.
dark-ness and per - plex - i - ty Point thou the heaven-ly way.

5 Lord Jesus, think on me,
That, when the flood is past,
I may the eternal brightness see,
And share thy joy at last.

6 Lord Jesus, think on me,
That I may sing above
To Father, Spirit, and to thee
The strains of praise and love.

TEXT: Synesius of Cyrene, c.375-430, translated by Allen W. Chatfield, 1808-1896
MELODY: *Damon's Psalter*, 1579
HARMONIZATION: Anonymous

SOUTHWELL
66.86

365 Parce, Domine/Spare thy people, Lord

Par-ce, Dó-mi-ne, par-ce pó-pu-lo tu - o:
Spare thy peo-ple, Lord, spare thy peo-ple; see us here be-fore thee;

Ne in ae - ter-num i - ra-scá - ris no - bis.
Be not an-gry, Lord, with thy peo-ple for - ev - er.

TEXT: Joel 2:17, translated by Charles W. Leland, copyright © 1958 by Ralph Jusko Publications, Inc., alt.
MELODY: Plainchant, Mode I
HARMONIZATION: Jean-Hébert Desrocquettes, O.S.B., copyright © 1958 by Ralph Jusko Publications, Inc.

PARCE DOMINE
Irregular

Attende, Domine/ Hear our entreaties, Lord

Refrain

At - tén - de, Dó - mi - ne, et mi - se - ré - re,
Hear our en - treat - ies, Lord, and show Thy mer - cy;

qui - a pec - cá - vi - mus ti - bi.
for we are sin - ners be - fore Thee.

Verses

1 Ad te Rex sum - me, ó - mni - um Red - émp - tor,
2 Ro - gá - mus, De - us, tu - am ma - je - stá - tem:
1 King high ex - alt - ed, all the world's Re - deem - er,
2 We, Thy e - ter - nal maj - es - ty en - treat - ing,

ó - cu - los no - stros sub - le - vá - mus flen - tes:
aú - ri - bus sa - cris gé - mi - tus ex - aú - di:
to Thee Thy chil - dren lift their eyes with weep - ing:
make lam - en - ta - tion in Thy ho - ly hear - ing:

ex - aú - di, Chri - ste, sup - pli - cán - tum pre - ces.
cri - mi - na no - stra plá - ci - dus in - dúl - ge.
Christ, we im - plore Thee, hear our sup - pli - ca - tion.
gra - cious - ly grant Thou to our sins in - dul - gence.

TEXT: Latin, 10th century, translation anonymous
MELODY: from *Paris Processional*, 1824
HARMONIZATION: Jean-Hébert Desrocquettes, O.S.B., copyright © 1958 by Ralph Jusko Publications, Inc.

ATTENDE DOMINE
1 1 . 1 1 . 1 1 with Refrain

380

Vexilla regis

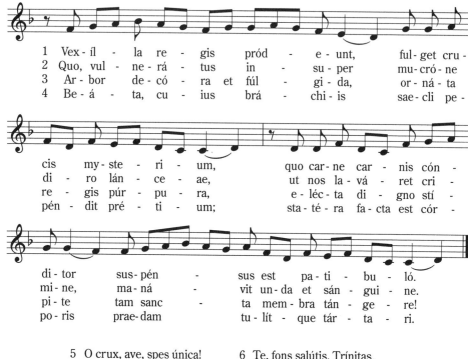

1 Vex-íl-la re-gis pród-e-unt, ful-get cru-
2 Quo, vul-ne-rá-tus in-su-per mu-cró-ne
3 Ar-bor de-có-ra et fúl-gi-da, or-ná-ta
4 Be-á-ta, cu-ius brá-chi-is sae-cli pe-

cis my-ste-ri-um, quo car-ne car-nis cón-
di-ro lán-ce-ae, ut nos la-vá-ret cri-
re-gis púr-pu-ra, e-léc-ta di-gno stí-
pén-dit pré-ti-um; sta-té-ra fa-cta est cór-

di-tor sus-pén- sus est pa-ti-bu-ló.
mi-ne, ma-ná- vit un-da et sán-gui-ne.
pi-te tam sanc- ta mem-bra tán-ge-re!
po-ris prae-dam tu-lít-que tár-ta-ri.

5 O crux, ave, spes única!
 hoc passiónis témpore
 piis adáuge grátiam
 reísque dela crímina.

6 Te, fons salútis, Trínitas,
 colláudet omnis spíritus;
 quos per crucis mystérium
 salvas, fove per saécula.

TEXT: Venantius Fortunatus, c.530-c.609
MELODY: Plainchant, Mode I
HARMONIZATION: Kurt Poterack, b.1962, copyright © Ignatius Press 1997

VEXILLA REGIS
88.88

The royal banners forward go

381

1 The roy - al ban - ners for - ward go, The cross shines
2 Ful - filled is all that Da - vid told In true pro -
3 O tree of beau - ty, tree most fair, Or - dained those
4 Blest tree, whose chos - en bran-ches bore The wealth that
5 O cross, our one re - li - ance, hail! Still may thy
6 To thee, e - ter - nal Three in One, Let hom - age

forth in mys - tic glow Where he, as man, who
phet - ic song of old; How God the na - tions'
ho - ly limbs to bear; Gone is thy shame, each
did the world re - store, The price of hu - man -
power with us a - vail More good for right - eous
meet by all be done: As by the cross thou

gave man breath, Now bows be - neath the yoke of death.
King should be, For God is reign - ing from the tree.
crim - son'd bough Pro - claims the King of glo - ry now.
kind to pay, And spoil the spoil - er of his prey.
souls to win, And save the sin - ner from his sin.
dost re - store, So rule and guide us ev - er - more.

TEXT: *Vexilla regis*, by Venantius Fortunatus, c.530-c.609,
    translated by John Mason Neale, 1818-1866, and compilers of *The Hymnal*, 1940, copyright © Church Publishing, Inc.
MELODY: Trinity College MS, 15th century
HARMONIZATION: Traditional

AGINCOURT
88.88

382

Ride on! ride on

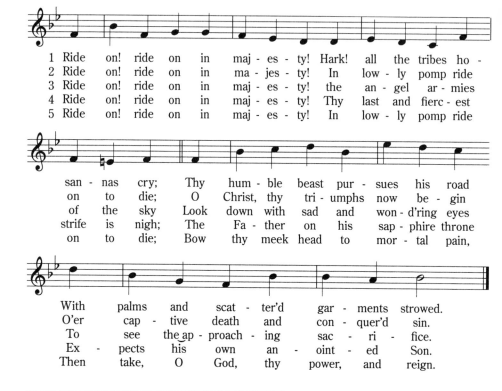

1 Ride on! ride on in maj - es - ty! Hark! all the tribes ho -
2 Ride on! ride on in ma - jes - ty! In low - ly pomp ride
3 Ride on! ride on in maj - es - ty! the an - gel ar - mies
4 Ride on! ride on in maj - es - ty! Thy last and fierc - est
5 Ride on! ride on in maj - es - ty! In low - ly pomp ride

san - nas cry; Thy hum - ble beast pur - sues his road
on to die; O Christ, thy tri - umphs now be - gin
of the sky Look down with sad and won - d'ring eyes
strife is nigh; The Fa - ther on his sap - phire throne
on to die; Bow thy meek head to mor - tal pain,

With palms and scat - ter'd gar - ments strowed.
O'er cap - tive death and con - quer'd sin.
To see the ap - proach - ing sac - ri - fice.
Ex - pects his own an - oint - ed Son.
Then take, O God, thy power, and reign.

TEXT: Henry Hart Milman, 1791-1868
MELODY: adapted from a chorale in *Musikalisches Handbuch*, Hamburg, 1690
HARMONIZATION: William Henry Monk, 1823-1889, alt.

WINCHESTER NEW
88.88

All glory, laud and honor

383

Refrain

All glo - ry, laud and hon - or To thee, Re - deem - er, King!

To whom the lips of chil - dren Made sweet ho - san - nas ring.

1 Thou art the King of Is - ra - el, Thou Da - vid's Roy - al Son,
2 The com - pan - y of an - gels Are prais - ing thee on high,
3 The peo - ple of the He - brews With palms be - fore thee went;
4 To thee be - fore thy pas - sion They sang their hymns of praise;
5 Thou didst ac - cept their prais - es, Ac - cept the pray'rs we bring.

Who in the Lord's name com - est, The King and Bless - ed One.
And mor - tal men and all things Cre - at - ed make re - ply.
Our praise and pray'r and an - thems Be - fore thee we pre - sent.
To thee, now high ex - alt - ed, Our mel - o - dy we raise.
Who in all good de - light - est, Thou kind and gra - cious King.

TEXT: St. Theodulph of Orleans, 760-821, translated by John Mason Neale, 1818-1866
MELODY: Melchior Teschner, 1584-1635
HARMONIZATION: Johann Sebastian Bach, 1685-1750

ST. THEODULPH
7 6 . 7 6 with Refrain

390 Ubi caritas

Antiphon

U - bi cá - ri - tas et a - mor, De - us i - bi est.

Verses

Con - gre - gá - vit nos in u - num Chri - sti a - mor,
E - xul - té - mus, et in ip - so ju - cun - dé - mur,

Ti - me - á - mus, et a - mé - mus De - um vi - vum,

Repeat Antiphon

Et ex cor - de di - li - gá - mus nos sin - cé - ro.

Final form of antiphon to follow last verse:

U - bi ca - ri - tas et a - mor, De - us i - bi est.

2 Simul ergo cum in unum cogregámur,
Ne nos mente dividámur caveámus.
Cessent júrgia malígna, cessent lites,
Et in médio nostri sit Christus Deus.

3 Simul quoque cum beátis videámus
Gloriánter vultum tuum, Christe Deus:
Gáudium quod est imménsum atque probum,
Saécula per infiníta saeculórum.

WHERE CHARITY IS

Antiphon: *Where charity and desire are one, there God is.*

Verses

1 *The love of Christ has united us,*
Let us both fear and yearn for the living God,
And from the heart let us devoutly love one another.

2 *Let us, therefore, be gathered together in unity*
And beware lest we be not of one mind.
Let us stop the malignant quarreling, cease our contentions
And let Christ, our God, be among us.

3 *And let us together with the Blessed Ones*
Exultingly behold thy face:
That which is an infinite joy
Throughout eternity.

TEXT: Hymn for the *mandatum* from the Holy Thursday Liturgy,
    translation by Richard Divozzo, b.1955. Used with permission.
MELODY: Plainchant, Mode VI
HARMONIZATION: Dominican Nuns of Summit, New Jersey
    Harmonization and final form of antiphon copyright © 1983 by the Dominican Nuns of Summit, New Jersey

UBI CARITAS
13.12.12.12.12

Pange lingua

1 Pan - ge lin - gua glo - ri - ó - si Cór - po - ris
2 No - bis da - tus, no - bis na - tus, Ex in - tá -
3 In su - pré - mae no - cte cae - nae, Re - cúm - bens
4 Ver - bum ca - ro, pa - nem ve - rum, Ver - bo car -
5 Tan - tum er - go sa - cra - mén - tum Ve - ne - ré -
6 Ge - ni - tó - ri ge - ni - tó - que Laus et ju -

my - sté - ri - um, San - gui - nís - que pre - ti - ó - si,
cta Vír - gi - ne, Et in mun - do con - ver - sá - tus,
cúm frá - tri - bus, Ob - ser - vá - ta le - ge ple - ne,
nem éf - fi - cit: Fit - que san - guis Chri - sti me - rum,
mur cér - nu - i: Et an - tí - quum do - cu - mén - tum
bi - lá - ti - o, Sa - lus, ho - nor, vir - tus quo - que,

Quem in mun - di pré - ti - um Fru - ctus ven - tris
Spar - so ver - bi sé - mi - ne, Su - i mo - ras
Ci - bis in le - gá - li - bus, Ci - bum tur - bae
Et si sen - sus dé - fi - cit, Ad fir - mán - dum
No - vo ce - dat rí - tu - i: Prae - stet fi - des
Sit et be - ne - di - cti - o: Pro - ce - dén - ti

ge - ne - ró - si Rex ef - fú - dit gén - ti - um.
in - co - lá - tus, Mi - ro clau - sit ór - di - ne.
du - o - dé - nae, Se dat su - is má - ni - bus.
cor sin - cé - rum, So - la fi - des súf - fi - cit.
sup - ple - mén - tum Sén - su - um de - fé - ctu - i.
ab u - tró - que Com - par sit lau - dá - ti - o. A - men.

TEXT: St. Thomas Aquinas, 1225-1274
MELODY: Plainchant, Mode III
HARMONIZATION: Jean-Hébert Desroquettes, O.S.B., copyright © 1958 by Ralph Jusko Publications, Inc.

PANGE LINGUA
87.87.87

392   Of the glorious Body telling

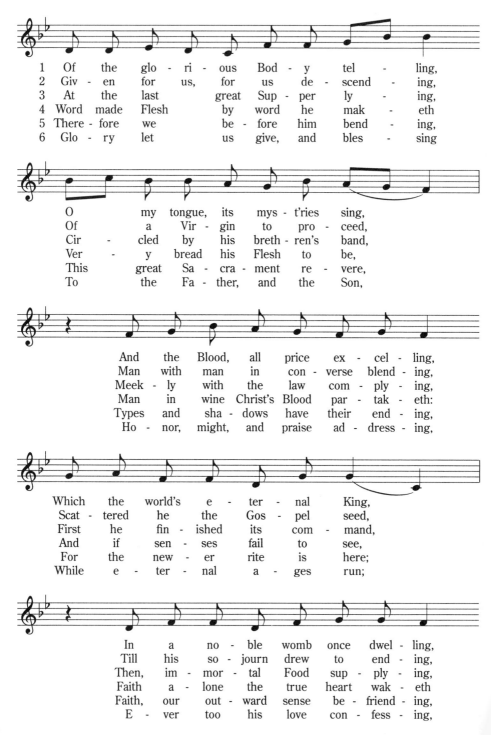

1 Of the glo - ri - ous Bod - y tel - ling,
2 Giv - en for us, for us de - scend - ing,
3 At the last great Sup - per ly - ing,
4 Word made Flesh by word he mak - eth
5 There - fore we be - fore him bend - ing,
6 Glo - ry let us give, and bles - sing

O my tongue, its mys - t'ries sing,
Of a Vir - gin to pro - ceed,
Cir - cled by his breth - ren's band,
Ver - y bread his Flesh to be,
This great Sa - cra - ment re - vere,
To the Fa - ther, and the Son,

And the Blood, all price ex - cel - ling,
Man with man in con - verse blend - ing,
Meek - ly with the law com - ply - ing,
Man in wine Christ's Blood par - tak - eth:
Types and sha - dows have their end - ing,
Ho - nor, might, and praise ad - dress - ing,

Which the world's e - ter - nal King,
Scat - tered he the Gos - pel seed,
First he fin - ished its com - mand,
And if sen - ses fail to see,
For the new - er rite is here;
While e - ter - nal a - ges run;

In a no - ble womb once dwel - ling,
Till his so - journ drew to end - ing,
Then, im - mor - tal Food sup - ply - ing,
Faith a - lone the true heart wak - eth
Faith, our out - ward sense be - friend - ing,
E - ver too his love con - fess - ing,

Shed for this world's ran - som - ing.
Which he closed in wond - rous deed.
Gave him - self with his own hand.
To be - hold the my - ster - y.
Makes the in - ward vi - sion clear.
Who, from both with both is one. A - men.

TEXT: St. Thomas Aquinas, 1225-1274,
   translated by John Mason Neale, 1818-1866, Edward Caswell, 1814-1878, and others;
   copyright © by Oxford University Press
MELODY: Plainchant, Mode III
HARMONIZATION: Kurt Poterack, b.1962, copyright © 1997 by Ignatius Press

PANGE LINGUA
87.87.87

HOLY THURSDAY

Tantum ergo/Down in adoration falling 393

1 Tan - tum er - go Sac - ra - mén - tum Ve - ne - ré - mur
2 Ge - ni - tó - ri, Ge - ni - tó - que Laus et ju - bi -
1 *Down in ad - or - a - tion fall - ing, Lo! the sac - red*
2 *To the ev - er - last - ing Fa - ther, And the Son who*

cér - nu - i: Et an - tí - quum do - cu - mén - tum
lá - ti - o, Sa - lus, ho - nor, vir - tus quo - que
Host we hail; Lo! o'er an - cient forms de - part - ing,
reigns on high, With the Spir - it Blest pro - ceed - ing

No - vo ce - dat rí - tu - i: Prae - stet fi - des
Sit et be - ne - dí - cti - o: Pro - ce - dén - ti
New - er rites of grace pre - vail; Faith for all de -
forth from each e - ter - nal - ly, Be sal - va - tion,

sup - ple - mén - tum Sén - su - um de - fé - ctu - i.
ab u - tró - que Com - par sit lau - dá - ti - o. A - men.
fects sup - ply - ing where the fee - ble sen - ses fail.
hon - or, bless - ing, might and end - less maj - es - ty. A - men.

TEXT: St. Thomas Aquinas, 1225-1274, translated by Edward Caswall, 1814-1878
MELODY: from *Cantus Diversi*, by John Francis Wade, 1711-1786
HARMONIZATION: attributed to Vincent Francis Novello, 1781-1861

ST. THOMAS
87.87.87

400

Stabat Mater

```
1  Sta - bat    Ma - ter    do - lo - ró - sa    Ju - xta   cru - cem
2  Cu - jus     a - ni -    mam ge - mén - tem,  Con - tri - stá - tam
3  O   quam     tris - tis  et   af - flí - cta  Fu - it    il - la
4  Quae moe - ré - bat,     et   do - lé - bat,  Pi - a     Ma - ter,
5  Quis est     ho - mo,    qui  non  fle - ret, Ma - trem  Chrí - sti
6  Quis non     pos - set   con - tri - stá - ri, Chri - sti Ma - trem
```

```
   la - cri - mó - sa,   Dum pen - dé - bat   Fi - li - us.
   et   do - lén - tem,  Per - tran - sí - vit glá - di - us.
   be - ne - dí - cta    Ma - ter  U - ni - gé - ni - ti!
   dum vi - dé - bat     Na - ti   poe - nas  ín - cly - ti.
   si   vi - dér - et    In  tan - to  sup - pli - ci - o?
   con - tem - plá - ri   Do - lén - tem cum  Fï - li - o?
```

7 Pro peccátis suae gentis
   Vidit Jesum in torméntis,
   Et flagéllis súbditum.

8 Vidit suum dulcem Natum
   Moriéndo desolátum,
   Dum emísit spíritum.

9 Eia Mater, fons amóris,
   Me sentíre vim dolóris
   Fac, ut tecum lúgeam.

10 Fac ut árdeat cor meum
   In amándo Christum Deum,
   Ut sibi compláceam.

11 Sancta Mater, istud agas,
   Crucifíxi fige plagas
   Cordi meo válide.

12 Tui nati vulneráti,
   Tam dignáti pro me pati,
   Poenas mecum dívide.

13 Fac me tecum pie flere,
   Crucifíxo condolére,
   Donec ego víxero.

14 Juxta crucem tecum stare,
   Et me tibi sociare
   In planctu desídero.

15 Virgo vírginum praeclára,
   Mihi jam non sis amára:
   Fac me tecum plángere;

16 Fac, ut portem Christi mortem,
   Passiónis fac consórtem,
   Et plagas recólere.

17 Fac me plagis vulnerári,
   Fac me cruce inebriári,
   Et cruóre Fílii;

18 Flammis ne urar succénsus,
   Per te, Virgo, sim defénsus
   In die judícii.

19 Christe, cum sit hinc exíre,
   Da per Matrem me veníre
   Ad palmam victóriae;

20 Quando corpus moriétur,
   Fac, ut ánimae donétur
   Paradísi glória. Amen.

TEXT: *Stabat mater*, ascribed to Jacopone da Todi, 1230-1306
MELODY: *Stabat mater*, from *Mainzisch Gesangbuch*, 1661

MAINZ
88.7

At the cross her station keeping

401

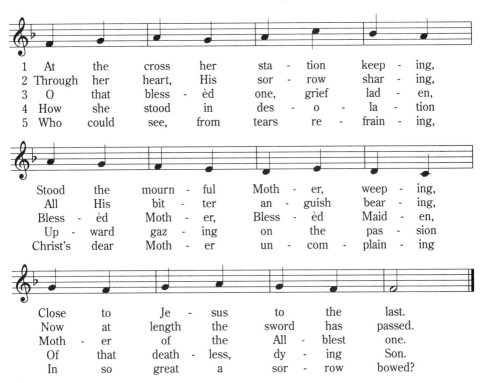

1	At	the	cross	her	sta -	tion	keep -	ing,
2	Through	her	heart,	His	sor -	row	shar -	ing,
3	O	that	bless - èd	one,	grief	lad -	en,
4	How	she	stood	in	des - o -	la -	tion
5	Who	could	see,	from	tears	re -	frain -	ing,

Stood	the	mourn - ful	Moth - er,	weep - ing,
All	His	bit - ter	an - guish	bear - ing,
Bless - èd	Moth - er,	Bless - èd	Maid - en,
Up - ward	gaz - ing	on	the	pas - sion
Christ's	dear	Moth - er	un - com - plain - ing

Close	to	Je - sus	to	the	last.
Now	at	length	the	sword	has	passed.
Moth - er	of	the	All - blest	one.
Of	that	death - less,	dy - ing	Son.
In	so	great	a	sor - row	bowed?

6 Who, unmoved, behold her languish
Underneath His Cross of anguish,
'Mid the fierce, unpitying crowd?

7 For His people's sins th'All-Holy
She beheld, a Victim lowly,
Bleed in torments, bleed and die.

8 Saw her well-beloved taken,
Saw her Child in death forsaken,
Heard His last expiring cry.

9 Fount of love and sacred sorrow,
Mother! may my spirit borrow
Sadness from thy holy woe.

10 May my spirit burn within me,
Love my God, and great love win me
Grace to please Him here below.

11 Those five Wounds on Jesus smitten,
Mother, in my heart be written,
Deep as in thine own they be.

12 Thou, my Savior's Cross who bearest,
Thou, Thy Son's rebuke who sharest,
Let me share them both with thee.

13 In the Passion of my Maker
Be my sinful soul partaker,
Weep till death, and weep with thee.

14 Mine with thee be that sad station,
There to watch the great Salvation,
Wrought upon th'atoning Tree.

15 Virgin thou of Virgins fairest,
May the bitter woe thou sharest
Make on me impression deep.

16 Thus Christ's dying may I carry,
With Him in His Passion tarry,
And His Wounds in mem'ry keep.

17 May His Wounds transfix me wholly,
May His Cross and Life Blood holy
Mortify my heart and mind:

18 Thus inflamed with pure affection,
In the Virgin's Son protection
May I at the judgement find.

19 When in death my limbs are failing,
Let Thy Mother's prayer prevailing
Lift me, Jesus, to Thy throne;

20 To my parting soul be given
Entrance through the gate of Heaven,
There confess me for Thine own.

TEXT: *Stabat mater*, ascribed to Jacopone da Todi, 1230-1306, translation by the St. Gregory Guild, Inc.

MELODY: *Stabat mater*, from *Mainzisch Gesangbuch*, 1661

MAINZ
8 8 . 7

GOOD FRIDAY

402   Ah, holy Jesus

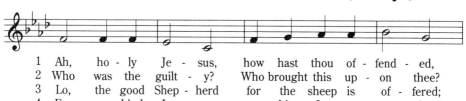

1 Ah, ho-ly Je-sus, how hast thou of-fend-ed,
2 Who was the guilt-y? Who brought this up-on thee?
3 Lo, the good Shep-herd for the sheep is of-fered;
4 For me, kind Je-sus, was thine In-car-na-tion,
5 There-fore, kind Je-sus, since I can-not pay thee,

That man to judge thee hath in hate pre-tend-ed? By foes de-
A-las, my trea-son, Je-sus hath un-done thee. 'Twas I, Lord
The slave hath sin-ned, and the Son hath suf-fered; For man's a-
Thy mor-tal sor-row, and thy life's ob-la-tion; Thy death of
I do a-dore thee, and will ev-er pray thee, Think on thy

rid-ed, by thine own re-ject-ed, O most af-flict-ed.
Je-sus, I it was de-nied thee: I cru-ci-fied thee.
tone-ment, while he noth-ing heed-eth, God in-ter-ceed-eth.
an-guish and thy bit-ter Pas-sion, For my sal-va-tion.
pi-ty and thy love un-swerv-ing, Not my de-serv-ing.

TEXT: Robert Bridges, 1844-1930, from a text by Johann Heerman, 1585-1647,
which was based on an 11th century Latin meditation

MELODY: Johann Crüger, 1598-1622

HARMONIZATION: Johann Crüger, 1598-1622

HERZLIEBSTER JESU
1 1 . 1 1 . 1 1 . 5

O Sacred Head surrounded

403

1 O Sa-cred Head sur-round-ed By crown of pierc-ing thorn!
2 I see thy strength and vig - or All fad-ing in the strife,
3 In this, thy bit - ter Pas - sion, Good Shep-herd, think of me,

O bleed-ing Head, so wound-ed, Re-viled and put to scorn!
And death with cru-el rig - or Be-reav-ing thee of life:
With thy most sweet com-pas - sion, Un-wor-thy though I be:

Death's pal - id hue comes o'er thee, The glow of life de - cays,
O ag - o - ny and dy - ing! O love to sin-ners free!
Be - neath thy Cross a - bid - ing For - ev - er would I rest,

Yet an - gel hosts a - dore thee, And trem-ble as they gaze.
Je - sus, all grace sup - ply - ing, O turn thy face on me.
In thy dear love con - fid - ing, And with thy pres-ence blest.

TEXT: Latin, attributed to St. Bernard of Clairvoux, 1091-1153, translated by Henry Williams Baker, 1821-1877
MELODY: Hans Leo Hassler, 1564-1612
HARMONIZATION: Johann Sebastian Bach, 1685-1750

PASSION CHORALE
7 6 . 7 6 . D

404 Sing, my tongue, the glorious battle

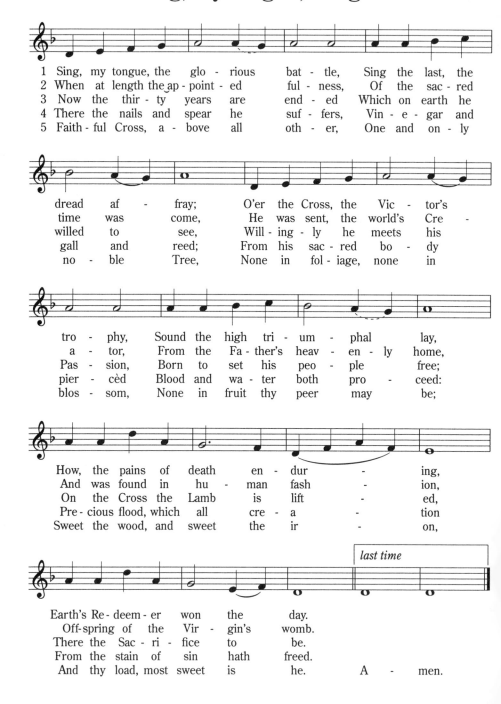

1 Sing, my tongue, the glo - rious bat - tle, Sing the last, the
2 When at length the ap - point - ed ful - ness, Of the sac - red
3 Now the thir - ty years are end - ed Which on earth he
4 There the nails and spear he suf - fers, Vin - e - gar and
5 Faith - ful Cross, a - bove all oth - er, One and on - ly

dread af - fray; O'er the Cross, the Vic - tor's
time was come, He was sent, the world's Cre -
willed to see, Will - ing - ly he meets his
gall and reed; From his sac - red bo - dy
no - ble Tree, None in fol - iage, none in

tro - phy, Sound the high tri - um - phal lay,
a - tor, From the Fa - ther's heav - en - ly home,
Pas - sion, Born to set his peo - ple free;
pier - cèd Blood and wa - ter both pro - ceed:
blos - som, None in fruit thy peer may be;

How, the pains of death en - dur - ing,
And was found in hu - man fash - ion,
On the Cross the Lamb is lift - ed,
Pre - cious flood, which all cre - a - tion
Sweet the wood, and sweet their - on,

last time

Earth's Re - deem - er won the day.
Off-spring of the Vir - gin's womb.
There the Sac - ri - fice to be.
From the stain of sin hath freed.
And thy load, most sweet is he. A - men.

6 Bend, O lofty Tree, thy branches, Thy too rigid sinews bend;
   And awhile the stubborn hardness, Which thy birth bestowed, suspend;
   And the limbs of heaven's high Monarch Gently on thine arms extend.

7 Thou alone wast counted worthy This world's Ransom to sustain,
   That a shipwrecked race for ever Might a port of refuge gain,
   With the sacred Blood anointed Of the Lamb for sinners slain.

8 Praise and honor to the Father, Praise and honor to the Son,
   Praise and honor to the Spirit, Ever Three and ever One:
   One in might, and One in glory, While eternal ages run.

TEXT: *Pange lingua gloriosi praelium certaminis,* Venantius Fortunatus, c.530-c.609,
   translated by John Mason Neale, 1818-1866, and compilers of *Hymns Ancient and Modern,*
   copyright © Proprietors of *Hymns Ancient and Modern*
MELODY: probably 17th century French carol, found in Tiersot's *Mélodies,* 1887
HARMONIZATION: after *Hymns Ancient and Modern*

PICARDY
8 7 . 8 7 . 8 7

410 Jesus Christ is risen today

1 Je - sus Christ is ris'n to - day, Al - le - lu - ia!
2 Hymns of praise then let us sing, Al - le - lu - ia!
3 But the pains that he en - dured, Al - le - lu - ia!
4 Sing we to our God a - bove, Al - le - lu - ia!

Our tri - um - phant ho - ly day, Al - le - lu - ia!
Un - to Christ, our heav'n - ly king, Al - le - lu - ia!
Our sal - va - tion have pro - cured; Al - le - lu - ia!
Praise e - ter - nal as his love; Al - le - lu - ia!

Who did once up - on the cross, Al - le - lu - ia!
Who en - dured the cross and grave, Al - le - lu - ia!
Now a - bove the sky he's king, Al - le - lu - ia!
Praise him, all ye heav'n - ly host, Al - le - lu - ia!

Suf - fer to re - deem our loss, Al - le - lu - ia!
Sin - ners to re - deem and save. Al - le - lu - ia!
Where the an - gels ev - er sing. Al - le - lu - ia!
Fa - ther, Son, and Ho - ly Ghost, Al - le - lu - ia! A - men.

TEXT: *Surrexit Christus hodie*, 14th century, paraphrase from *Lyra Davidica*, 1708,
  translated by Nahum Tate, 1652-1715, and Nicholas Brady, 1659 -1726; v. 4, Charles Wesley, 1707-1788
MELODY: altered from a melody in *Lyra Davidica*, 1708
HARMONIZATION: Traditional

LYRA DAVIDICA (EASTER HYMN)
7 7 . 7 7 with Alleluias

At the Lamb's high feast

1 At the Lamb's high feast we sing   Praise to our vic - tor - ious King:
2 Where the Pas- chal blood is poured, Death's dark an - gel sheathes his sword;
3 Might- y Vic - tim from on high, Powers of hell be - neath thee lie;
4 Pas- chal tri- umph, Pas - cal joy,   On - ly sin can this des - troy;

Who hath washed us in the tide   Flow - ing from his pier - céd side;
Is - rael's hosts tri - um- phant go Through the wave that drowns the foe.
Death is brok - en in the fight, Thou hast brought us life and light.
From sin's death do those set free, Souls re - born, dear Lord, in thee.

Praise we him whose love di - vine Gives the guests his blood for wine,
Christ, the Lamb whose blood was shed, Pas - chal vic - tim, Pas- chal bread!
Now thy ban - ner thou dost wave, Con- quering Sa - tan and the grave.
Hymns of glo - ry, songs of praise, Fa - ther, un - to thee we raise.

Gives his bo - dy for the feast, Love the Vic - tim, Love the Priest.
With sin- cer - i - ty and love Eat we Man - na from a- bove.
See the prince of darkness quelled; Heav'n's bright gates are op - en held.
Ris - en Lord, all praise to thee, Ev - er with the Spir- it be.   A-men.

TEXT: *Ad regias agni dapes*, attributed to St. Ambrose, 340-397, altered in 1632, translated by Robert Campbell, 1814-1868
MELODY: Jakob Hintze, 1622-1702
HARMONIZATION: Johann Sebastian Bach, 1685-1750

SALZBURG
7 7 . 7 7 . D

412 Ye sons and daughters of the Lord

Refrain

Al - le - lu - ia, Al - le - lu - ia, Al - le - lu - ia!

1 Ye sons and daugh - ters of the Lord, The King of
2 All in the ear - ly morn - ing grey, Went ho - ly
3 Of spi - ces pure a pre - cious store, In their pure
4 An an - gel clad in white they see, Who sat and
5 That night th'A - pos - tles met in fear, But Christ did

Glo - ry, King a - dored, This day him -
wom - en on their way To see the
hands these wo - men bore, To a - noint the
spake un - to the three: "Your Lord hath
in their midst ap - pear: "My peace," he

self from death re - stored. Al - le - lu - ia!
tomb where Je - sus lay. Al - le - lu - ia!
sac - red bo - dy o'er. Al - le - lu - ia!
gone to Gal - i - lee." Al - le - lu - ia!
saith, "be on all here." Al - le - lu - ia!

6 When Thomas first the tidings heard,
How they had seen the risen Lord,
He doubted the disciples' word. Alleluia! *Refrain*

7 "My piercéd side, O Thomas, see:
My hands, my feet, I show to thee:
Not faithless, but believing be." Alleluia! *Refrain*

8 No longer Thomas then denied,
He saw the feet, the hands, the side:
"Thou art my Lord and God," he cried. Alleluia! *Refrain*

9 How blest are they who have not seen,
And yet whose faith has constant been,
For they eternal life shall win. Alleluia! *Refrain*

10 On this most holy day of days,
To God your hearts and voices raise,
In laud, and jubilee, and praise. Alleluia. *Refrain*

After the last stanza

Al - le - lu - ia, Al - le - lu - ia, Al - le - lu - ia!

TEXT: Jean Tisserand, ?-1494, vv. 1-5, trans. from Edward Caswall, 1814-1878, vv. 6-10, John Mason Neale, 1818-1866
MELODY: 15th century French melody
HARMONIZATION: John Rodgers, copyright © 1966 by Benziger Editions, Inc., alt.

O FILII ET FILIAE
8 8 8 with Alleluias

The strife is o'er, the battle done 413

Al - le - lu - ia! Al - le - lu - ia! Al - le - lu - ia!

1 The strife is o'er, the bat - tle done, The vic - to -
2 The powers of death have done their worst, But Christ their
3 The three sad days are quick - ly sped, He ri - ses
4 He closed the yawn - ing gates of hell, The bars from
5 Lord! by the stripes which wound - ed thee, From death's dread

ry of life is won; The song of tri - umph
le - gions hath dis - persed: Let shout of ho - ly
glo - rious from the dead: All glo - ry to our
heav'n's high por - tals fell; Let hymns of praise his
sting thy ser - vants free, That we may live and

hath be - gun. Al - le - lu - ia!
joy out - burst. Al - le - lu - ia!
ris - en Head! Al - le - lu - ia!
tri - umphs tell! Al - le - lu - ia!
sing to thee. Al - le - lu - ia!

TEXT: from *Sinfonia Sirenum*, Cologne, 1695, translated by Francis Pott, 1832-1909, alt.
MELODY: adapted from the Gloria Patri of a Magnificat on Tone III
   by Giovanni Pierluigi da Palestrina, c. 1525 -1594, by William Henry Monk, 1823 -1889
HARMONIZATION: William Henry Monk, 1823 -1889

VICTORY
8 8 8 with Alleluias

414

Hail thee, festival day!

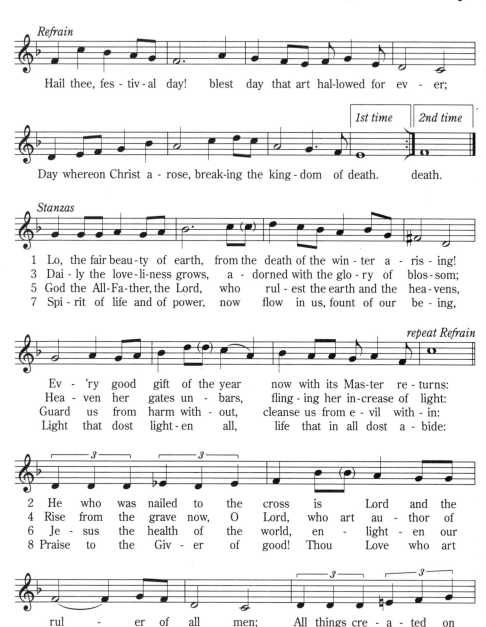

Refrain

Hail thee, fes - tiv - al day! blest day that art hal-lowed for ev - er;

1st time | *2nd time*

Day whereon Christ a - rose, break-ing the king - dom of death. death.

Stanzas

1 Lo, the fair beau-ty of earth, from the death of the win - ter a - ris - ing!
3 Dai - ly the love-li-ness grows, a - dorned with the glo - ry of blos-som;
5 God the All-Fa-ther, the Lord, who rul - est the earth and the hea-vens,
7 Spi - rit of life and of power, now flow in us, fount of our be - ing,

repeat Refrain

Ev - 'ry good gift of the year now with its Mas-ter re - turns:
Hea - ven her gates un - bars, fling - ing her in-crease of light:
Guard us from harm with - out, cleanse us from e - vil with - in:
Light that dost light - en all, life that in all dost a - bide:

2 He who was nailed to the cross is Lord and the
4 Rise from the grave now, O Lord, who art au - thor of
6 Je - sus the health of the world, en - light - en our
8 Praise to the Giv - er of good! Thou Love who art

rul - er of all men; All things cre - a - ted on
life and cre - a - tion. Tread-ing the path - way of
minds, thou Re - deem - er, Son of the Fa - ther su -
au - thor of con - cord, Pour out thy balm on our

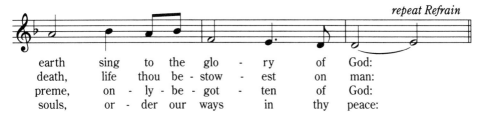

repeat Refrain

earth	sing	to	the	glo - ry	of	God:
death,	life	thou	be - stow - est		on	man:
preme,	on - ly - be - got - ten				of	God:
souls,	or - der	our	ways		in	thy peace:

TEXT: *Salve Festa Dies,* Venantius Honorius Fortunatus, 530-609, translated by Maurice F. Bell, 1862-1947,
    adapted from the translation in the *English Hymnal,* copyright © by Oxford University Press,
    text altered by permission of Oxford University Press.
MELODY: Ralph Vaughn Williams, 1872-1958, from the *English Hymnal* by permission of Oxford University Press.
HARMONIZATION: Ralph Vaughn Williams, 1872-1958, copyright © by Oxford University Press,
    from the *English Hymnal* by permission of Oxford University Press.

SALVE FESTA DIES
Irregular with Refrain

EASTER

Christc the Lord is risen today

415

1 Christ the Lord is ris'n to - day, Al - le - lu - ia!
2 Lives a - gain our glo - rious King; Al - le - lu - ia!
3 Love's re - deem - ing work is done, Al - le - lu - ia!
4 Soar we now where Christ has led, Al - le - lu - ia!

Sons of men and an - gels say. Al - le - lu - ia!
Where, O death, is now thy sting? Al - le - lu - ia!
Fought the fight, the bat - tle won. Al - le - lu - ia!
Foll'w- ing our ex - alt - ed head; Al - le - lu - ia!

Raise your joys and tri - umphs high, Al - le - lu - ia!
Once he died our souls to save, Al - le - lu - ia!
Death in vain for - bids him rise: Al - le - lu - ia!
Made like him, like him we rise, Al - le - lu - ia!

Sing ye heav'ns and earth re - ply, Al - le - lu - ia!
Where thy vic - to - ry, O grave? Al - le - lu - ia!
Christ has o - pen'd par - a - dise. Al - le - lu - ia!
Ours the cross, the grave, the skies. Al - le - lu - ia!

TEXT: Charles Wesley, 1707-1788
MELODY: Robert Williams, 1781-1821
HARMONIZATION: John Roberts, 1822-1877

LLANFAIR
7 7 . 7 7 with Alleluias

416

Ye watchers and ye holy ones

1 Ye watch-ers and ye ho-ly ones, Bright ser-aphs, cher-u-bim, and thrones, Raise the glad strain, Al-le-lu-ia! Cry out, do-min-ions, prince-doms, powers, Vir-tues, arch-an-gels, an-gels' choirs, Al-le-lu-ia, Al-le-lu-ia, Al-le-lu-ia, Al-le-lu-ia, Al-le-lu-ia!

2 O high-er than the cher-u-bim, More glo-rious than the ser-a-phim, Lead their prais-es, Al-le-lu-ia! Thou bear-er of the e-ter-nal Word, Most gra-cious, mag-ni-fy the Lord, Al-le-...

3 Re-spond, ye souls in end-less rest, Ye pat-ri-archs and pro-phets blest, Al-le-lu-ia, Al-le-lu-ia! Ye ho-ly twelve, ye mar-tyrs strong, All saints tri-um-phant, raise the song: Al-le-...

4 O friends, in glad-ness let us sing, Su-per-nal an-thems ech-o-ing, Al-le-lu-ia, Al-le-lu-ia! To God the Fa-ther, God the Son, And God the Spir-it, Three in One, Al-le-...

TEXT: John Athelstan Riley, 1858-1945, from the *English Hymnal* by permission of Oxford University Press.
MELODY: *Auserlesene Katholische Geistliche Kirchengesänge*, Cologne, 1623
HARMONIZATION: Ralph Vaughan Williams, 1872-1958, copyright © by Oxford University Press,
    from the *English Hymnal* by permission of Oxford University Press.

LASST UNS ERFREUEN
8 8 . 4 4 . 8 8 with Refrain

Come, ye faithful, raise the strain

1 Come, ye faith - ful, raise the strain Of tri - um - phant glad - ness;
2 'Tis the spring of souls to - day; Christ hath burst his pris - on,
3 Now the queen of sea - sons, bright With the day of splen - dor,
4 Nei - ther might the gates of death, Nor the tomb's dark por - tal,

God hath brought his Is - ra - el In - to joy from sad - ness;
And from three days' sleep in death As a sun has ris - en;
With the roy - al feast of feasts, Comes its joy to ren - der;
Nor the watch - ers, nor the seal Hold thee as a mor - tal:

Loosed from Phar - oah's bit - ter yoke Ja - cob's sons and daugh - ters;
All the win - ter of our sins, Long and dark, is fly - ing
Comes to glad Je - ru - sa - lem, Who with true af - fec - tion
But to - day a - midst thine own Thou didst stand, be - stow - ing

Led them with un - mois - tened foot Through the Red Sea wa - ters.
From his light, to whom we give Laud and praise un - dy - ing.
Wel - comes in un - wea - ried strains Je - sus' res - ur - rec - tion.
That thy peace which ev - er - more Pass - eth hu - man know - ing.

TEXT: St. John of Damascus, c.696-c.754, translated by John Mason Neale, 1818-1866
MELODY: Johann Roh, d.1547, who was also known as Johann Cornu and Johann Horn
HARMONIZATION: Traditional

GAUDEAMUS PARITER
76.76.D

Victimae Paschali laudes

1 Vi - cti - mae Pa - schá - li lau - des
im - mo - lent Chri - sti - á - ni.

2 A - gnus red - é - mit o - ves: Chri - stus in - no - cens Pa - tri
3 Mors et vi - ta du - él - lo con - fli - xé - re mi - rán - do:

re - con - cil - i - á - vit pec - ca - tó - res.
dux vi - tae mór - tu - us, re - gnat vi - vus.

4 Dic no - bis, Ma - ri - a, quid vi - dí - sti in vi - a?
6 An - gé - li - cos te - stes, su - dá - ri - um, et ve - stes.

5 Se - púl - crum Chri - sti vi - vén - tis,
7 Sur - ré - xit Chri - stus spes me - a:

et gló - ri - am vi - di re - sur - gén - tis:
prae - cé - det su - os in Ga - li - laé - am.

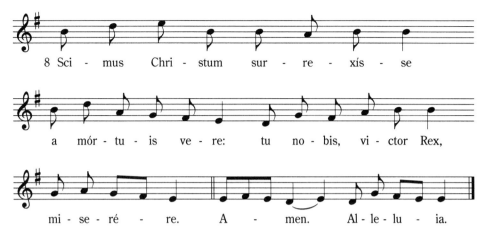

8 Sci - mus Chri - stum sur - re - xís - se a mór - tu - is ve - re: tu no - bis, vi - ctor Rex, mi - se - ré - re. A - men. Al - le - lu - ia.

PRAISES TO THE PASCHAL VICTIM

1 *Let Christians offer praises to the Paschal Victim.*

2 *The Lamb has redeemed the sheep:*
   the innocent Christ has reconciled sinners to the Father.

3 *Death and Life have struggled in a marvelous conflict:*
   the One who died is the Lord of life and the living One reigns.

4 *Tell us, Mary, what did you see on the way?*

5 *I have seen the tomb of the living Christ and the glory of the risen One:*

6 *Angelic witnesses, the funeral veil, and the shroud.*

7 *Christ, my hope, has risen:*
   He precedes them into Galilee.

8 *We know that truly Christ has risen from the dead:*
   Thou, triumphant king, have mercy on us.

TEXT: Attributed to Wipo of Burgundy, ?-c.1048,
    translation by Richard Divozzo, b.1955. Used with permission.
MELODY: Attributed to Wipo of Burgundy, ?-c.1048
HARMONIZATION: Jean-Hébert Desroquettes, O.S.B., copyright © 1958 by Ralph Jusko Publications, Inc.

VICTIMAE PASCHALI LAUDES
Irregular

419 Good Christian men, rejoice and sing

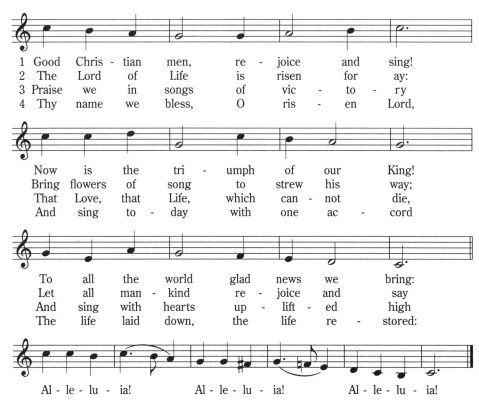

1 Good Chris - tian men, re - joice and sing!
2 The Lord of Life is risen for ay:
3 Praise we in songs of vic - to - ry
4 Thy name we bless, O ris - en Lord,

Now is the tri - umph of our King!
Bring flowers of song to strew his way;
That Love, that Life, which can - not die,
And sing to - day with one ac - cord

To all the world glad news we bring:
Let all man - kind re - joice and say
And sing with hearts up - lift - ed high
The life laid down, the life re - stored:

Al - le - lu - ia! Al - le - lu - ia! Al - le - lu - ia!

TEXT: Cyril A. Alington, 1872-1955
MELODY: Melchior Vulpius, c.1560-1616
HARMONIZATION: Friedrich Layritz, 1808-1859

GELOBT SEI GOTT
8 8 8 with Alleluias

Hail the day that sees him rise

430

1 Hail the day that sees him rise, Al - le - lu - ia!
2 There the glo - rious tri - umph waits; Al - le - lu - ia!
3 See! he lifts his hands a - bove; Al - le - lu - ia!
4 Lord be - yond our mor - tal sight, Al - le - lu - ia!

Glo - rious to his na - tive skies; Al - le - lu - ia!
Lift your heads, e - ter - nal gates! Al - le - lu - ia!
See! he shows the prints of love: Al - le - lu - ia!
Raise our hearts to reach thy height, Al - le - lu - ia!

Christ, a - while to mor - tals giv'n, Al - le - lu - ia!
Wide un - fold the ra - diant scene; Al - le - lu - ia!
Hark! his gra - cious lips be - stow, Al - le - lu - ia!
There thy face un - cloud - ed see, Al - le - lu - ia!

En - ters now the high - est heav'n! Al - le - lu - ia!
Take the King of glo - ry in! Al - le - lu - ia!
Bless - ings on his Church be - low. Al - le - lu - ia!
Find our heav'n of heav'ns in thee. Al - le - lu - ia!

TEXT: Charles Wesley, 1707-1788, alt.
MELODY: Robert Williams, 1781-1821
HARMONIZATION: John Roberts, 1822-1877

LLANFAIR
7 7 . 7 7 with Alleluias

431   See the Conqueror mounts in triumph

1 See the Con - qu'ror mounts in tri - umph;
2 He who on the cross did suf - fer,
3 Thou hast raised our hu - man na - ture

See the King in roy - al state,
He who from the grave a - rose,
On the clouds to God's right hand:

Rid - ing on the clouds, his char - iot,
He has van - quished sin and Sa - tan;
There we sit in heav'n - ly pla - ces,

To his heav'n - ly pal - ace gate!
He by death has spoiled his foes.
There with thee in glo - ry stand.

Hark! the choirs of an - gel voic - es
While he lifts his hands in bless - ing,
Je - sus reigns, a - dored by an - gels;

Joy - ful al - le - lu - ias sing,
He is part - ed from his friends;
Man with God is on the throne;

And the por - tals high are lift - ed
While their ea - ger eyes be - hold him,
Migh - ty Lord, in thine as - cen - sion,

To	re	-	ceive	their		heav'n	-	ly		King.
He	up	-	on	the		clouds	as	-		cends.
We	by		faith	be	-	hold	our			own.

TEXT: Christopher Wordsworth, 1807-1885
MELODY: Traditional Dutch melody from *Oude en Neiwe Hollantse Boerenlites en Contradanseu*, c.1710
HARMONIZATION: Charles Winfred Douglas, 1867-1944, copyright by Church Publishing, Inc.

IN BABILONE
87.87.D

432

Hail thee, festival day!

Refrain

Hail thee, fes-tiv-al day! blest day that art hal-lowed for ev-er;

1st time | *2nd time*

Day whereon Christ a-rose, break-ing the king-dom of death. death.

Stanzas

1 He who was nailed to the cross is Lord and the rul-er of all men;
3 God the All-Fa-ther, the Lord, who rul-est the earth and the hea-vens,
5 Spi-rit of life and of power, now flow in us, fount of our be-ing,

repeat Refrain

All things cre-a-ted on earth sing to the glo-ry of God:
Guard us from harm with-out, cleanse us from e-vil with-in:
Light that dost light-en all, life that in all dost a-bide:

2 Dai-ly the love-li-ness grows, a-dorned with the
4 Je-sus the health of the world, en-light-en our
6 Praise to the Giv-er of good! Thou Love who art

glo-ry of blos-som; Hea-ven her gates un-
minds, thou Re-deem-er, Son of the Fa-ther su-
au-thor of con-cord, Pour out thy balm on our

repeat Refrain

bars, fling-ing her in-crease of light:
preme, on-ly be-got-ten of God:
souls, or-der our ways in thy peace:

TEXT: *Salve Festa Dies*, Venantius Honorius Fortunatus, c.530-c.609, translated by Maurice F. Bell, 1862-1947,
  adapted from the translation in the *English Hymnal*, copyright © by Oxford University Press,
  text altered by permission of Oxford University Press.
MELODY: Ralph Vaughan Williams, 1872-1958, from the *English Hymnal* by permission of Oxford University Press.
HARMONIZATION: Ralph Vaughan Williams, 1872-1958, copyright © by Oxford University Press,
  from the *English Hymnal* by permission of Oxford University Press.

SALVE FESTA DIES
Irregular with Refrain

Come down, O Love divine

440

1 Come down, O Love di - vine, Seek thou this soul of mine,
2 O let it free - ly burn, Till earth-ly pas - sions turn
3 Let ho - ly char - i - ty Mine out-ward ves - ture be,
4 And so the yearn - ing strong, With which the soul will long,

And vis - it it with thine own ar - dour glow - ing;
To dust and ash - es in its heat con - sum - ing;
And low - li - ness be - come mine in - ner cloth - ing;
Shall far out - pass the power of hu - man tell - ing;

O Com-fort - er, draw near, With - in my heart ap - pear,
And let thy glo - rious light Shine ev - er on my sight,
True low - li - ness of heart, Which takes the hum - bler part,
For none can guess its grace, Till he be - come the place

And kin - dle it, thy ho - ly flame be - stow - ing.
And clothe me round, the while my path il - lum - ing.
And o'er its own short - com - ings weeps with loath - ing.
Where - in the Ho - ly Spi - rit makes his dwell - ing.

TEXT: Bianco da Siena, d.1434, translated by Richard Frederick Littledale, 1833-1890
MELODY: Ralph Vaughan Williams, 1872-1958, from the *English Hymnal* by permission of Oxford University Press.
HARMONIZATION: Ralph Vaughan Williams, 1872-1958, copyright © by Oxford University Press,
  from the *English Hymnal* by permission of Oxford University Press.

DOWN AMPNEY
66.11.D

441

Veni Creator Spiritus

1 Ve - ni Cre - á - tor Spi - ri - tus, Men - tes tu - ó -
2 Qui dí - ce - ris Pa - rá - cli - tus, Do - num De - i
3 Tu se - pti - fór - mis mú - ne - re, Dex - trae De - i
4 Ac - cén - de lu - men sén - si - bus, In - fún - de a - mó -
5 Ho - stem re - pél - las lón - gi - us, Pa - cém - que do -
6 Per te sci - á - mus da Pa - trem, No - scá - mus at -
7 De - o Pa - tri sit gló - ri - a, Et Fí - li - o,

rum ví - si - ta; Im - ple su - pér - na grá - ti - a
al - tís - si - mi, Fons vi - vus, i - gnis cá - ri - tas,
tu dí - gi - tus, Tu ri - te pro - mís - sum Pa - tris,
rem cór - di - bus, In - fír - ma no - stri cór - po - ris
nes pró - ti - nus; Du - ctó - re sic te praé - vi - o,
que Fí - li - um, Te u - tri - ús - que Spí - ri - tum
quia mór - tu - is, Sur - ré - xit, ac Pa - rá - cli - to,

Quae tu cre - á - sti pé - cto - ra.
Et spi - ri - tá - lis ún - cti - o.
Ser - mó - ne di - tans gút - tu - ra.
Vir - tú - te fir - mans pér - pe - ti.
Vi - té - mus o - mne nó - xi - um.
Cre - dá - mus o - mni tém - po - re.
In sae - cu - ló - rum saé - clu - la. A - men.

TEXT: ascribed to Rabanus Maurus, 776-856
MELODY: Plainchant, Mode VIII, 9th century
HARMONIZATION: Theodore Marier, copyright © 1979 by International Committee on English in the Liturgy

VENI CREATOR SPIRITUS
88.88

Come, Holy Ghost

442

1 Come, Ho - ly Ghost, Cre - a - tor blest, Vouch - safe with - in our
2 To Thee, the Com - fort - er, we cry, To Thee, the Gift of
3 The sev'n - fold gifts of grace are Thine, O Fin - ger of the
4 Thy light to ev - 'ry thought im - part And shed Thy love in
5 Drive far a - way our wi - ly Foe And Thine a - bid - ing

souls to rest; Come with Thy grace and heav'n - ly
God Most High, The Fount of life, the Fire of
Hand Di - vine; True Pro - mise of the Fa - ther
ev - 'ry heart; The weak - ness of our mor - tal
peace be - stow; If Thou be our pro - tect - ing

aid And fill the hearts which Thou hast made.
love, The soul's A - noint - ing from a - bove.
Thou, Who dost the tongue with speech en - dow.
state With death - less might in - vig - or - ate.
Guide, No ev - il can our steps be - tide.

6 Make Thou to us the Father known,
Teach us the eternal Son to own
And Thee, whose name we ever bless,
Of both the Spirit, to confess.

7 Praise we the Father and the Son
And Holy Spirit, with them One;
And may the Son on us bestow
The gifts that from the Spirit flow!

TEXT: *Veni creator spiritus*, ascribed to Rabanus Maurus, 776-856,
translated by Edward Caswall, 1814-1878, alt.
MELODY: Joseph Klug, b. 1500?, *Geistliche Lieder, 1533*, based on *Veni Creator Spiritus*
HARMONIZATION: Joseph Klug, b. c.1500, *Geistliche Lieder*, 1533

KOMM, GOTT SCHÖPFER
88.88

443 Come, Holy Ghost, Creator blest

1 Come, Ho - ly Ghost, Cre - a - tor blest, And in our
2 O Com - fort - er, to thee we cry, Thou heav'n - ly
3 O Ho - ly Ghost, Through thee a - lone, Know we the
4 Praise we the Lord, Fa - ther and Son, And Ho - ly

hearts take up thy rest: Come with thy grace and heav'n - ly
gift of God most high; Thou fount of life, and fire of
Fa - ther and the Son; Be this our firm un - chang - ing
Spir - it with them one; And may the Son on us be -

aid To fill the hearts which thou hast made,
love. And sweet a - noint - ing from a - bove.
creed. That thou dost from them both pro - ceed.
stow All gifts that from the Spir - it flow,

To fill the hearts which thou hast made.
And sweet a - noint - ing from a - bove.
That thou dost from them both pro - ceed.
All gifts that from the Spir - it flow. A - men.

TEXT: *Veni Creator Spiritus,* ascribed to Rabanus Maurus, 776-856, translated by Edward Caswall, 1814-1878, alt.
MELODY: Louis Lambillotte, S.J., 1796-1855
HARMONIZATION: Richard Proulx, b.1937, copyright © 1986 by G.I.A. Publications, Inc.

LAMBILLOTTE
8 8 . 8 8 with Repeat

Holy Spirit, Lord of Light

1 Ho - ly Spir - it, Lord of Light, From the clear ce - les - tial height,
2 Thou, of all con - sol - ers best, Thou, the soul's de - light - ful guest,
3 Light im - mor - tal, Light di - vine, Vis - it thou these hearts of thine,
4 Heal our wounds, our strength re - new; On our dry - ness pour thy dew;
5 Thou, on us who ev - er - more Thee con - fess and thee a - dore,

Thy pure beam - ing ra - diance give. Come, thou Fa - ther of the poor,
Dost re - fresh - ing peace be - stow. Thou in toil art com - fort sweet;
And our in - most be - ing fill. If thou take thy grace a - way,
Wash the stains of guilt a - way. Bend the stub - born heart and will;
With thy sev'n - fold gifts des - cend. Give us com - fort when we die;

Come with treas - ures which en - dure; Come, thou Light of all that live.
Pleas - ant cool - ness in the heat; Sol - ace in the midst of woe.
Noth - ing pure in man will stay; All his good is turned to ill.
Melt the fro - zen, warm the chill; Guide the steps that go a - stray;
Give us life with thee on high; Give us joys that nev - er end.

TEXT: *Veni Sancte Spiritus*, attributed to Pope Innocent III, c.1160-1216,
    translated by Edward Caswall, 1814-1878
MELODY: Attributed to Samuel Webbe the Elder, 1740-1816
HARMONIZATION: Attributed to Samuel Webbe the Elder, 1740-1816

VENI, SANCTE SPIRITUS
7 7 7 . D

445

Hail thee, festival day!

Refrain

Hail thee, fes - tiv - al day! blest day that art hal - lowed for ev - er;

1st time *2nd time*

Day where-on Christ a - rose, break-ing the king - dom of death. death.

Stanzas

1 He who was nailed to the cross is Lord and the rul - er of all men;
3 God the All-Fa-ther, the Lord, who rul - est the earth and the hea - vens,
5 Spi - rit of life and of power, now flow in us, fount of our be - ing,

repeat Refrain

All things cre - a - ted on earth sing to the glo - ry of God:
Guard us from harm with - out, cleanse us from e - vil with - in:
Light that dost light - en all, life that in all dost a - bide:

2 Lo, in the like - ness of fire, on them that a -
4 Je - sus the health of the world, en - light - en our
6 Praise to the Giv - er of good! Thou Love who art

wait, his ap - pear - ing. He, whom the Lord had fore -
minds, thou Re - deem - er, Son of the Fa - ther su -
au - thor of con - cord, Pour out thy balm on our

repeat Refrain

told, sud - den - ly, swift - ly, de - scends:
preme, on - ly be - got - ten of God:
souls, or - der our ways in thy peace:

TEXT: *Salve Festa Dies*, Venantius Honorius Fortunatus, c.530-c.609, translated by Maurice F. Bell, 1862-1947,
  adapted from the translation in the *English Hymnal*, copyright © by Oxford University Press,
  text altered by permission of Oxford University Press.
MELODY: Ralph Vaughan Williams, 1872-1958, from the *English Hymnal* by permission of Oxford University Press.
HARMONIZATION: Ralph Vaughan Williams, 1872-1958, copyright © by Oxford University Press,
  from the *English Hymnal* by permission of Oxford University Press.

SALVE FESTA DIES
Irregular with Refrain

Holy, Holy, Holy!

460

1 Ho - ly, Ho - ly, Ho - ly! Lord God Al - migh - ty!
2 Ho - ly, Ho - ly, Ho - ly! all the saints a - dore thee,
3 Ho - ly, Ho - ly, Ho - ly! though the dark-ness hide thee,

Ear - ly in the morn - ing our song shall rise to thee:
Cast - ing down their gold - en crowns a - round the glass - y sea;
Though the eye of sin - ful man thy glo - ry may not see,

Ho - ly, Ho - ly, Ho - ly! mer - ci - ful and migh - ty,
Cher - u - bim and ser - a - phim fall - ing down be - fore thee,
On - ly thou art ho - ly; there is none be - side thee,

God in three Per - sons, bless- ed Tri - ni - ty.
Which wert, and art, and ev - er- more shalt be.
Per - fect in power, in love, and pu - ri - ty. A - men.

TEXT: Reginald Heber, 1783-1826
MELODY: John Bacchus Dykes, 1823-1876
HARMONIZATION: John Bacchus Dykes, 1823-1876

NICAEA
11.12.12.10

461 Holy God, we praise thy name!

1 Ho - ly God, we praise thy name! Lord of
2 Hark! the loud ce - les - tial hymn An - gel
3 Lo! the Bless - ed Twelve pro - claim To the
4 Ho - ly Fa - ther, Ho - ly Son, Ho - ly

all, we bow be - fore thee. All on earth thy
choirs a - bove are rais - ing, Cher - u - bim and
Fa - ther hymns of glo - ry; Proph - ets sing in
Spir - it, Three we name thee; While in es - sence

scep - tre claim; All in heav'n a - bove a -
ser - a - phim In un - ceas - ing cho - rus
loud ac - claim; Mar - tyrs tell the won - drous
on - ly One, Un - di - vid - ed God we

dore thee. In - fi - nite thy vast do -
prais - ing, Fill the heav'ns with sweet ac -
sto - ry; And from morn to set of
claim thee; And a - dor - ing bend the

main, Ev - er - last - ing is thy reign.
cord: Ho - ly, Ho - ly, Ho - ly Lord.
sun, Through the Church they sing as one.
knee, While we own the mys - ter - y.

In - fi - nite thy vast do - main, Ev - er -
Fill the heav'ns with sweet ac - cord: Ho - ly,
And from morn to set of sun, Through the
And a - dor - ing bend the knee, While we

last - ing	is	thy	reign.
Ho - ly,	Ho - ly	Lord.	
Church	they sing	as	one.
own	the mys - ter - y.	A - men.	

TEXT: *Te Deum*, ascribed to St. Nicetas, ?-415,
  paraphrase translation by Clarence Augustus Walworth, 1820-1900, alt.
MELODY: from *Katholisches Gesangbuch*, Vienna 1774
HARMONIZATION: Anonymous

GROSSER GOTT (TE DEUM)
7 8 . 7 8 . 7 7 with Repeat

TRINITY SUNDAY

All hail, adored Trinity! 462

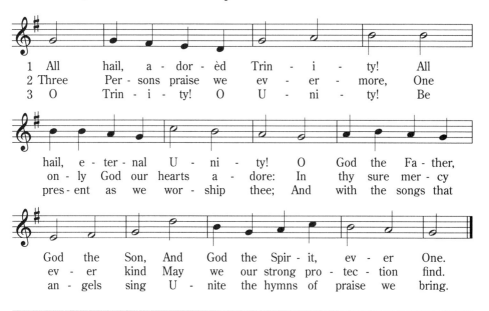

1 All hail, a - dor - èd Trin - i - ty! All
2 Three Per - sons praise we ev - er - more, One
3 O Trin - i - ty! O U - ni - ty! Be

hail, e - ter - nal U - ni - ty! O God the Fa - ther,
on - ly God our hearts a - dore: In thy sure mer - cy
pres - ent as we wor - ship thee; And with the songs that

God the Son, And God the Spir - it, ev - er One.
ev - er kind May we our strong pro - tec - tion find.
an - gels sing U - nite the hymns of praise we bring.

TEXT: *Ave, colenda Trinitas*, anonymous Latin hymn, 11th century, translated by John David Chambers, 1805-1893,
  and compilers of *Hymns Ancient and Modern*
MELODY: Louis Bourgeois, c.1510-c1561
HARMONIZATION: Louis Bourgeois, c.1510-c1561

OLD HUNDREDTH
8 8 . 8 8

463

I bind unto myself today

1 I bind un - to my - self to - day The strong Name
2 I bind this day to me for ev - er, By power of
3 I bind un - to my - self the power Of the great
4 I bind un - to my - self to - day The vir - tues
5 I bind un - to my - self to - day The power of

of the Tri - ni - ty, By in - vo - ca - tion
faith, Christ's In - car - na - tion; His bap - tism in the
love of cher - u - bim; The sweet "Well done" in
of the star - lit heav'n, The glo - rious sun's life -
God to hold and lead, His eye to watch, his

of the same, The Three in One, and One in Three.
Jor - dan riv - er; His death on cross for my sal - va - tion;
judg - ment hour; The ser - vice of the ser - a - phim;
giv - ing ray, The white - ness of the moon at even,
might to stay, His ear to heark - en to my need;

2 His burst - ing from the spi - cèd tomb; His ri - ding
3 Con - fess - ors' faith, a - pos - tles' word, The pa - triarchs'
4 The flash - ing of the light - ning free, The whirl - ing
5 The wis - dom of my God to teach, His hand to

up the heav'n - ly way; His com - ing at the
prayers, the pro - phets' scrolls; All good deeds done un -
wind's tem - pes - tuous shocks, The sta - ble earth, the
guide, his shield to ward; The word of God to

day of doom: I bind un - to my - self to - day.
to the Lord, And pu - ri - ty of vir - gin souls.
deep salt sea, A - round the old e - ter - nal rocks.
give me speech, His heav'n - ly host to be my guard.

6 Christ be with me, Christ with-in me, Christ be-hind me, Christ be-fore me,
Christ be-neath me, Christ a-bove me, Christ in qui-et, Christ in dan-ger,

Christ be-side me, Christ to win me, Christ to com-fort and re-store me,
Christ in hearts of all that love me, Christ in mouth of friend and stran-ger.

7 I bind un-to my-self the Name, The strong Name

of the Tri-ni-ty; By in-vo-ca-tion

of the same, The Three in One, and One in Three.

Of whom all na-ture hath cre-a-tion; E-ter-nal

Fa-ther, Spi-rit, Word: Praise to the Lord of my sal-

va-tion, Sal-va-tion is of Christ the Lord. A-men.

TEXT: Ascribed to St. Patrick, c.389-461, metrical paraphrase translation by Cecil Frances Alexander, 1823-1895,
    copyright by Arthur C. H. Alexander, Executor for Mrs. Alexander
MELODY: Irish melody found in an 11th century manuscript
HARMONIZATION: Charles Villiers Stanford, 1852-1924, copyright © 1913 by Stainer and Bell, Ltd.

ST. PATRICK
88.88.D

464 God Father, praise and glory

1 God Fa - ther, praise and glo - ry Thy chil - dren bring to thee.
2 And thou, Lord co - e - ter - nal, God's sole - be - got - ten Son,
3 O Ho - ly Ghost, Cre - a - tor, Thou gift of God most high;

Thy grace and peace to man - kind Shall now for - ev - er be.
O Je - sus, King a - noint - ed, Who hast re - demp - tion won.
Life, love and ho - ly wis - dom, Our weak - ness now sup - ply.

O most ho - ly Trin - i - ty, Un - di - vid - ed U - ni - ty;

Ho - ly God, might - y God, God im - mor - tal, be a - dored.

TEXT: German, anonymous, translated by John Rothensteiner, 1860-1936
MELODY: *Limburg Gesangbuch,* 1838
HARMONIZATION: Healey Willan, 1880-1968, copyright © 1958 by Ralph Jusko Publications, Inc.

GOTT VATER SEI GEPRIESEN
7 6 . 7 6 with Refrain

Love divine, all loves excelling 470

1 Love di - vine, all loves ex - cel - ling, Joy of
2 Je - sus, thou art all com - pas - sion, Pure un -
3 Come, al - migh - ty to de - liv - er, Let us
4 Thee we would be al - ways bless - ing, Serve thee
5 Fin - ish then thy new cre - a - tion: Pure and
6 Changed from glo - ry in - to glo - ry, Till in

heav'n, to earth come down, Fix in us thy hum - ble
bound - ed love thou art; Vis - it us with thy sal -
all thy grace re - ceive; Sud - den - ly re - turn, and
as thy hosts a - bove; Pray, and praise thee, with - out
spot - less let us be; Let us see thy great sal -
heav'n we take our place, Till we cast our crowns be -

dwell - ing, All thy faith - ful mer - cies crown.
va - tion, En - ter ev - ery trem - bling heart.
nev - er, Nev - er more thy tem - ples leave.
ceas - ing, Glo - ry in thy per - fect love.
va - tion, Per - fect - ly re - stored in thee;
fore thee, Lost in won - der, love, and praise.

This hymn may also be sung to the tune HYFRYDOL, no. 601

TEXT: Charles Wesley, 1707-1788
MELODY: Sir John J. Stainer, 1840-1901
HARMONIZATION: Sir John J. Stainer, 1840-1901

LOVE DIVINE
8 7 . 8 7

471   To Christ, the prince of peace

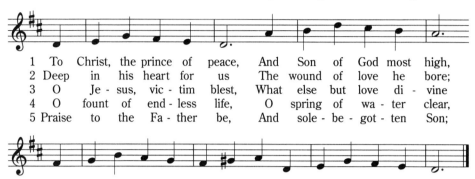

1 To Christ, the prince of peace, And Son of God most high,
2 Deep in his heart for us The wound of love he bore;
3 O Je - sus, vic - tim blest, What else but love di - vine
4 O fount of end - less life, O spring of wa - ter clear,
5 Praise to the Fa - ther be, And sole - be - got - ten Son;

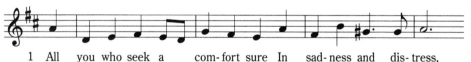

The fa - ther of the world to come, Sing we with ho - ly joy.
That love where-with he still in-flames The hearts that him a - dore.
Could thee con-strain to o - pen thus That sa - cred heart of thine?
O flame cel - es - tial, cleans-ing all Who un - to thee draw near!
Praise, ho - ly Par - a - clete, to thee, While end-less a - ges run.

TEXT: *Summi parentis filio*, from *Catholicum Hymnologium Germanicum*, 1587,
   translated by Edward Caswall, 1814-1878
MELODY: Anonymous,
   founded on Fugue in E, *Well-tempered Clavier*, Part II, No. 9, by Johann Sebastian Bach, 1685-1750
HARMONIZATION: Anonymous

POTSDAM
6 6 . 8 6

472   All you who seek a comfort sure

1 All you who seek a com-fort sure In sad-ness and dis-tress,
2 Je - sus, who gave him - self for you Up - on the cross to die,
3 Now hear him as he speaks to us Those words for ev - er blest:
4 O Heart a-dored by saints on high, And hope of sin - ners here,

What - ev - er sor - row bur-dens you, What - ev - er griefs op - press,
Un - folds to you his Sa - cred Heart: O to that Heart draw nigh.
"All you who la - bor, come to me, And I will give you rest."
We place our hum - ble trust in you And lift to you our prayer.

TEXT: *Quicumque certum quaeritis*, anonymous 18th century hymn,
   translated by Edward Caswall, 1814-1878, alt.
MELODY: from *Tochter Sion*, Cologne, 1741
HARMONIZATION: Traditional

ST. BERNARD
8 6 . 8 6

To Jesus Christ, our sov'reign King 480

1 To Jesus Christ, our sov-'reign King, Who is the world's sal-
2 Thy reign ex-tend, O King be-nign, To ev-'ry land and
3 To thee and to thy Church, great King, We pledge our hearts' ob-
4 Thy maj-es-ty shall be the praise And thanks of ev-'ry
5 May God the Fa-ther, God the Son And God the Spir-it

va-tion, All praise and hom-age do we bring And thanks and ad-o-
na-tion, For in thy king-dom, Lord di-vine, A-lone we find sal-
la-tion, Un-til be-fore thy throne we sing In end-less ju-bi-
na-tion; To thee the world with joy shall raise The voice of ex-ul-
bless us! Let all the world praise him a-lone, Let sol-emn awe pos-

ra-tion.
va-tion.
la-tion. Christ Je-sus, Vic-tor! Christ Je-sus,
ta-tion.
sess us.

Rul-er! Christ Je-sus, Lord and Re-deem-er!

TEXT: Martin B. Hellriegel, 1890-1981, copyright © 1941 by Martin B. Hellriegel;
 assigned 1978 to Irene C. Mueller.
MELODY: *Mainz Gesangbuch*, 1870
HARMONIZATION: Calvert Shenk, b.1940, copyright © 1997 by Calvert Shenk

CHRISTUS REX (ICH GLAUB AN GOTT)
8 7 . 8 7 with Refrain

481   Crown him with many crowns

1 Crown	him with man - y	crowns,	The Lamb	up - on	his	throne;
2 Crown	him the Vir - gin's	Son,	The God	in - car - nate	born,
3 Crown	him the Lord of	love:	Be - hold	his hands and	side,
4 Crown	him the Lord of	peace,	Whose pow'r a	scep - tre	sways
5 Crown	him the Lord of	life,	Who tri-umphed o'er	the	grave,
6 Crown	him the Lord of	years,	The Po - ten - tate	of	time,

Hark, how the heav'n-ly an - them drowns All mu - sic but its own;
Whose arm those crim-son tro - phies won Which now his brow a - dorn;
Rich wounds yet vis - i - ble a - bove In beau-ty glo - ri - fied:
From pole to pole, that wars may cease, Ab-sorbed in prayer and praise:
And rose vic - to - rious in the strife For those he came to save.
Cre - a - tor of the roll-ing spheres, In - ef - fa - bly sub - lime.

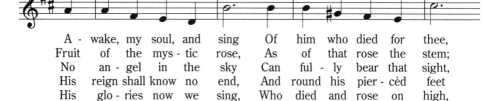

A - wake, my soul, and sing Of him who died for thee,
Fruit of the mys - tic rose, As of that rose the stem;
No an - gel in the sky Can ful - ly bear that sight,
His reign shall know no end, And round his pier - cèd feet
His glo - ries now we sing, Who died and rose on high,
All hail, Re - deem - er, hail! For thou hast died for me;

And hail him as thy match-less King Through all e - ter - ni - ty.
The root, whence mer-cy ev - er flows, The Babe of Beth - le - hem.
But down-ward bends his burn - ing eye At mys - ter - ies so bright.
Fair flowers of Par - a - dise ex - tend Their fra-grance ev - er sweet.
Who died, e - ter - nal life to bring, And lives that death may die.
Thy praise and glo - ry shall not fail Through-out e - ter - ni - ty.

TEXT: Verses 1-4 by Matthew Bridges, 1800-1894, verses 5-6 by Godfrey Thring, 1823-1903
MELODY: Sir George Job Elvey, 1816-1893
HARMONIZATION: Sir George Job Elvey, 1816-1893

DIADEMATA
66.86.D

Hail, Redeemer, King divine!

482

1 Hail, Re- deem- er, King di - vine! Priest and Lamb, the throne is thine,
2 King, whose name cre - a - tion thrills, Rule our minds, our hearts, our wills,
3 King most ho - ly, King of truth, Guide the low - ly, guide the youth;
4 Shep - herd- King, o'er moun-tains steep, Home- ward bring the wan- d'ring sheep;

King, whose reign shall nev - er cease, Prince of ev - er - last- ing peace.
Till in peace each na - tion rings With thy prais- es, King of kings,
Christ thou King of glo - ry bright, Be to us e - ter - nal light.
Shel - ter in one roy - al fold States and king-doms, new and old.

An - gels, saints and na - tions sing "Praised be Je - sus Christ, our King;

Lord of life, earth, sky and sea, King of love on Cal - va - ry."

TEXT: Patrick Brennan, C.SS.R., copyright © by Burns and Oates, Ltd.
MELODY: George Job Elvey, 1816-1893
HARMONIZATION: George Job Elvey, 1816-1893

ST. GEORGE'S WINDSOR
77.77.77.77

483   O worship the King

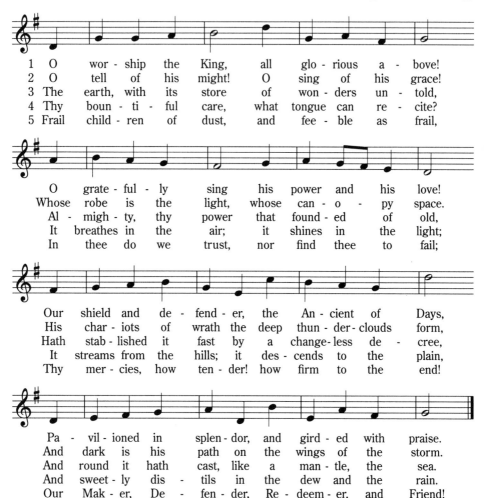

1 O wor-ship the King, all glo-rious a - bove!
2 O tell of his might! O sing of his grace!
3 The earth, with its store of won-ders un - told,
4 Thy boun-ti-ful care, what tongue can re - cite?
5 Frail child-ren of dust, and fee-ble as frail,

O grate-ful-ly sing his power and his love!
Whose robe is the light, whose can-o - py space.
Al - migh-ty, thy power that found-ed of old,
It breathes in the air; it shines in the light;
In thee do we trust, nor find thee to fail;

Our shield and de - fend-er, the An - cient of Days,
His char-iots of wrath the deep thun - der- clouds form,
Hath stab-lished it fast by a change-less de - cree,
It streams from the hills; it des - cends to the plain,
Thy mer - cies, how ten - der! how firm to the end!

Pa - vil-ioned in splen-dor, and gird-ed with praise.
And dark is his path on the wings of the storm.
And round it hath cast, like a man - tle, the sea.
And sweet-ly dis - tils in the dew and the rain.
Our Mak-er, De - fen-der, Re - deem-er, and Friend!

TEXT: Robert Grant, 1779-1838, based on Psalm 104
MELODY: attributed to William Croft, 1678-1727
HARMONIZATION: Traditional

HANOVER
10.10.11.11

Come, Thou almighty King

484

1 Come, Thou al - might - y King, Help us Thy
2 Come, Thou In - car - nate Word, Gird on Thy
3 Come, ho - ly Com - fort - er, Thy sa - cred
4 To the great One in Three E - ter - nal

name to sing, Help us to praise. Fa - ther all
might - y sword, Our prayer at - tend. Come and Thy
wit - ness bear In this glad hour. Thou, who al -
prais - es be Hence ev - er - more! His sov- 'reign

glo - ri - ous, O'er all vic - to - ri - ous, Come and reign
peo - ple bless and give Thy Word suc- cess; Stab - lish Thy
might - y art, Now rule in ev - 'ry heart And ne'er from
maj - es - ty May we in glo - ry see And to e -

o - ver us, An - cient of Days.
righ - teous-ness, Sav - ior and Friend!
us de - part, Spir - it of Pow'r!
ter - ni - ty Love and a - dore! A - men.

TEXT: from an anonymous British tract, c.1757
MELODY: Felice de Giardini, 1716-1796
HARMONIZATION: Traditional

ITALIAN HYMN (MOSCOW)
6 6 4 . 6 6 6 4

485   Lift up your heads, ye mighty gates

1 Lift up your heads, ye migh - ty gates; Be -
2 O blest the land, the ci - ty blest, Where
3 Fling wide the por - tals of your heart; Make
4 So come, my Sov - 'reign; en - ter in! Let

hold the King of glo - ry waits! The
Christ the rul - er is con - fest! O
it a tem - ple, set a - part From
new and no - bler life be - gin; Thy

King of kings is draw - ing near; The
hap - py hearts and hap - py homes To
earth - ly use for heav'n's em - ploy, A -
Ho - ly Spir - it guide us on,   Un -

Sa - vior of the world is here.
whom this King of tri - umph comes!
dorned with prayer and love and joy.
til the glo - rious crown be won.

TEXT: based on Psalm 24, by Georg Weissel, 1590-1635, translated by Catherine Winkworth, 1827-1878, alt.
MELODY: from *Psalmodia Evangelica*, 1789
HARMONIZATION: Anonymous

TRURO
88.88

Sing praise to our Creator

1 Sing praise to our Cre - a - tor, O you of Ad - am's race —
2 To Je - sus Christ give glo - ry, God's co - e - ter - nal Son;
3 And praise the Ho - ly Spi - rit poured forth up - on the earth;

God's chil - dren by a - dop - tion, bap - tized in - to his grace.
as mem - bers of his Bo - dy we live in him as one.
who sanc - ti - fies and guides us, made strong in our re - birth.

TEXT: Mark Evans, b.1916, alt., copyright © 1962 by World Library Publications,
   a division of J.S. Paluch Company, Inc., 3825 N. Willow Road, Schiller Park, IL 60176.
   All rights reserved. Used by permission.
MELODY: Melchior Vulpius, c.1560-1616
HARMONIZATION: After Melchior Vulpius, c.1560-1616

CHRISTUS, DER IST MEIN LEBEN
76.76

510

Adoro te devote

1 A - dó - ro te de - vó - te, la - tens Dé - i - tas,
2 Vi - sus, tá - ctus, gú - stus in te fál - li - tur,
3 In crú - ce la - té - bat só - la Dé - i - tas,
4 Plá - gas, si - cut Thó - mas, non in - tú - e - or:
5 O me - mo - ri - á - le mór - tis Dó - mi - ni,

Quae sub his fi - gú - ris ve - re lá - ti - tas:
Sed au - dí - tu só - lo tu - to cré - di - tur:
At hic lá - tet si - mul et hu - má - ni - tas:
Dé - um ta - men mé - um te con - fí - te - or:
Pá - nis vi - vus ví - tam praé - stans hó - mi - ni,

Ti - bi se cor me - um to - tum súb - ji - cit,
Cré - do quíd - quid di - xit Dé - i Fí - li - us:
Am - bo ta - men cré - dens at - que cón - fi - tens,
Fac me tí - bi sem - per ma - gis cré - de - re,
Praé - sta mé - ae mén - ti de te ví - ve - re,

Qui - a te con - tem - plans to - tum dé - fi - cit.
Nil hoc vér - bo ve - ri - tá - tis vér - ri - us.
Pé - to quod pe - tí - vit lá - tro paé - ni - tens.
In te spem ha - bé - re, te di - lí - ge - re.
Et te íl - li sem - per dúl - ce sá - pe - re. A - men.

6 Píe pellicáne Jésu Dómine,
Me immúndum múnda túo sánguine,
Cújus úna stilla sálvum fácere,
Tótum múndum quit ab ómni scélere.

7 Jésu, quem velátum nunc aspício,
Oro fíat íllud quod tam sítio:
Ut te reveláta cérnens fácie,
Vísu sim beátus túae glóriae. *Amen.*

TEXT: St. Thomas Aquinas, 1225-1274
MELODY: Plainchant, Mode V
HARMONIZATION: Theodore Marier, copyright © 1963 by Summy-Birchard Music division of Birch Tree Group, Ltd.

ADORO TE DEVOTE
11.11.11.11

Godhead here in hiding

511

1 God-head here in hid - ing Whom I do a - dore
2 See - ing, touch-ing, tast - ing are in Thee de - ceived;
3 On the cross Thy God - head made no sign to men;
4 I am not like Thom - as, wounds I can - not see,
5 O Thou, our re - mind - er of the Cru - ci - fied,

Masked by these bare sha - dows, shape and noth-ing more,
How says trust - y hear - ing? that shall be be-lieved;
Here Thy ver - y man - hood steals from hu - man ken:
But I plain - ly call Thee Lord and God as he:
Liv - ing Bread, the life of us for whom He died,

See, Lord, at Thy ser - vice low lies here a heart
What God's Son has told me, take for truth I do;
Both are my con - fes - sion, both are my be - lief,
This faith each day deep - er be my hold - ing of,
Lend this life to me, then; feed and feast my mind,

Lost, all lost in won - der at the God Thou art.
Truth Him-self speaks tru - ly or there's noth-ing true.
And I pray the prayer of the dy - ing thief.
Dai - ly make me hard - er hope and dear - er love.
There be Thou the sweet-ness man was meant to find. A - men.

6 Like what tender tales tell of the Pelican,
Bathe, Jesus Lord, in what Thy bosom ran—
Blood that but one drop of has the pow'r to win
All the world forgiveness of its world of sin.

7 Jesus, Whom I look at shrouded here below,
I beseech Thee, send me what I thirst for so,
Some day to gaze on Thee face to face in light
And be blest forever with Thy glory's sight. Amen.

TEXT: St. Thomas Aquinas, 1225-1274, translated by Gerard Manley Hopkins, S.J., 1844-1889, alt.
MELODY: Plainchant, Mode V
HARMONIZATION: Theodore Marier, copyright © 1963 by Summy-Birchard Music division of Birch Tree Group, Ltd.

ADORO TE DEVOTE
11.11.11.11

512

O Lord, I am not worthy

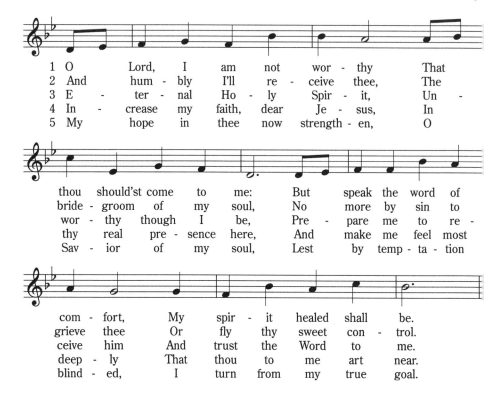

1 O Lord, I am not wor - thy That thou should'st come to me: But speak the word of com - fort, My spir - it healed shall be.

2 And hum - bly I'll re - ceive thee, The bride - groom of my soul, No more by sin to grieve thee, Or fly thy sweet con - trol.

3 E - ter - nal Ho - ly Spir - it, Un - wor - thy though I be, Pre - pare me to re - ceive him And trust the Word to me.

4 In - crease my faith, dear Je - sus, In thy real pre - sence here, And make me feel most deep - ly That thou to me art near.

5 My hope in thee now strength - en, O thy Sav - ior of my soul, Lest by temp - ta - tion blind - ed, I turn from my true goal.

6 And let me love thee only With all my heart and mind;
In thee alone my spirit True rest and joy can find.

7 O Sacrament most holy, O Sacrament divine,
All praise and all thanksgiving Be every moment thine.

TEXT: probably based on "O Herr, ich bin nicht würdig," *Landshuter Gesangbuch*, 1777
MELODY: Traditional
HARMONIZATION: Frank Campbell-Watson, copyright © 1966 by Benziger Editions, Inc.

CLARIBEI
76.76

O Lord Jesus, I adore thee

513

1 O Lord Je - sus, I a - dore thee For the bread of
2 Make thou of my soul an or - chard Quick-ened in - to
3 Ah, Lord Je - sus, go not from me, Stay, ah, stay with
4 Would that I could keep thee al - ways In mine in - most

worth un - told Free - ly giv'n in thy Com - mun - ion,
fruit - ful - ness; Come, O come, life giv - ing Man - na,
me, my Lord; Make me shrink from what - so - ev - er
heart to be, Thou and on - ly thou sug - gest - ing

Won - der - ful a thou - sand - fold, Giv'n to - day in
Mak - ing glad my wild - er - ness: Sweet - er far than
Will not with thy name ac - cord; Act through me in
Ev - ery thought and wish in me; All my soul, with

lov - ing boun - ty More than my poor heart can hold.
an - y sweet-ness Tongue can taste, or words ex - press.
ev - ery ac - tion, Speak through me in ev - ery word.
sing - ing, of - fered For a sac - ri - fice to thee.

TEXT: *Eia, Jesu adorande,* by John Maubern in his *Rosetum excercitiorum in spiritualium,* 1494,
    translated by J.M.C. Crum for the *Plainsong Hymn Book,* 1932
MELODY: from *Cantus Diversi* by John Francis Wade, c.1711-1786
HARMONIZATION: attributed to Vincent Francis Novello, 1781-1861, alt.

ST. THOMAS
87.87.87

514

Ave verum Corpus

A - ve ve-rum Cor-pus na-tum de Ma-rí - a Vír - gi-
Ve - re pas-sum, im-mo-lá-tum in cru-ce pro hó - mi-

1. ne:
2. ne:

Cu-jus la-tus per-fo-rá - tum
Es-to no-bis prae-gu-stá - tum

flu - xit a-qua et sán - gui-ne.
mor-tis in ex-á-mi- ne:

O Je-su dul - cis! O Je-su pi - e!

O Je - su, fi-li Ma-rí - ae!

Hail, true body, born of the Virgin Mary:
Truly suffered, died on the cross for mankind:
From whose pierced side flowed water and blood!
Be for us a foretaste of death in the last hour!
O gentle Jesus! O holy Jesus!
O Jesus, Son of Mary!

TEXT: Ascribed to Innocent VI, ?-1362.
MELODY: Plainchant, Mode VI, ascribed to Innocent VI, ?-1362

AVE VERUM
Irregular

Father, we thank thee who hast planted 515

1 Fa - ther, we thank thee who hast plant - ed Thy ho - ly
2 Watch o'er thy Church, O Lord, in mer - cy, Save it from

Name with - in our hearts. Know - ledge and faith and life im -
e - vil, guard it still, Per - fect it in thy love, u -

mor - tal Je - sus thy Son to us im - parts.
nite it, Cleansed and con - formed un - to thy will.

Thou, Lord, didst make all for thy plea - sure, Didst give man food for
As grain, once scat - ter'd on the hill - sides, Was in this bro - ken

all his days, Giv - ing in Christ the Bread e -
bread made one, So from all lands thy Church be

ter - nal; Thine is the power, be thine the praise.
gath - er'd In - to thy king - dom by thy Son.

TEXT: Greek, from *the Didache*, c.110, translated by F. Bland Tucker, 1895-1984
MELODY: Louis Bourgeois, c.1510-1561
HARMONIZATION: Louis Bourgeois, c.1510-c.1561

RENDEZ A DIEU
9 8 . 9 8 . D

516   Jesus, my Lord, my God, my all!

1 Je - sus, my Lord, my God, my all!
2 Had I but Mar - y's sin - less heart
3 Thy bod - y, soul and God - head, all!
4 Sound, then his prais - es high - er still,
5 Thou art with us, O dear - est Lord,
6 Je - sus, dear Pas - tor of the flock,

How can I love thee as I ought?
With which to love thee, dear - est King,
O mys - ter - y of love di - vine!
And come, ye an - gels, to our aid;
Ev - er our guest and food to be;
We crowd in love a - bout thy feet;

And how re - vere this won - drous gift.
O with what bursts of fer - vent praise,
I can - not com - pass all I have,
For this is God, the ver - y God
Strength - en the faith of lov - ing hearts
Our voic - es yearn to praise thee, Lord,

So far sur - pass - ing hope or thought?
Thy good - ness, Je - sus, would I sing!
For all thou hast and art is mine!
Who has both men and an - gels made!
Who put their hope and trust in thee.
And joy - ful - ly thy pre - sence greet.

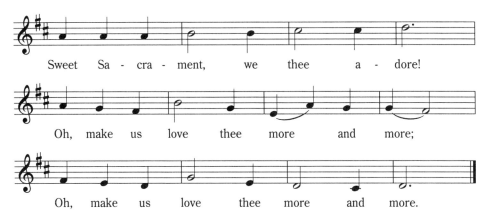

Sweet Sa - cra - ment, we thee a - dore!

Oh, make us love thee more and more;

Oh, make us love thee more and more.

TEXT: Frederick Faber, 1814-1863, alt.
MELODY: *Römischkatholisches Gesangbüchlein,* 1826
HARMONIZATION: Traditional

SWEET SACRAMENT
8 8 . 8 8 with Refrain

517

O Jesus, we adore thee

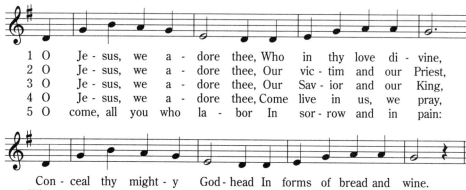

1 O Je - sus, we a - dore thee, Who in thy love di - vine,
2 O Je - sus, we a - dore thee, Our vic - tim and our Priest,
3 O Je - sus, we a - dore thee, Our Sav - ior and our King,
4 O Je - sus, we a - dore thee, Come live in us, we pray,
5 O come, all you who la - bor In sor - row and in pain:

Con - ceal thy might - y God - head In forms of bread and wine.
Whose pre - cious blood and bod - y Be - come our sa - cred feast.
And with the saints and an - gels A hum - ble hom - age bring.
That all our thoughts and ac - tions Be thine a - lone to - day.
Come, eat this bread from heav - en, Your peace and strength re - gain.

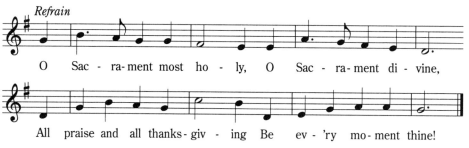

Refrain

O Sac - ra - ment most ho - ly, O Sac - ra - ment di - vine,

All praise and all thanks - giv - ing Be ev - 'ry mo - ment thine!

TEXT: Irvin Udulutsch, O.F.M. Cap., b.1920, copyright © 1959, renewed 1977 by The Order of St. Benedict
MELODY: from *Gebet und Gesangbuch*, Fulda, 1891, adapted by Roger Nachtwey, b.1930
HARMONIZATION: Roger Nachtwey, b.1930, copyright © 1959, renewed 1977 by The Order of St. Benedict

FULDA MELODY
7 6 . 7 6 with Refrain

O Jesus Christ, remember

518

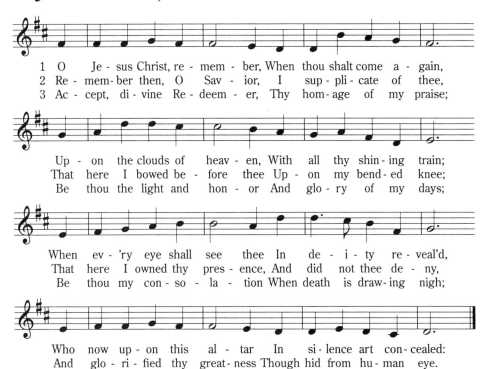

1 O Je - sus Christ, re - mem - ber, When thou shalt come a - gain,
2 Re - mem - ber then, O Sav - ior, I sup - pli - cate of thee,
3 Ac - cept, di - vine Re - deem - er, Thy hom - age of my praise;

Up - on the clouds of heav - en, With all thy shin - ing train;
That here I bowed be - fore thee Up - on my bend - ed knee;
Be thou the light and hon - or And glo - ry of my days;

When ev - 'ry eye shall see thee In de - i - ty re - veal'd,
That here I owned thy pres - ence, And did not thee de - ny,
Be thou my con - so - la - tion When death is draw - ing nigh;

Who now up - on this al - tar In si - lence art con - cealed:
And glo - ri - fied thy great - ness Though hid from hu - man eye.
Be thou my on - ly treas - ure Through all e - ter - ni - ty.

TEXT: Edward Caswall, 1814-1878
MELODY: Samuel Sebastian Wesley, 1810-1876
HARMONIZATION: Samuel Sebastian Wesley, 1810-1876

AURELIA
7 6 . 7 6 . D

519   O salutaris Hostia/O saving Victim

1 O sa - lu - tá - ris Hó - sti - a,
2 U - ni tri - nó - que Dó - mi - no
1 O sav - ing Vic - tim, o - pening wide
2 To thy great name be end - less praise,

Quae cae - li pan - dis ó - sti - um,
Sit sem - pi - tér - na gló - ri - a:
The gate of heav'n to man be - low!
Im - mor - tal God - head, One in Three:

Bel - la - pre - munt ho - stí - li - a,
Qui - vi - tam si - ne tér - mi - no
Our foes press on from ev - 'ry side:
Oh, grant us end - less length of days

Da ro - bur fer au - xí - li - um.
No - bis do - net in pá - tri - a. A - men.
Thine aid sup - ply, Thy strength be - stow.
When our true na - tive land we see. A - men.

TEXT: St. Thomas Aquinas, 1225-1274, translated by Edward Caswall, 1814-1878, alt.
MELODY: attributed to Abbé Dieudonne Duguet, 1794-1849
HARMONIZATION: Traditional

DUGUET
88.88

O salutaris Hostia/O saving Victim   520

1 O sa - lu - tá - ris Hó - sti - a,
2 U - ni tri - nó - que Dó - mi - no
1 O sav - ing Vic - tim, o - pening wide
2 To thy great name be end - less praise,

Quae cae - li pan - dis ó - sti - um,
Sit sem - pi - tér - na gló - ri - a:
The gate of heav'n to man be - low!
Im - mor - tal God - head, One in Three:

Bel - la - pre - munt ho - sti - li - a,
Qui - vi - tam si - ne tér - mi - no
Our foes press on from ev - 'ry side:
Oh, grant us end - less length of days

Da ro - bur fer au - xí - li - um.
No - bis do - net in pá - tri - a. A - men.
Thine aid sup - ply, Thy strength be - stow.
When our true na - tive land we see. A - men.

TEXT: St. Thomas Aquinas, 1225-1274, translated by Edward Caswall, 1814-1878, alt.
MELODY: Anthony Werner, 19th century
HARMONIZATION: Edward C. Currie, copyright © 1958 by Ralph Jusko Publications, Inc.

WERNER
88.88

521 O Thou, who at thy Eucharist didst pray

1 O Thou, who at thy Euch - ar - ist didst pray
2 We pray thee too for wan - derers from thy fold;
3 So, Lord, at length when sac - ra - ments shall cease,

That all thy Church might be for ev - er one,
O bring them back, Good Shep - herd of the sheep,
May we be one with all thy Church a - bove,

Grant us at ev - ery Euch - ar - ist to say
Back to the faith which saints be - lieved of old,
One with thy saints in one un - brok - en peace,

With long - ing heart and soul, 'Thy will be done:'
Back to the Church which still that faith doth keep:
One with thy saints in one un - bound - ed love:

O may we all one Bread, one Bo - dy be,
Soon may we all one Bread, one Bo - dy be,
More bless - ed still, in peace and love to be

Through this blest Sac - ra - ment of u - ni - ty.
Through this blest Sac - ra - ment of u - ni - ty.
One with the Tri - ni - ty in U - ni - ty.

TEXT: William Harry Turton, 1856-1938
MELODY: William Henry Monk, 1823-1889
HARMONIZATION: William Henry Monk, 1823-1889, alt.

UNDE ET MEMORES
10.10.10.10.10.10

Soul of my Savior

522

1 Soul of my Sav - ior, sanc - ti - fy my breast!
2 Strength and pro - tec - tion may his Pas - sion be;
3 Guard and de - fend me from the foe ma - lign;

Bod - y of Je - sus, be my sav - ing guest!
O bless - ed Je - sus, hear and an - swer me!
In life's last mo - ments make me on - ly thine;

Blood of my Sav - ior, bathe me in thy tide!
Deep in thy wounds, Lord, hide and shel - ter me;
Call me and bid me come to thee on high,

Wash me, ye wa - ters, gush - ing from his side.
So shall I nev - er, nev - er part from thee.
When I may praise thee with thy saints for aye.

TEXT: *Anima Christi*, attributed to Pope John XXII, 1249-1334, translation anonymous
MELODY: Lorenzo Dobici
HARMONIZATION: Nicola Aloysius Montani, 1880-1948

ST. GREGORY ANIMA
10.10.10.10

523

Panis angelicus

1 Pa - nis an - gé - li - cus   fit   pa - nis hó - mi - num;
2 Te   tri - na Dé - i - tas   ú - na - que pó - sci - mus,

Dat   pa - nis cóe - li - cus   fi - gú - ris tér - mi - num:
Sic   nos tu ví - si - ta,   sic - ut te có - li - mus;

O   res mi - rá - bi - lis!   man - dú - cat Do - mi - num
Per   tu - as sé - mi - tas   duc nos quo tén - di - mus,

Pau - per,   ser - vus, et hu - mi - lis.
Ad   lu - cem quám in - há - bi - tas.   A - men.

The Bread of angels was made the Bread of man;
He confined the heavenly Bread to a thing of size and shape:
O marvelous thing! That a poor man,
A humble servant, should eat the Lord.

We beseech thee, O God, Three in One,
Visit us, thus, even as we worship thee.
Lead us into thy ways; and by them
May we direct our course to the Light in which thou dwellest.
Amen.

TEXT: St. Thomas Aquinas, 1225-1274, translation by Richard Divozzo, b.1955. Used with permission.
MELODY: Louis Lambilotte, 1796-1855
HARMONIZATION: Nicola A. Montani, 1880-1948

LAMBILOTTE PANIS
12.12.12.8

Hail, holy Queen enthroned above 530

1 Hail! ho - ly Queen en - throned a - bove, O Ma - ri - a!
2 Our life, our sweet - ness here be - low, O Ma - ri - a!
3 To thee we cry, poor sons of Eve, O Ma - ri - a!
4 This earth is but a vale of tears, O Ma - ri - a!

Hail! Mother of mer - cy and of love, O Ma - ri - a!
Our hope in sor - row and in woe, O Ma - ri - a!
To thee we sigh, we mourn, we grieve, O Ma - ri - a!
A place of ban - ish - ment, of fears, O Ma - ri - a!

Refrain

Tri - umph, all ye cher - u - bim, Sing with us, ye

ser - a - phim. Heav'n and earth re - sound the hymn.

Sal - ve, sal - ve, sal - ve Re - gi - na!

5 Turn then, most gracious advocate,
    O Maria!
  Toward us thine eyes compassionate,
    O Maria! *Refrain*

6 When this our exile is complete,
    O Maria!
  Show us thy Son, our Jesus sweet,
    O Maria! *Refrain*

7 O clement, gracious, Mother sweet,
    O Maria!
  O Virgin Mary, we entreat,
    O Maria! *Refrain*

TEXT: *Salve Regina*, probably Aimor, Bishop of Le Puy (11th cent.),
    this anonymous translation appeared in *The Roman Hymnal*, New York, 1884
MELODY: from M.L. Herold's *Choralmelodien zum Heiligen Gesänge*, 1808
HARMONIZATION: John Rodgers, copyright © 1966 by Benziger Editions, Inc.

SALVE REGINA
8 4 . 8 4 with Refrain

531

Ave María

A - ve Ma - rí - a grá - ti - a plé - na Dó - mi - nus té - cum,

be - ne - dí - cta tu in mu - li - é - ri bus, et

be - ne - dí - ctus frú - ctus vén - tris tú - i, Jé - sus.

Sán - cta Ma - rí - a, Má - ter Dé - i, ó - ra pro nó - bis pec -

ca - tó - ri - bus, nunc et in hó - ra mór - tis nó - strae. A - men.

Hail, Mary, full of grace, the Lord is with thee;
blessed art thou among women,
and blessed is the fruit of thy womb, Jesus.
Holy Mary, Mother of God,
pray for us sinners,
now and at the hour of our death. Amen.

TEXT: Luke 1:28, 42
MELODY: Plainchant, Mode I, c.13th century
HARMONIZATION: Achille Bragers, copyright © 1939 by McLaughlin and Reilly Co.

AVE MARIA
Irregular

Immaculate Mary

532

1 Im - mac - u - late Mar - y, thy prais - es we sing,
2 In heav - en, the bles - sed thy glo - ry pro - claim;
3 Thy name is our pow - er, thy vir - tues our light,
4 We pray for our moth - er, the Church up - on earth;

Who reign - est in splen - dor with Je - sus our King.
On earth, we thy chil - dren in - voke thy fair name.
Thy love is our com - fort, thy plead - ing our might.
And bless, dear - est La - dy, the land of our birth.

Refrain

A - ve, A - ve, A - ve Ma - ri - a,

A - ve, A - ve Ma - ri - a.

TEXT: Anonymous
MELODY: Traditional French Cantique with Refrain added
HARMONIZATION: Calvert Shenk, b.1940, copyright © 1997 by Calvert Shenk

LOURDES HYMN
6 5 . 6 5 with Refrain

533

Ave, maris stella

1 A - ve, ma - ris stel - la, De - i
2 Su - mens il - lud A - ve Ga - bri -
3 Sol - ve vin - cla re - is, Pro - fer
4 Mon - stra te es - se ma - trem: Su - mat
5 Sit laus De - o Pa - tri, Sum - mo

Ma - ter al - ma, At - que sem - per Vir - go,
é - lis o - re, Fun - da nos in pa - ce,
lu - men cae - cis: Ma - la no - stra pel - le,
per te pre - ces, Qui pro no - bis na - tus
Chri - sto de - cus, Spi - rí - tu - i San - cto,

Fe - lix cae - li por - ta.
Mu - tans He - vae no - men.
Bo - na cun - cta po - sce.
Tu - lit es - se tu - us.
Tri - bus ho - nor u - nus. A - men.

Hail Star of the Sea,
Gracious and ever-virgin Mother of God,
Blessed Gate of Heaven.

Pray [for us], thou who received
That "Ave" from Gabriel, [and] establish us in peace,
Transforming the name of Eve.

Dissolve the chains [that bind us] to things,
Shine forth the Light of Heaven:
Cast out from us what is evil [and] beseech [God] all good things [for us].

Show thyself to be [our] Mother;
Let [him] receive [our] prayers through thee,
Who, being thy Son, has borne our sins.

Praise be to God the Father,
Glory be to Christ in the highest and to the Holy Spirit,
[And] honor to the One in Three. Amen.

TEXT: Anonymous, 9th century, translation by Richard Divozzo, b.1955. Used with permission.
MELODY: Plainchant, Mode I, 9th century
HARMONIZATION: Jean-Hébert Desrocquettes, O.S.B., copyright © 1958 by Ralph Jusko Publications, Inc.

AVE MARIS STELLA
66.66

The God whom earth and sea and sky
534

1 The God whom earth and sea and sky A -
2 O Moth - er blest! and chos - en shrine Where -
3 Blest in the mes - sage Gab - riel brought; Blest
4 O Lord, the Vir - gin - born, to thee E -

dore and laud and mag - ni - fy, Whose
in the Ar - chi - tect di - vine, Whose
in the work the Spir - it wrought; Most
ter - nal praise and glo - ry be, Whom

might they own, whose praise they tell, In
hand con - tains the earth and sky, Vouch -
blest, to bring to hu - man birth The
with the Fa - ther we a - dore And

Ma - ry's bod - y deigned to dwell.
safed in hid - den guise to lie:
long de - sired of all the earth.
Ho - ly Ghost for ev - er - more. A - men.

TEXT: Venantius Fortunatus, c.530-c.609, translated by John Mason Neale, 1818-1866
MELODY: Johann H. Schein, 1586-1630
HARMONIZATION: Johann Sebastian Bach, 1685-1750

EISENACH
88.88

535

Concordi laetitia

1 Con - cór - di lae - tí - ti - a, Pro - púl - sa mae -
2 Quam con - cén - tu pá - ri - li Cho - ri lau - dant
3 O Re - gí - na vír - gi - num, Vo - tis fa - ve
4 Glo - ri - ó - sa Trí - ni - tas, In - di - ví - sa

stí - ti - a. Ma - rí - ae prae - có - ni - a
caé - li - ci, Et nos cum cae - lé - sti - bus,
sup - pli - cum, Et post mor - tis stá - di - um,
U - ni - tas, Ob Ma - rí - ae mé - ri - ta,

Ré - co - lat Ec - clé - si - a: Vir - go Ma - rí - a.
No - vum me - los pán - gi - mus: Vir - go Ma - rí - a.
Vi - tae con - fer praé - mi - um: Vir - go Ma - rí - a.
Nos sal - va per saé - cu - la: Vir - go Ma - rí - a.

TEXT: Latin, anonymous, 13th century
MELODY: Pierre de Corbeil, d.1222
HARMONIZATION: Jean-Hébert Desrocquettes, O.S.B., copyright © 1958 by Ralph Jusko Publications, Inc.

CONCORDI LAETITIA CHANT
7 7 . 7 7 . 5

Sounds of joy have put to flight

536

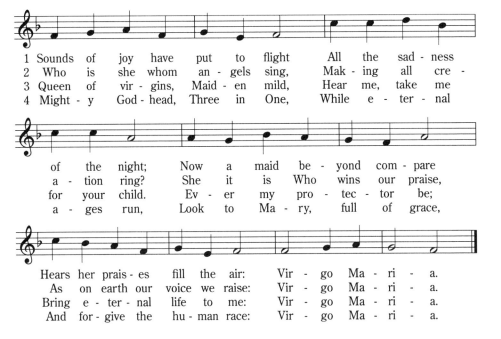

1 Sounds of joy have put to flight All the sad - ness
2 Who is she whom an - gels sing, Mak - ing all cre -
3 Queen of vir - gins, Maid - en mild, Hear me, take me
4 Might - y God - head, Three in One, While e - ter - nal

of the night; Now a maid be - yond com - pare
a - tion ring? She it is Who wins our praise,
for your child. Ev - er my pro - tec - tor be;
a - ges run, Look to Ma - ry, full of grace,

Hears her prais - es fill the air: Vir - go Ma - ri - a.
As on earth our voice we raise: Vir - go Ma - ri - a.
Bring e - ter - nal life to me: Vir - go Ma - ri - a.
And for - give the hu - man race: Vir - go Ma - ri - a.

TEXT: Latin, Anonymous, 13th century, *Concordi laetitia,*
translated by M. Owen Lee, C.S.B., b.1930, copyright © 1958 by Ralph Jusko Publications, Inc.
MELODY: Pierre de Corbeil, d.1222
HARMONIZATION: Sister Mary Florian, S.S.J., copyright © 1958 by Ralph Jusko Publications, Inc.

CONCORDI LAETITIA
7 7.7 7.5

537   Alma Redemptoris Mater

Cantor(s) ... **All**

Al - ma Red-em-ptó-ris Ma-ter, quae pér-vi-a cae-

li por-ta ma-nes, Et stel-la ma-ris, suc-cúr-re ca-dén-ti

súr-ge-re qui cu-rat pó-pu-lo: Tu quae ge-nu-í-sti,

na-tú-ra mi-rán-te, tu-um san-ctum Ge-ni-tó-rem:

Vir-go pri-us ac po-sté-ri-us, Ga-bri-é-lis ab o-re

su-mens il-lud A-ve, pec-ca-tó-rum mi-se-ré-re.

Marian Antiphon for Advent

Loving Mother of our Savior,
thou open gate leading us to heaven,
and Star of the Sea, help thy fallen people,
help all those who seek to rise again.

Maiden who didst give birth,
all nature wondering, to thy holy Lord Creator:
Virgin before and virgin always who received from
Gabriel's mouth this message from heaven,
take pity on us poor sinners.

TEXT: Ascribed to Hermannus Contractus, 1013-1054, translated by Theodore Marier.
  copyright © 1953 Summy-Birchard Music division of Birch Tree Group, Ltd.
MELODY: Ascribed to Hermannus Contractus, 1013-1054

ALMA REDEMPTORIS MATER
Irregular

Ave, Regina caelórum

A - ve, Re - gi - na cae - ló - rum, A - ve,

Dó - mi - na an - ge - ló - rum: Sal - ve ra - dix,

sal - ve por - ta, Ex qua mun - do lux est or - ta:

Gau - de Vir - go glo - ri - ó - sa, Su - per

o - mnes spe - ci - ó - sa: Va - le, O val - de

de - có - ra, Et pro no - bis Chri- stum ex - ó - ra.

Marian Antiphon for Candlemas to Wednesday of Holy Week

Hail, Queen of the Heavens. Hail, Ruler of Angels.
Hail Root, Hail Gate,
From whom the Light is rising on the world.
Rejoice, O glorious Virgin,
Of all mankind, the fairest:
Thou art worthy, O Lady of exceeding beauty,
Pray to Christ for us.

TEXT: Latin, Anonymous, 12th century, translated by Richard Divozzo, b.1955. Used with permission.
MELODY: Plainchant, Mode VI, 12th century
HARMONIZATION: Jean-Hébert Desrocquettes, O.S.B., copyright © 1958 by Ralph Jusko Publications, Inc.

AVE REGINA CAELORUM
Irregular

539 Hail, Queen of heaven, the ocean star

1 Hail, Queen of heav'n, the o - cean star,
2 O gen - tle, chaste, and spot - less maid,
3 So - jour - ners in this vale of tears,
4 And while to him who reigns a - bove,

Guide of the wan - d'rer here be - low; Thrown on life's
We sin - ners make our prayers through thee; Re - mind thy
To thee, blest ad - vo - cate, we cry: Pit - y our
In God-head One, in Per - sons Three, The source of

surge, we claim thy care: Save us from per - il
son that he has paid The price of our in -
sor - rows, calm our fears, And soothe with hope our
life, of grace, of love. Hom - age we pay on

and from woe Moth - er of Christ, star of the
i - qui - ty. Vir - gin most pure, star of the
mis - er - y. Re - fuge in grief, star of the
bend - ed knee. Do thou, bright Queen, star of the

sea. Pray for the wan - d'rer, pray for me.
sea, Pray for the sin - ner, pray for me.
sea, Pray for the mourn - er, pray for me.
sea, Pray for the chil - dren, pray for me.

TEXT: John Lingard, 1771-1851   STELLA
MELODY: Henri Frédéric Hemy, 1818-1888   88.88.88
HARMONIZATION: Henri Frédéric Hemy, 1818-1888

Maiden, yet a Mother

540

1 Maid - en, yet a Moth - er, Daugh-ter of thy Son,
2 Thus his place pre - par - èd, He who all things made
3 Noon on Si - on's moun - tain Is thy char - i - ty;
4 Nor a - lone thou hear - est When thy name we hail;
5 La - dy, lest our vi - sion, Striv- ing heav'n-ward, fail,

High be - yond all oth - er— Low - li - er is none;
'Mid his crea-tures tar - ried, In thy bo - som laid;
Hope its liv - ing foun - tain Finds, on earth, in thee:
Of - ten thou art near - est When our voic - es fail;
Still let thy pe - ti - tion With thy Son pre - vail,

Thou the con - sum - ma - tion Planned by God's de - cree,
There his love he nour - ished— Warmth that gave in - crease
La - dy, such thy pow - er, He, who grace would buy
Mir - rored in thy fash - ion All cre - a - tion's good,
Un - to whom all mer - it Power and ma - jes - ty

When our lost cre - a - tion Nob - ler rose in thee!
To the Root whence flour- ished Our e - ter - nal peace.
Not as of thy dow - er, With- out wings would fly.
Mer - cy, might, com - pas - sion Grace thy wo - man - hood.
With the Ho - ly Spir - it And the Fath - er be. A - men.

TEXT: Dante Alighieri, 1265-1321, translated by Ronald Arbuthknott Knox, 1909-1958
MELODY: French Noël
HARMONIZATION: A. Gregory Murray, O.S.B., copyright © by Burns & Oates, Ltd., alt.

UNE VAINE CRAINTE
65.65.D

541

Mary the Dawn

1. Mar - y the Dawn, Christ the Per - fect Day;
2. Mar - y the Root, Christ the Mys - tic Vine;
3. Mar - y the Wheat - sheaf, Christ the Liv - ing Bread;
4. Mar - y the Font, Christ the Cleans - ing Flood;
5. Mar - y the Tem - ple, Christ the Tem - ple's Lord;
6. Mar - y the Bea - con, Christ the Ha - ven's Rest;

Mar - y the Gate, Christ the Heav'n - ly Way!
Mar - y the Grape, Christ the Sa - cred Wine!
Mar - y the Rose - tree, Christ the Rose blood - red!
Mar - y the Chal - ice, Christ the Sav - ing Blood!
Mar - y the Shrine, Christ the God a - dored!
Mar - y the Mir - ror, Christ the Vi - sion Blest!

Mar - y the Moth - er, Christ the Moth - er's Son;

Both ev - er blest while end - less a - ges run. A - men.

TEXT: Justin Mulcahy, C.P., under the pseudonym "Paul Cross," first appearing in the Pius X Hymnal, 1953
MELODY: Justin Mulcahy, C.P.

MARY THE DAWN
Irregular

O sanctissima/O most holy one

542

1 O san - ctís - si - ma, O pi - ís - si - ma,
2 Vir - go, ré - spi - ce, Ma - ter, á - spi - ce,
1 O most ho - ly one, O most low - ly one,
2 Vir - gin ev - er fair, Moth - er, hear our prayer,

Dul - cis Vir - go, Ma - ri - a!
Au - di nos, O Ma - ri - a!
Lov - ing Vir - gin, Ma - ri - a!
Look up - on us, Ma - ri - a!

Ma - ter a - má - ta, In - te - me -
Tu me - di - ci - nam Por - tas di -
Moth - er, Maid of fair - est love, La - dy, Queen of
Bring to us your treas - ure, Grace be - yond all

rá - ta,
vi - nam, O - ra, o - ra pro no - bis!
all a - bove,
mea - sure;

TEXT: Anonymous, translated by Charles W. Leland, copyright © 1958 by Ralph Jusko Publications, Inc.
MELODY: "Sicilian melody," *Tattersall's Improved Psalmody*, 1794
HARMONIZATION: Healey Willan, 1880-1968, copyright © 1958 by Ralph Jusko Publications, Inc., alt.

O DU FRÖHLICHE
55.7.55.7

543   Sing of Mary, pure and lowly

1 Sing of Ma - ry, pure and low - ly, Vir - gin –
2 Sing of Je - sus, Son of Ma - ry, In the
3 Joy - ful Mo - ther, full of glad - ness, In Thine
4 Glo - ry be to God the Fa - ther; Glo - ry

moth - er un - de - filed, Sing of God's own
home at Na - za - reth. Toil and la - bour
arms thy Lord was borne. Mourn - ful Mo - ther,
be to God the Son; Glo - ry be to

Son most ho - ly, Who be - came her lit - tle Child.
can - not wea - ry Love en - dur - ing un - to death.
full of sad - ness, All thy heart with pain was torn.
God the Spir - it; Glo - ry to the Three in One.

Fair - est Child of fair - est moth - er, God the
Con - stant was the love He gave her, Though He
Glo - rious Mo - ther, now re - ward - ed With a
From the heart of bless - ed Ma - ry, From all

Lord Who came to earth. Word made flesh, our ver - y
went forth from her side. Forth to preach, and heal, and
crown at Je - sus' hand, Age to age thy name re -
saints the song as - cends, And the Church and strain re -

Broth - er, Takes our na - ture by His birth.
suf - fer, Till on Cal - va - ry He died.
cord - ed Shall be blest in ev - 'ry land.
ech - oes Un - to earth's re - mo - test ends. A - men.

TEXT: Roland Ford Palmer, 1891-1985, *Canadian Book of Common Praise*, 1938, alt.
    Copyright by the Estate of Roland F. Palmer, S.S.J.E. (1891-1985)
MELODY: *Plymouth Collection*, New York, 1855
HARMONIZATION: Traditional

PLEADING SAVIOR (SALTASH)
87.87.D

Daily, daily sing to Mary

544

1 Dai - ly, dai - ly sing to Mar - y. Sing, my soul, her
2 She is might - y in her plead - ing, Ten - der in her
3 Sing, my tongue, the Vir - gin's tro - phies, Who, for us, her
4 All my sens - es, heart, af - fec - tions, Strive to sound her
5 All our joys do fall from Ma - ry, All then join her

prais - es due: All her feasts, her ac - tions hon - or
lov - ing care; Ev - er watch - ful, un - der - stand - ing,
Mak - er bore; For the curse of old in - flict - ed,
glo - ry forth: Spread a - broad the sweet me - mor - ials
praise to sing; Trem - bling sing the Vir - gin Moth - er,

With the heart's de - vo - tion true. Lost in won - d'ring
All our sor - rows she will share. Gifts of heav - en
Peace and bless - ings to re - store. Sing in songs of
Of the Vir - gin's price - less worth. Where the voice of
Moth - er of our Lord and King. While we sing her

con - tem - pla - tion. Be her maj - es - ty con - fessed: Call her Moth - er,
she has giv - en. No - ble La - dy, to our race; She the Queen, who
praise un - end - ing. Call up - on her lov - ing - ly: Seat of wis - dom,
mu - sic thrill - ing, Where the tongues of el - o - quence, That can ut - ter
awe - ful glo - ry, Far a - bove our fan - cy's reach, Let our hearts be

call her Vir - gin, Gra - cious Moth - er, Vir - gin blest.
decks her sub - jects With the light of God's own grace.
Gate of heav - en, Morn - ing star up - on the sea.
hymns be - seem - ing All her match - less ex - cel - lence?
quick to of - fer Love the heart a - lone can teach.

TEXT: ascribed to St. Bernard of Cluny, d.1150, translated by Henry Bittleston, 1818-1866, alt.
MELODY: *Trier Gesangbuch*, 1695
HARMONIZATION: Traditional

SUNRISE
87.87.D

545

Salve, Mater misericordiae

Sal - ve, Ma - ter mi - se - ri - cór - di - ae,

Ma - ter De - i et Ma - ter vé - ni - ae,

Ma - ter spe - i et Ma - ter grá - ti - ae,

Ma - ter ple - na san - ctae lae - tí - ti - ae, O Ma - ri - a!

1 Sal - ve, de - cus hu - má - ni gé - ne - ris.
2 Sal - ve, fe - lix Vir - go pu - ér - pe - ra:

Sal - ve, Vir - go dí - gni - or cé - te - ris,
Nam qui se - det in Pa - tris déx - te - ra.

Quae vir - gi - nes o - mnes trans - gré - de - ris,
Cae - lum re - gens, ter - ram et áe - the - ra.

Et ál - ti - us se - des in sú - pe - ris, O Ma - ri - a!
In - tra tu - a se clau - sit ví - sce - ra, O Ma - ri - a!

Refrain

Hail, Mother of Mercy, Mother of God and Mother of Pardon,
Mother of Hope and Mother of Grace,
Plentiful Mother of the Blessed Saints, O Mary!

Verses

1 *Hail, Glory of the Human Race.*
Hail, Worthiest of Virgins,
you who have exceeded all others
and have taken the higher seat in highest Heaven, O Mary!

2 *Hail Blessed Virgin Mother.*
For He who sits at the right hand of the Father,
ruling in Heaven the whole created universe,
enclosed Himself within your body, O Mary!

TEXT: Ancient Carmelite Hymn, translated by Richard Divozzo, b.1955
MELODY: Plainchant, Mode V
HARMONIZATION: Jean-Hébert Desrocquettes, O.S.B., copyright © 1958 by Ralph Jusko Publications, Inc.

SALVE, MATER MISERICORDIAE
Irregular

Regina caeli

546

Re - gí - na cae - li, lae - tá - re, Al - le - lú - ia: Qui - a quem

me - ru - í - sti por - tá - re, Al - le - lú - ia:

Re - sur - réx - it sic - ut di - xit, Al - le - lú - ia:

O - ra pro no - bis De - um, al - le - lú - ia.

Marian Antiphon for Eastertide

Mary, Queen of Heav'n, be joyful, Alleluia.
For he whom thou hast merited to bear, Alleluia,
He is risen as he foretold, Alleluia.
Plead with God our sins to spare, alleluia.

TEXT: Anonymous, 14th century, translated by Theodore Marier. Reprinted from *Hymns, Psalms and Spiritual Canticles*,
© 1974, by Theodore Marier (Belmont, Mass.: BACS Publishing Company, 1974). Used by permission.
Copyright © 1953 by Summy-Birchard Music division of Birch Tree Group Ltd.
MELODY: Plainchant, Mode VI, 14th century

REGINA CAELI
Irregular

547

Salve Regína

Sal - ve Re - gí - na, Ma - ter mi - se - ri - cór - di - ae:

Ví - ta, dul - cé - do, et spes no - stra, sal - ve. Ad te cla - má - mus,

éx - su - les, fí - li - i He - vae. Ad te su - spi - rá - mus,

ge - mén - tes et flen - tes in hac la - cri - má - rum val - le.

E - ia er - go, Ad - vo - cá - ta no - stra, il - los tu -

os mi - se - ri - cór - des ó - cu - los ad nos con - vér - te.

Et Je - sum, be - ne - dí - ctum fru - ctum ven - tris tu - i,

no - bis post hoc ex - sí - li - um os - tén - de.

O cle - mens; O pi - a;

O   dul - cis Vir - go Ma - rí - a.

Marian Antiphon for Ordinary Time

Hail, O holy Queen! Hail, O Mother all merciful,
* our life, our sweetness, and our hope, we hail thee!*
To thee do we cry, poor banished children of Eve.
To thee we send our sighs while mourning
* and weeping in this lowly valley of tears.*
Turn then thine eyes, most gracious Advocate,
O turn thine eyes, so loving and compassionate,
* upon us sinners.*
And Jesus, the most blessed fruit of thy virgin womb,
* show us when this earthly exile is ended.*
O clement. O loving. O most sweet, Virgin Mary.

TEXT: Attributed to Hermannus Contractus, 1013-1054, English translated by Theodore Marier.
Reprinted from *Hymns, Psalms and Spiritual Canticles,* by Theodore Marier
(Belmont, Mass.: BACS Publishing Company, 1974) © 1974. Used by permission.
Copyright © 1953 by Summy-Birchard Music division of Birch Tree Group, Ltd.
MELODY: attributed to Hermannus Contractus, 1013-1054

SALVE REGINA CHANT
Irregular

560

The Church's one foundation

1 The Chur-ch's one foun - da - tion Is Je - sus Christ her Lord;
2 E - lect from ev - 'ry na - tion, Yet one o'er all the earth,
3 Though with a scorn-ful won - der Men see her sore op - prest,

She is his new cre - a - tion By wa - ter and the word:
Her char - ter of sal - va - tion, One Lord, one faith, one birth;
By schi-sms rent a - sun - der, By her - e - sies dis - trest;

From heav'n he came and sought her To be his ho - ly bride;
One ho - ly Name she bless - es, Par - takes one ho - ly food,
Yet saints their watch are keep - ing, Their cry goes up, "How long?"

With his own blood he bought her, And for her life he died.
And to one hope she press - es, With ev - 'ry grace en - dued.
And soon the night of weep - ing Shall be the morn of song.

TEXT: Samuel John Stone, 1839-1900
MELODY: Samuel Sebastian Wesley, 1810-1876
HARMONIZATION: from *Hymns, Ancient and Modern*, 1904 edition

AURELIA
76.76.D

Christ is made the sure foundation

561

1 Christ is made the sure foun-da-tion, Christ the head and
2 To this tem - ple, where we call thee, Come, O Lord of
3 Grant, we pray, to all thy peo - ple, All the grace they

cor - ner - stone; Cho - sen of the Lord, and pre - cious,
hosts, to - day; With thy wont - ed lov - ing - kind - ness
ask to gain; What they gain from thee, for - ev - er

Bind - ing all the Church in one; Ho - ly Zi - on's
Hear thy ser - vants as they pray, And thy full - est
With the bless - ed to re - tain, And here - af - ter

help for - ev - er, And her con - fi - dence a - lone.
ben - e - dic - tion Shed in all its bright ar - ray.
in thy glo - ry Ev - er - more with thee to reign.

TEXT: Latin, 6th-7th century, stanzas 5-8 and doxology, *Urbs Jerusalem beata*,
    translated by John Mason Neale, 1818-1866, alt.
MELODY: adapted by Ernest Hawkins, 1802-1868, from an anthem of Henry Purcell, 1659-1695
HARMONIZATION: adapted by Ernest Hawkins, 1802-1868, from an anthem of Henry Purcell, 1659-1695

WESTMINSTER ABBEY (BELVILLE)
87.87.87

562   O Love, who drew from Jesus' side

1 O Love, who drew from Je - sus' side,   One bo - dy
2 Round Pe - ter's chair may all u - nite;   From blind - ed
3 While Chris - tians pray for u - ni - ty,   Pour forth the
4 Spoiled chil - dren, we, so blest with sight,   Re - deemed by

freed from A - dam's shame,   One Church sent forth to serve and guide,
eyes the veil with - draw;   The minds of rul - ers set a - right
light your saints have seen;   Dis - pel the dark of en - mi - ty:
love sur - pass - ing all;   Lest we who glo - ry in your light

One faith con - firmed by gifts of flame; When world - ly schemes our
Who bind your Church be - neath their law; Where faith grows dim and
Make known to all what love can mean, Where brood - ing minds old
Share not our gift, heed not your call, In Chris - tian hearts that

hopes as - sail   Thy king - dom come, thy truth pre - vail.
hearts are frail,   Thy king - dom come, thy truth pre - vail.
wounds be - wail,   Thy king - dom come, thy truth pre - vail.
faint and fail,   Thy king - dom come, thy truth pre - vail.

TEXT: Richard J. Wojcik, b. 1923, copyright © 1977 by American Catholic Press
MELODY: Georg Neumark, 1621-1681
HARMONIZATION: Johann Sebastian Bach, 1685-1750

NEUMARK (alt.)
8 8 . 8 8 . 8 8 (alt.)

Glorious things of thee are spoken 563

1 Glo-rious things of thee are spo-ken, Zi - on, ci - ty of our God!
2 See, the streams of liv-ing wa-ters, Spring-ing from e - ter - nal love,
3 Sav - ior, if of Zi-on's ci - ty I, through grace, a mem-ber am,

He whose word can - not be bro - ken Formed thee for his own a - bode:
Well sup - ply thy sons and daugh-ters, And all fear of want re - move:
Let the world de - ride or pi - ty, I will glo-ry in thy name:

On the Rock of A - ges found-ed, What can shake thy sure re - pose?
Who can faint while such a riv - er Ev - er flows their thirst to as-suage?
Fad-ing is the world-ling's plea - sure, All his boast-ed pomp and show;

With sal - va-tion's walls sur-round-ed, Thou may'st smile at all thy foes.
Grace, which like the Lord the Giv - er, Ne - ver fails from age to age.
Sol - id joys and last-ing trea-sure None but Zi - on's chil-dren know.

TEXT: John Newton, 1725-1807
MELODY: Franz Joseph Haydn, 1732-1809
HARMONIZATION: from *The English Hymnal*, 1906

AUSTRIA
8 7 . 8 7 . D

570 All the world is God's own field

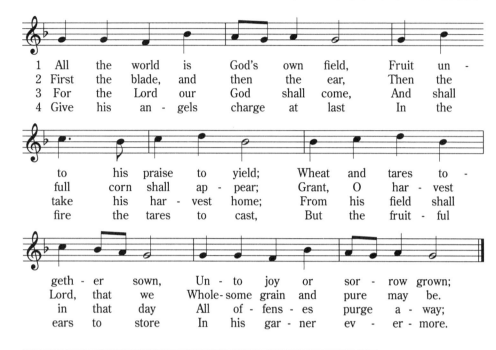

1 All the world is God's own field, Fruit un -
2 First the blade, and then the ear, Then the
3 For the Lord our God shall come, And shall
4 Give his an - gels charge at last In the

to his praise to yield; Wheat and tares to -
full corn shall ap - pear; Grant, O har - vest
take his har - vest home; From his field shall
fire the tares to cast, But the fruit - ful

geth - er sown, Un - to joy or sor - row grown;
Lord, that we Whole- some grain and pure may be.
in that day All of - fens - es purge a - way;
ears to store In his gar - ner ev - er - more.

TEXT: Henry Alford, 1810-1871, alt.
MELODY: *Erfurt Enchiridion*, 1524
HARMONIZATION: Melchior Vulpius, 1560?-1616, from *Erfurt Enchiridion*, 1524, alt.

NUN KOMM, DER HEIDEN HEILAND
7 7. 7 7

Help, Lord, the souls that thou has made 571

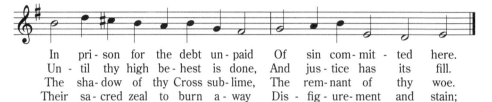

1 Help, Lord, the souls that thou hast made, The souls to thee so dear,
2 These ho - ly souls, they suf - fer on, Re - sign'd in heart and will,
3 For dai - ly falls, for par - don'd crime, They joy to un - der - go
4 Oh, by their pa - tience of de - lay, Their hope a - mid their pain,
5 Oh, by their fire of love, not less In keen - ness than the flame;
6 Good Je - sus, help! sweet Je - sus, aid The souls to thee most dear,

In pri - son for the debt un - paid Of sin com - mit - ted here.
Un - til thy high be - hest is done, And jus - tice has its fill.
The sha - dow of thy Cross sub - lime, The rem - nant of thy woe.
Their sa - cred zeal to burn a - way Dis - fig - ure - ment and stain;
Oh, by their ver - y help - less - ness, Oh, by thy own great Name;
In pri - son for the debt un - paid Of sins com - mit - ted here.

TEXT: John Henry Newman, 1801-1890
MELODY: A. Gregory Murray, O.S.B., b.1905, copyright © by Burns & Oates, Ltd.
HARMONIZATION: A. Gregory Murray, O.S.B., b.1905, copyright © by Burns & Oates, Ltd.

REQUIEM
86.86

572

In paradisum

In pa-ra-dí-sum de-dú-cant te án-ge-li: in tu-o ad-vén-tu

su - scí-pi-ant te már-ty - res, et per-dú-cant te in ci-vi-

tá-tem san - ctam Je - rú-sa-lem. Cho-rus an - ge-ló - rum

te su - sci-pi-at, et cum Lá - za-ro quon-dam páu-pe-re

ae - tér - nam há-be-as ré - qui-em.

May the Angels conduct you to Paradise:
And at your coming may the Martyrs receive you.
May they lead you to the holy City of Jerusalem.
May a choir of Angels receive you
And may you, with Lazarus — once a poor man —
Possess eternal peace.

TEXT: Antiphons from *Last Farewell of the Requiem Mass*, translation by Richard Divozzo, b.1955. Used with permission.
MELODY: Plainchant, Mode VII, antiphons from *Last Farewell of the Requiem Mass*

IN PARADISUM
Irregular

May flights of angels lead you on your way 573

May flights of an - gels lead you on your way To pa - ra - dise, and heav'n's e - ter - nal day! May mar - tyrs greet you af - ter death's dark night, And bid you en - ter in - to Zi - on's light! May choirs of an - gels sing you to your rest With once poor Laz - 'rus, now for ev - er blest!

TEXT: James Quinn, S.J., copyright © 1969 by Geoffrey Chapman, Ltd.
MELODY: from *Genevan Psalter*, 1551, alt.
HARMONIZATION: Louis Bourgeois, c.1510-1561

TOULON (alt.)
10 . 10 . 10 . 10 . 10 . 10

574

Requiem aeternam

All:

Ré - qui-em * ae - tér - nam do - na

e - is, Dó - mi - ne:

et lux per-pé - tu - a lú - ce - at

Cantor or Choir only
Psalm (64) 65

e - is. Te de - cet hy-mnus, De-us, in Si - on,

et ti - bi red-dé - tur vo - tum in Je - rú - sa - lem:

ex-áu - di o-ra-ti-ó-nem me-am, ad te o-mnis ca-ro vé-ni-et.

Antiphon

Grant him, O Lord,
eternal rest and may thy perpetual light shine upon him.

Psalm verse

It is right, O God,
to sing to thee a hymn in Zion and in Jerusalem render thee a vow.

[Antiphon]

Thou who hearest our prayers, to thee all flesh must come.

[Antiphon]

TEXT: Requiem Mass, Introit, 4 Esdras 2:34-35,
   translation by Richard Divozzo, b.1955. Used with permission.
MELODY: Plainchant, Mode VI, Requiem Mass, Introit
HARMONIZATION: Jean-Hébert Desrocquettes, O.S.B., copyright © 1958 by Ralph Jusko Publications.

REQUIEM AETERNAM
Irregular

Remember those, O Lord

575

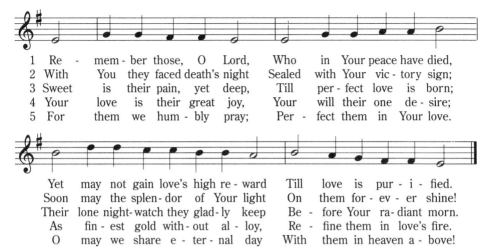

1 Re - mem - ber those, O Lord, Who in Your peace have died,
2 With You they faced death's night Sealed with Your vic - tory sign;
3 Sweet is their pain, yet deep, Till per - fect love is born;
4 Your love is their great joy, Your will their one de - sire;
5 For them we hum - bly pray; Per - fect them in Your love.

Yet may not gain love's high re - ward Till love is pur - i - fied.
Soon may the splen- dor of Your light On them for - ev - er shine!
Their lone night-watch they glad- ly keep Be - fore Your ra - diant morn.
As fin - est gold with- out al - loy, Re - fine them in love's fire.
O may we share e - ter - nal day With them in heaven a - bove!

TEXT: James Quinn, S.J., copyright © 1969 by Geoffrey Chapman, Ltd.
MELODY: from the *Psalms of David in English Meter*, 1579, by William H. Damon, c.1540-1591
HARMONIZATION: Composite

SOUTHWELL
6 6 . 8 6

576   Day of wrath! O Day of mourning!

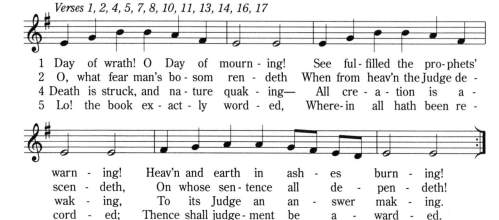

Verses 1, 2, 4, 5, 7, 8, 10, 11, 13, 14, 16, 17

1 Day of wrath! O Day of mourn - ing!   See ful - filled the pro - phets'
2 O, what fear man's bo - som ren - deth   When from heav'n the Judge de -
4 Death is struck, and na - ture quak - ing—   All cre - a - tion is a -
5 Lo! the book ex - act - ly word - ed,   Where - in all hath been re -

warn - ing!   Heav'n and earth in ash - es burn - ing!
scen - deth,   On whose sen - tence all de - pen - deth!
wak - ing,   To its Judge an an - swer mak - ing.
cord - ed;   Thence shall judge - ment be a - ward - ed.

Verses 3, 6, 9, 12, 15, 18, 19

3 Won - drous sound the trum - pet fling - eth,   Thru' earth's se - pul - chres it
6 When the Judge his seat at - tain - eth,   And each hid - den deed ar -

ring - eth,   All be - fore the throne it bring - eth!
raign - eth,   No - thing un - a - venged re - main - eth.

7 What shall I, frail man, be pleading,
Who for me be interceding,
When the just are mercy needing?

8 King of majesty tremendous,
Who dost free salvation send us,
Fount of pity, then befriend us!

9 Think, king Jesus! — my salvation
Caus'd thy wondrous Incarnation;
Leave me not to reprobation.

10 Faint and weary thou has sought me,
On the Cross of suffering bought me:
Shall such grace be vainly brought me?

11 Righteous Judge of retribution,
Grant thy gift of absolution,
Ere that reckoning-day's conclusion.

12 Guilty, now I pour my moaning,
All my shame with anguish owning;
Spare, O God, thy suppliant groaning.

13 Thou the sinful woman savedst;
Thou the dying thief forgavest;
And to me a hope vouchsafest.

14 Worthless are my prayers and sighing,
Yet, good Lord, in grace complying,
Rescue me from fires undying!

15 With thy favoured sheep O place me,
Nor among the goats abase me:
But to thy right hand upraise me.

16 While the wicked are confounded,
Doom'd to flames of woe unbounded,
Call me, with thy saints surrounded.

17 Low I kneel, with heart-submission;
    See, like ashes, my contrition—
    Help me, in my last condition!

18 Ah! that day of tears and mourning!
    From the dust of earth returning,
    Man for judgement must prepare him!

19 Spare, O God, in mercy spare him!
    Lord, who didst our souls redeem,
    Grant a blessèd Requiem.

TEXT: Thomas of Celano, O.F.M., 13th century, translated by William Josiah Irons, 1812-1883   **DIES IRAE**
MELODY: H. Stanley Taylor, b.1905, copyright © by Burns & Oates, Ltd.   **888.888.888**
HARMONIZATION: H. Stanley Taylor, b.1905, copyright © by Burns & Oates, Ltd.

577

Dies irae, dies illa

1 Di - es i - rae, di - es il - la, Sol - vet sae - clum
2 Quan-tus tre-mor est fu - tú - rus Quan-do ju - dex

in fa - víl - la: Te - ste Da - vid cum Si - byl - la.
est ven - tú - rus, Cun - cta stri - cte dis - cu - sú - rus!

3 Tu - ba mi - rum spar - gens so - num Per se - púl - cra
4 Mors stu- pé - bit et na - tú - ra, Cum re - súr-get

re - gi - ó - num Co - get o - mnes an - te thro - num.
cre - a - tú - ra, Ju - di cán - ti re - spon-sú - ra.

5 Li - ber scri - ptus pro - fe - ré - tur, In quo to-tum
6 Ju - dex er - go cum se - dé - bit, Quid - quid la - tet

con - ti - né - tur, Un - de mun-dus ju - di - cé - tur.
ap - pa - ré - bit: Nil in - úl - tum re - ma - né - bit.

7 Quid sum mi - ser tunc di - ctú-rus? Quem pa - tró - num
8 Rex tre-mén-dae ma - je - sta - tis, Qui sal - ván - dos

ro - ga - tú - rus? Cum vix ju - stus sit se - cú - rus.
sal - vas gra - tis, Sal - va me, fons pi - e - tá - tis.

qua - si ci - nis: Ge - re cu - ram me - i fi - nis.

La - cri - mó - sa di - es il - la, Qua re - súr - get

ex fa - víl - la. 19 Ju - di - cán - dus ho - mo re - us:

Hu - ic er - go par - ce, De - us. 20 Pi - e Je - su

Dó - mi - ne, do - na e - is ré - qui - em. A - men.

TEXT: Thomas of Celano, O.F.M., 13th century
MELODY: Plainchant, Mode I, 13th century, Thomas of Celano
HARMONIZATION: Jean-Hébert Desrocquettes, O.S.B., copyright © 1958 by Ralph Jusko Publications, Inc.

DIES IRAE CHANT
888.888.888

Lead, kindly Light

578

1 Lead, kind-ly Light, a-mid the en-cir-cling gloom, Lead thou me
2 I was not ev - er thus, nor prayed that thou Shouldst lead me
3 So long thy power hath blest me, sure it still Will lead me

on; The night is dark, and I am far from home; Lead
on; I love to choose and see my path; but no Lead
on O'er moor and fen, o'er crag and tor-rent, till The

thou me on: Keep thou my feet; I do not ask to
thou me on. I loved the ga - rish day, and, spite of
night is gone; And with the morn those an - gel fa - ces

see The dis - tant scene; one step e- nough for me.
fears, Pride ruled my will: re - mem-ber not past years.
smile Which I have loved long since, and lost a - while.

TEXT: John Henry Newman, 1801-1890
MELODY: Charles Henry Purday, 1799-1885
HARMONIZATION: Charles Henry Purday, 1799-1885

SANDON
10.4.10.4.10.10

579   I heard the voice of Jesus say

1 I heard the voice of Je - sus say, 'Come un - to me and rest;
2 I heard the voice of Je - sus say, 'Be - hold, I free - ly give
3 I heard the voice of Je - sus say, 'I am this dark world's light;

lay down, thou wea - ry one, lay down thy head up - on my breast.'
the liv - ing wa - ter; thirst - y one, stoop down, and drink, and live.'
look un - to me, thy morn shall rise, and all thy day be bright.'

I came to Je - sus as I was wea - ry and worn and sad:
I came to Je - sus, and I drank of that life - giv - ing stream;
I looked to Je - sus, and I found in him my star, my sun;

I found in him a rest - ing place, and he has made me glad.
my thirst was quenched, my soul re - vived, and now I live in him.
and in that light of life I'll walk till trav - elling days are done.

TEXT: Horatius Bonar, 1808-1889
MELODY: Traditional English melody
HARMONIZATION: coll. Lucy Broadwood, arr. Ralph Vaughan Williams, 1872-1858,
    copyright © by Oxford University Press, from the *English Hymnal* by permission of Oxford University Press.

KINGSFOLD
86.86.D

The King of love my shepherd is

580

1 The King of love my shep - herd is, Whose good - ness
2 Where streams of liv - ing wa - ter flow My ran - somed
3 Per - verse and fool - ish oft I strayed, But yet in
4 In death's dark vale I fear no ill With thee, dear
5 Thou spread'st a ta - ble in my sight; Thy unc - tion,
6 And so through all the length of days Thy good - ness

fail - eth nev - er; I noth - ing lack if
soul he lead - eth, And where the ver - dant
love he sought me, And on his shoul - der
Lord, be - side me, Thy rod and staff my
grace be - stow - eth: And O what trans - port
fail - eth nev - er; Good Shep - herd, may I

I am his, And he is mine for - ev - er.
pas - tures grow With food ce - les - tial feed - eth.
gent - ly laid, And home, re - joic - ing, brought me.
com - fort still, Thy Cross be - fore to guide me.
and de - light From thy pure chal - ice flow - eth!
sing thy praise With - in thy house for - ev - er.

TEXT: Henry Williams Baker, 1821-1877, paraphrase of Psalm 22(23)
MELODY: Traditional Gaelic hymn
HARMONIZATION: from *The English Hymnal*, 1906

ST. COLUMBA
8 7 . 8 7

590

For all the saints

1 For all the saints, who from their la - bors rest,
2 Thou wast their rock, their fort - ress, and their might:
3 O may thy sol - diers, faith - ful, true, and bold,
4 From earth's wide bounds, from o - cean's far - thest coast,

Who thee by faith be - fore the world con - fessed, Thy
Thou, Lord, their Cap - tain in the well-fought fight;
Fight as the saints who no - bly fought of old, And
Through gates of pearl streams in the count-less host,

Name, O Je - sus, be for ev - er blest. Al -
Thou, in the dark - ness drear, their one true light. Al -
win, with them, the vic - tor's crown of gold. Al -
Sing - ing to Fa - ther, Son and Ho - ly Ghost. Al -

- le - lu - ia, al - le - lu - ia!

TEXT: William Walsham How, 1823-1897, alt.
MELODY: Ralph Vaughan Williams, 1872-1958, copyright © by Oxford University Press, alt.,
  from the *English Hymnal* by permission of Oxford University Press.
HARMONIZATION: Ralph Vaughan Williams, 1872-1958, copyright © by Oxford University Press, alt.,
  from the *English Hymnal* by permission of Oxford University Press.

SINE NOMINE
1 0 . 1 0 . 1 0 with Alleluias

Ye holy angels bright

591

1 Ye ho - ly an - gels bright, who wait at God's right
2 Ye bless - ed souls at rest, who ran this earth - ly
3 Ye saints, who toil be - low, a - dore your heaven - ly
4 My soul, bear thou thy part, tri - umph in God a -

hand, or through the realms of light fly at your
race and now, from sin re - leased, be - hold the
King, and on - ward as ye go some joy - ful
bove: and with a well - tuned heart sing thou the

Lord's com - mand, as - sist our song, for
Sa - vior's face, God's prais - es sound, as
an - them sing; take what he gives and
songs of love! Let all thy days till

else the theme too high doth seem for mor - tal tongue.
in his sight with sweet de - light ye do a - bound.
praise him still, through good or ill, who ev - er lives!
life shall end, what - e'er he send, be filled with praise.

TEXT: Richard Baxter, 1615-1691, and John Hampden Gurney, 1802-1862
MELODY: John Darwall, 1731-1789
HARMONIZATION: William Henry Monk, 1823-1889, alt.

DARWALL'S 148th
66.66.44.44

592

From all thy saints in warfare

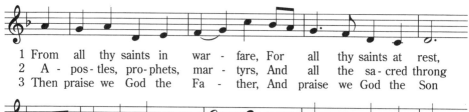

1 From all thy saints in war - fare, For all thy saints at rest,
2 A - pos - tles, pro - phets, mar - tyrs, And all the sa - cred throng
3 Then praise we God the Fa - ther, And praise we God the Son

To thee, O bless - ed Je - sus, All prais - es be ad - dressed.
Who wear the spot - less rai - ment, Who raise the cease - less song—
And God the Ho - ly Spir - it, E - ter - nal Three in One,

Thou, Lord, didst win the bat - tle That they might con - querors be;
For these, passed on be - fore us, Sav - ior, we thee a - dore,
Till all the ran - somed num - ber Fall down be - fore the throne

Their crowns of liv - ing glo - ry Are lit with rays from thee.
And walk - ing in their foot - steps, Would serve thee more and more.
And hon - or, pow'r, and glo - ry As - cribe to God a - lone.

ANDREW

Praise, Lord, for thine apostle,
The first to welcome thee,
The first to lead his brother
The very Christ to see.
With hearts for thee made ready,
May we throughout the year
Still watch to lead our brethren
To own thine advent near.

CONVERSION OF ST. PAUL

Praise for the light from heaven,
Praise for the voice of awe,
Praise for the glorious vision
The persecutor saw.
Thee, Lord, for his conversion
We glorify today;
Enlighten all our darkness
With thy true Spirit's ray.

HOLY INNOCENTS

Praise for thine infant martyrs,
By thee with tenderest love
Called early from the warfare
To share the rest above.
O Rachel, cease your weeping;
They rest from pains and cares.
Lord, grant us hearts as guileless
And crowns as bright as theirs.

JAMES THE ELDER

For him, O Lord, we praise thee,
Who, slain by Herods sword,
Drank of thy cup of suffering,
Fulfilling thus thy word.
Curb we all vain impatience
To read thy veiled decree,
And count it joy to suffer
If so brought nearer thee.

JOHN THE EVANGELIST

Praise for the loved disciple,
Exile on Patmos' shore;
Praise for the faithful record
He to thy Godhead bore.

Praise for the mystic vision
Through him to us revealed;
May we, in patience waiting,
With thine elect be sealed.

BARTHOLOMEW

All praise for thine apostle,
The faithful, pure and true,
Whom underneath the fig tree
Thine eye all-seeing knew;
Like him may we be guileless
True Israelites indeed
That thine abiding presence
Our longing souls may feed.

MATTHEW

Praise, Lord, for him whose Gospel
Thy human life declared,
Who, worldly gains forsaking,
Thy path of suffering shared.
From all unrighteous mammon,
O give us hearts set free
That we, whate'er our calling,
May rise and follow thee.

MATTHIAS THE APOSTLE

Lord, thine abiding presence
Directs the wondrous choice;
For one in place of Judas
The faithful now rejoice.
The Church from false apostles
Forevermore defend,
And by thy parting promise
Be with her to the end.

PETER

Praise for thy great apostle,
The eager and the bold;
Thrice falling, yet repentant,
Thrice charged to feed thy fold.
Lord, make thy pastors faithful
To guard their flocks from ill,
And grant them dauntless courage
With humble earnest will.

LUKE THE EVANGELIST

For that beloved physician
All praise, whose Gospel shows
The Healer of the nations,
The Sharer of our woes,
Thy wine and oil, O Savior,
On bruised hearts deign to pour,
And with true balm of Gilead
Anoint us evermore.

MARK THE EVANGELIST

For him, O Lord, we praise thee,
The weak by grace made strong,
Whose labors and whose Gospel
Enrich our triumph song.
May we in all our weakness
Find strength from thee supplied
And all as fruitful branches
In thee, the Vine, abide.

STEPHEN THE MARTYR

Praise for the first of martyrs,
Who saw thee ready stand
To aid in midst of torment,
To plead at Gods right hand.
Share we with him, if summoned
By death our Lord to own,
On earth the faithful witness,
In heaven the martyr-crown.

PHILIP AND JAMES

All praise for thine apostle
Blest guide to Greek and Jew,
And him surnamed thy brother;
Keep us thy brethren true.
And grant the grace to know thee,
The Way, the Truth, the Life,
To wrestle with temptations
Till victors in the strife.

SIMON AND JUDE

Praise, Lord, for thine apostles
Who sealed their faith today;
One love, one zeal impelled them
To tread the sacred way.
May we with zeal as earnest
The faith of Christ maintain
And, bound in love as brethren,
At length thy rest attain.

THOMAS

All praise for thine apostle,
Whose short-lived doubtings prove
Thy perfect twofold nature,
The fullness of thy love.
On all who wait thy coming
Shed forth thy peace, O Lord,
And grant us faith to know thee,
True Man, true God, adored.

NATIVITY OF JOHN THE BAPTIST

We praise thee for the Baptist,
Forerunner of the Word,
Our true Elias, making
A highway for the Lord.
Of prophets last and greatest,
He saw thy dawning ray,
Make us the rather blessed,
Who love thy glorious day.

TEXT: Horatio Earl Nelson, 1823-1913
MELODY: Traditional English melody
HARMONIZATION: Ralph Vaughan Williams, 1872-1958, copyright © by Oxford University Press,
  from the *English Hymnal* by permission of Oxford University Press.

KING'S LYNN
76.76.D

600 All creatures of our God and King

1 All crea-tures of our God and King, Lift
2 Thou rush-ing wind that art so strong, Ye
3 Thou flow-ing wa-ter, pure and clear, Make
4 Dear moth-er earth, who day by day Un -
5 And all ye men of ten-der heart, For -

up your voice and with us sing Al - le - lu - ia! Al - le -
clouds that sail in heaven a - long, O praise him! Al - le -
mu - sic for thy Lord to hear, Al - le - lu - ia! Al - le -
fold-est bless-ings on our way, O praise him! Al - le -
giv-ing oth-ers, take your part, O sing ye! Al - le -

lu - ia! Thou burn-ing sun with gold-en beam, Thou
lu - ia! Thou ris-ing morn, in praise re - joice, Ye
lu - ia! Thou fire so mas-ter-ful and bright, Thou
lu - ia! The flowers and fruits that in thee grow, Let
lu - ia! Ye who long pain and sor-row bear, Praise

Refrain

sil-ver moon with soft-ter gleam!
lights of eve-ning, find a voice!
giv-est man both warmth and light! } O praise him, O praise him,
them his glo-ry al-so show!
God and on him cast your care!

after last verse

Al-le-lu - ia, Al-le-lu - ia, Al-le-lu - ia! A - men.

6 And thou, most kind and gentle death,
Waiting to hush our latest breath,
O praise him! Alleluia!
Thou leadest home the child of God,
And Christ our Lord the way hath trod. *Refrain*

7 Let all things their creator bless,
And worship him in humbleness,
O praise him! Alleluia!
Praise, praise the Father, praise the Son,
And praise the Spirit, Three in One! *Refrain*

TEXT: St. Francis of Assisi, 1182-1226,
Enlish translation and musical arrangement by William H. Draper, 1855-1933,
copyright © 1923 (renewed) by J. Curwen and Sons, Ltd.
All rights for the U.S. and Canada controlled by G. Schirmer, Inc. (ASCAP)
International copyright secured. All rights reserved. Reprinted by permission.
MELODY: from *Auserlesene Katholische Geistliche Kirchengesange*, 1623, Cologne
HARMONIZATION: Ralph Vaughan Williams, 1872-1958, copyright © by Oxford University Press,
from the *English Hymnal* by permission of Oxford University Press.

LASST UNS ERFREUEN
88.44.88 with Refrain

Alleluia! sing to Jesus

1 Al - le - lu - ia! sing to Je - sus! His the
2 Al - le - lu - ia! not as or - phans Are we
3 Al - le - lu - ia! Bread of An - gels, Thou on
4 Al - le - lu - ia! King e - ter - nal, Thee the

scep - ter, his the throne; Al - le - lu - ia!
left in sor - row now; Al - le - lu - ia!
earth our food, our stay! Al - le - lu - ia!
Lord of lords we own; Al - le - lu - ia!

his the tri - umph, His the vic - to - ry a - lone;
he is near us, Faith be - lieves, nor ques - tions how;
here the sin - ful Flee to thee from day to day;
born of Ma - ry, Earth thy foot - stool, heav'n thy throne;

Hark! the songs of peace - ful Zi - on Thun - der
Though the cloud from sight re - ceived him, When the
In - ter - ces - sor, friend of sin - ners, Earth's re -
Thou, with - in the veil hast en - tered, Robed in

like a might - y flood; Je - sus out of ev - 'ry
for - ty days were o'er, Shall our hearts for - get his
deem - er, plead for me, Where the songs of all the
flesh, our great high priest; Thou on earth both priest and

na - tion Hath re - deemed us by his blood.
prom - ise, "I am with you ev - er - more"?
sin - less Sweep a - cross the crys - tal sea.
vic - tim In the Eu - cha - ris - tic feast.

TEXT: William Chatterton Dix, 1837-1898
MELODY: Rowland Hugh Prichard, 1811-1887
HARMONIZATION: Traditional

HYFRYDOL
8 7. 8 7. D

602 At the Name of Jesus

1 At the Name of Je - sus Ev - 'ry knee shall bow,
2 Hum-bled for a sea - son, To re - ceive a Name
3 Bore it up tri - umph - ant, With its hu - man light,
4 In your hearts en - throne him; There let him sub - due
5 Broth-ers, this Lord Je - sus Shall re - turn a - gain,

Ev - 'ry tongue con - fess him King of glo - ry now;
From the lips of sin - ners, Un - to whom he came,
Through all ranks of crea - tures, To the cen - tral height,
All that is not ho - ly, All that is not true:
With his Fa - ther's glo - ry O'er the earth to reign;

'Tis the Fa - ther's plea - sure We should call him Lord,
Faith - ful - ly he bore it Spot-less to the last,
To the throne of God - head, To the Fa - ther's breast;
Crown him as your Cap - tain In temp - ta - tion's hour;
For all wreaths of em - pire Meet up - on his brow,

Who from the be - gin - ning Was the migh - ty Word.
Brought it back vic - to - rious, When from death he passed;
Filled it with the glo - ry Of that per - fect rest.
Let his will en - fold you In its light and power.
And our hearts con - fess him King of glo - ry now.

TEXT: Caroline Maria Noel, 1817-1877
MELODY: Ralph Vaughan Williams, 1872-1958, copyright © by Oxford University Press
HARMONIZATION: Ralph Vaughan Williams, 1872-1958, copyright © by Oxford University Press

KING'S WESTON
65.65.D

Faith of our fathers!

603

1 Faith of our fa - thers! liv - ing still In spite of
2 Our fa - thers, chained in pris - ons dark, Were still in
3 Faith of our fa - thers! Ma - ry's prayers Shall win all
4 Faith of our fa - thers! We will love Both friend and

dun - geon, fire and sword: O how our hearts beat high with
heart and con - science free: And tru - ly blest would be our
na - tions un - to thee: And thro' the truth that comes from
foe in all our strife: And preach thee, too, as love knows

joy When-e'er we hear that glo - rious word: Faith of our
fate If we, like them, should die for thee. Faith of our
God Man-kind shall then in - deed be free. Faith of our
how, By kind - ly deeds and vir - tuous life. Faith of our

fa - thers, ho - ly faith! We will be true to thee till death.

TEXT: Frederick W. Faber, 1814-1863, alt.
MELODY: Henri Frédéric Hemy, 1818-1888
HARMONIZATION: James George Walton, 1821-1905

ST. CATHERINE (TYNEMOUTH)
88.88.88

604 Jesus, Lover of my soul

1 Je - sus Lov - er of my soul, Let me to thy bo - som fly,
2 Oth - er re - fuge have I none, Hangs my help- less soul on thee;
3 Plen- teous grace with thee is found, Grace to cleanse from ev - 'ry sin;

While the near - er wa - ters roll, While the tem-pest still is high:
Leave, ah! leave me not a - lone, Still sup - port and com-fort me!
Let the heal - ing streams a - bound, Make and keep me pure with - in.

Hide me, O my Sa - viour, hide, Till the storm of life be past;
All my trust on thee is stayed; All my help from thee I bring;
Thou of life the foun - tain art, Free- ly let me take of thee:

Safe in - to the ha - ven guide, O re - ceive my soul at last.
Cov- er my de- fence- less head With the sha - dow of thy wing.
Spring thou up with - in my heart, Rise to all e - ter- ni - ty. A- men.

TEXT: Charles Wesley, 1707-1788, alt.
MELODY: Joseph Parry, 1841-1903
HARMONIZATION: Traditional

ABERYSTWYTH
7 7 . 7 7 . D

Let all mortal flesh keep silence

605

1 Let all mor - tal flesh keep si - lence And with fear and
2 King of kings, yet born of Ma - ry, As of old on
3 Rank on rank the host of heav - en Spreads its van - guard
4 At his feet the six - wing - ed ser - aph; Cher - u - bim with

trem - bling stand; Pon - der noth - ing earth - ly -
earth he stood, Lord of lords, in hu - man
on the way, As the Light of light de -
sleep - less eye, Veil their fac - es to the

mind - ed, For with bless - ing in his hand
ves - ture, In the bo - dy and the blood:
scend - eth From the realms of end - less day,
Pres - ence, As with cease - less voice they cry,

Christ our God to earth de - scend - eth,
He will give to all the faith - ful
That the powers of hell may van - ish
Al - le - lu - ia, al - le - lu - ia,

Our full hom - age to de - mand.
His own self for heav - en - ly food.
As the dark - ness clears a - way.
Al - le - lu - ia, Lord most high!

TEXT: Liturgy of St. James, translated by Gerard Moultrie, 1829-1885
MELODY: probably 17th century French carol, found in Tiersot's *Mélodies*, 1887
HARMONIZATION: after *Hymns, Ancient and Modern*, alt.

PICARDY
87.87.87

606

Lift high the cross

Lift high the cross, the love of Christ pro - claim Till
all the world a - dore his sa - cred name.

1 Come, breth - ren, fol - low where our cap - tain trod, Our
2 Led on their way by this tri - um - phant sign, The
3 Each new - born sol - dier of the Cru - ci - fied Bears
4 This is the sign which Sa - tan's le - gions fear And
5 Saved by this cross where - on their Lord was slain, The

King vic - tor - ious, Christ the Son of God.
hosts of God in con - quering ranks com - bine.
on his brow the seal of him who died.
an - gels veil their fa - ces to re - vere.
sons of A - dam their lost home re - gain.

6 From north and south, from east and west they raise
In growing unison their songs of praise. *Lift high the cross, etc.*

7 O Lord, once lifted on the glorious Tree,
As thou hast promised, draw men unto thee. *Lift high the cross, etc.*

8 Let every race and every language tell
Of him who saves our souls from death and hell. *Lift high the cross, etc.*

9 From farthest regions let them homage bring,
And on his cross adore their Saviour King. *Lift high the cross, etc.*

10 Set up thy throne, that earth's despair may cease
Beneath the shadow of its healing peace. *Lift high the cross, etc.*

11 For thy blest cross which doth for all atone
Creation's praises rise before thy throne. *Lift high the cross, etc.*

TEXT: George William Kitchin, 1827-1912, and Michael Robert Newbolt, 1874-1956,
    copyright © 1974 by Hope Publishing Co., Carol Stream, IL 60188. All rights reserved. Used with permission.
MELODY: Sydney Hugo Nicholson, 1875-1947
HARMONIZATION: Sydney Hugo Nicholson, 1875-1947,
    copyright © 1974 by Hope Publishing Co., Carol Stream, IL 60188. All rights reserved. Used with permission.

CRUCIFER
1 0 . 1 0, with Refrain

Now thank we all our God

607

1 Now thank we all our God   With heart and hands and voic - es,
2 O may this gra - cious God   Through all our life be near us,
3 All praise and thanks to God   The Fa - ther now be giv - en,

Who won - drous things hath done,   In whom his world re - joic - es;
With ev - er joy - ful hearts   And bless - ed peace to cheer us;
The Son, and Spir - it blest,   Who reigns in high - est heav - en,

Who, from our moth - ers' arms,   Hath blessed us on our way
Pre - serve us in his grace,   And guide us in dis - tress,
E - ter - nal, Tri - une God,   Whom earth and heav'n a - dore;

With count - less gifts of love,   And still is ours to - day.
And free us from all sin,   Till heav - en we pos - sess.
For thus it was, is now,   And shall be ev - er - more.   A - men.

TEXT: Martin Rinkart, 1586-1649, translated by Catherine Winkworth, 1827-1878
MELODY: Johann Crüger, 1598-1662
HARMONIZATION: Felix Mendelssohn, 1809-1847

NUN DANKET ALLE GOTT
67.67.66.66

608

O God of loveliness

1 O God of love - li - ness, O Lord of heav'n a - bove,
2 Thou art blest Three in One, Yet un - di - vid - ed still;
3 O Love - li - ness su - preme, And Beau - ty in - fi - nite!

How wor - thy to pos - sess My heart's de - vot - ed
Thou art that one a - lone Whose love my heart can
O ev - er - flow - ing stream And o - cean of de -

love. So sweet thy coun - te - nance, So gra - cious
fill. The heav'ns and earth be - low, Were fash - ioned
light! O Life by which I live, My tru - est

to be - hold, That on - ly glance were bliss un - told.
by thy word; How great thou art, O ho - ly Lord!
life a - bove, I give thee un - di - vid - ed love.

TEXT: St. Alphonsus Ligouri, 1696-1787, translated by Edmund Vaughn, 1827-1908, alt.
MELODY: Silesian melody, published in Leipzig, 1892
HARMONIZATION: T. Tertius Noble, 1867-1953, copyright © H.W. Gray, Inc.

SCHÖNSTER HERR JESU
66.66.668

O Lord, the Giver of all life

609

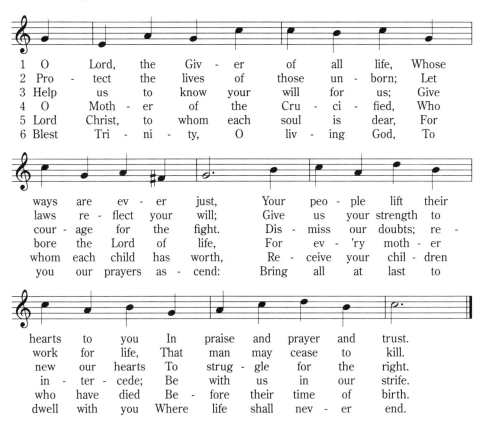

1 O Lord, the Giv - er of all life, Whose
2 Pro - tect the lives of those un - born; Let
3 Help us to know your will for us; Give
4 O Moth - er of the Cru - ci - fied, Who
5 Lord Christ, to whom each soul is dear, For
6 Blest Tri - ni - ty, O liv - ing God, To

ways are ev - er just, Your peo - ple lift their
laws re - flect your will; Give us your strength to
cour - age for the fight. Dis - miss our doubts; re -
bore the Lord of life, For ev - 'ry moth - er
whom each child has worth, Re - ceive your chil - dren
you our prayers as - cend: Bring all at last to

hearts to you In praise and prayer and trust.
work for life, That man may cease to kill.
new our hearts To strug - gle for the right.
in - ter - cede; Be with us in our strife.
who have died Be - fore their time of birth.
dwell with you Where life shall nev - er end.

TEXT: Calvert Shenk, b.1940, copyright © by Calvert Shenk
MELODY: William Croft, 1678-1727
HARMONIZATION: William Croft, 1678-1727

ST. ANNE
8 8 . 8 8

610 On this day, the first of days

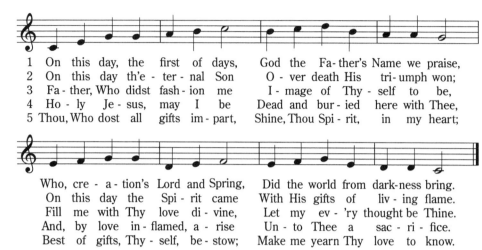

1 On this day, the first of days, God the Fa-ther's Name we praise,
2 On this day th'e - ter - nal Son O - ver death His tri - umph won;
3 Fa - ther, Who didst fash - ion me I - mage of Thy - self to be,
4 Ho - ly Je - sus, may I be Dead and bur - ied here with Thee,
5 Thou, Who dost all gifts im - part, Shine, Thou Spi - rit, in my heart;

Who, cre - a - tion's Lord and Spring, Did the world from dark-ness bring.
On this day the Spi - rit came With His gifts of liv - ing flame.
Fill me with Thy love di - vine, Let my ev - 'ry thought be Thine.
And, by love in - flamed, a - rise Un - to Thee a sac - ri - fice.
Best of gifts, Thy - self, be - stow; Make me yearn Thy love to know.

TEXT: *Die parente temporum,* Le Mans Breviary, 1748, translated by Henry Williams Baker, 1821-1877
MELODY: Johann Anastasius Freylinghausen, 1670-1739, from *Neues Geistreiches Gesangbuch,* Halle, 1704
HARMONIZATION: William Henry Havergal, 1793-1870

GOTT SEI DANK (LÜBECK)
7 7 . 7 7

Praise, my soul, the King of heaven 611

1 Praise, my soul, the King of hea - ven; to his feet thy
2 Praise him for his grace and fa - vor to his peo - ple
3 Fa - ther - like he tends and spares us; well our fee - ble
4 An - gels, help us to a - dore him; ye be - hold him

trib - ute bring; ran - somed, healed, re - stored, for - giv - en,
in dis - tress; praise him still, the same as ev - er,
frame he knows; in his hand he gen - tly bears us,
face to face; sun and moon, bow down be - fore him,

ev - er - more his prais - es sing: Al - le - lu - ia,
slow to chide, and swift to bless: Al - le - lu - ia,
res - cues us from all our foes. Al - le - lu - ia,
dwell - ers all in time and space. Al - le - lu - ia,

al - le - lu - ia! Praise the ev - er - last - ing King.
al - le - lu - ia! Glo - rious in his faith - ful - ness.
al - le - lu - ia! Wide - ly yet his mer - cy flows.
al - le - lu - ia! Praise with us the God of grace.

TEXT: Henry Francis Lyte, 1793-1847, based on Psalm 103, alt.
MELODY: John Goss, 1800-1880
HARMONIZATION: Traditional

LAUDA ANIMA
8 7 . 8 7 . 8 7

612

Praise to the Lord, the Almighty

1 Praise to the Lord, the Al - might - y, the King of cre -
2 Praise to the Lord, who o'er all things so won - drous - ly
3 Praise to the Lord, who doth pros - per thy work and de -
4 Praise to the Lord, O let all that is in me a -

a - tion; O my soul, praise him, for he is thy
reign - eth, Who, as on wings of an ea - gle up -
fend thee; Sure - ly his good - ness and mer - cy here
dore him; All that hath life and breath, come now with

health and sal - va - tion; Join the great throng, Psal - ter - y,
lift - ed, sus - tain - eth. Hast thou not seen? All that is
dai - ly at - tend thee. Pon - der a - new What the Al -
prais - es be - fore him. Let the A - men Sound from his

or - gan, and song, Sound - ing in glad ad - o - ra - tion.
need - ful hath been Grant - ed in what he or - dain - eth.
might - y can do, Who with his love doth be - friend thee.
peo - ple a - gain; Glad - ly for aye we a - dore him.

TEXT: *Lobe den Herren,* Joachim Neander, 1650-1680, translated by Catherine Winkworth, 1827-1878
MELODY: *Erneuertes Gesangbuch,* Stralsund, 1665
HARMONIZATION: *The Chorale Book for England,* 1863

LOBE DEN HERREN
1 4 14.4 7 8

There's a wideness in God's mercy 613

1 There's a wide-ness in God's mer-cy Like the wide-ness
2 For the love of God is broad-er Than the meas-ures
3 Souls of men, why will you scat-ter Like a crowd of

of the sea; There's a kind-ness in his jus-tice
of man's mind, And the heart of the E-ter-nal
fright-ened sheep? Fool-ish hearts, why will you wan-der

Which is more than lib-er-ty. There is plen-ti-
Is most won-der-ful-ly kind. If our love were
From a love so true and deep? There is wel-come

ful re-demp-tion In the blood that has been shed;
but more sim-ple We should take him at his word,
for the sin-ner And more grac-es for the good;

There is joy for all the mem-bers In the sor-rows of the Head.
And our lives would be all sun-shine In the sweet-ness of our Lord.
There is mer-cy with the Sav-ior, There is heal-ing in his blood.

TEXT: Frederick William Faber, 1814-1863
MELODY: Traditional Dutch melody from *Oude en Niewe Hollantse Boerenlites en Contradanseu*, c.1710
HARMONIZATION: Traditional

IN BABILONE
87.87.D

614   When morning gilds the skies

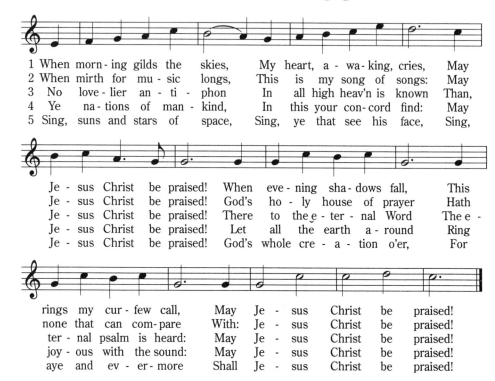

1 When morn-ing gilds the skies, My heart, a-wa-king, cries, May
2 When mirth for mu-sic longs, This is my song of songs: May
3 No love-lier an-ti-phon In all high heav'n is known Than,
4 Ye na-tions of man-kind, In this your con-cord find: May
5 Sing, suns and stars of space, Sing, ye that see his face, Sing,

Je-sus Christ be praised! When eve-ning sha-dows fall, This
Je-sus Christ be praised! God's ho-ly house of prayer Hath
Je-sus Christ be praised! There to the e-ter-nal Word The e-
Je-sus Christ be praised! Let all the earth a-round Ring
Je-sus Christ be praised! God's whole cre-a-tion o'er, For

rings my cur-few call, May Je-sus Christ be praised!
none that can com-pare With: Je-sus Christ be praised!
ter-nal psalm is heard: May Je-sus Christ be praised!
joy-ous with the sound: May Je-sus Christ be praised!
aye and ev-er-more Shall Je-sus Christ be praised!

TEXT: from *Würzburg Katholiches Gesangbuch*, 1828, translated by Robert Bridges, 1844-1930,
from the *Yattendon Hymnal* by permission of Oxford University Press.
MELODY: Joseph Barnby, 1838-1896
HARMONIZATION: Traditional

LAUDES DOMINI
666.666

Praise to the Holiest in the height

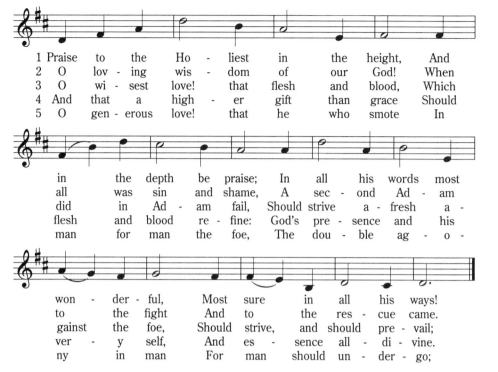

1 Praise to the Holiest in the height, And
in the depth be praise; In all his words most
won - der - ful, Most sure in all his ways!

2 O lov - ing wis - dom of our God! When
all was sin and shame, A sec - ond Ad - am
to the fight And to the res - cue came.

3 O wi - sest love! that flesh and blood, Which
did in Ad - am fail, Should strive a - fresh a -
gainst the foe, Should strive, and should pre - vail;

4 And that a high - er gift than grace Should
flesh and blood re - fine: God's pre - sence and his
ver - y self, And es - sence all - di - vine.

5 O gen - erous love! that he who smote In
man for man the foe, The dou - ble ag - o -
ny in man For man should un - der - go;

6 And in the garden secretly,
And on the cross on high,
Should teach his brethren, and inspire
To suffer and to die.

7 Praise to the Holiest in the height,
And in the depth be praise;
In all his words most wonderful,
Most sure in all his ways!

TEXT: John Henry Newman, 1801-1890
MELODY: Richard Runciman Terry, 1865-1938
HARMONIZATION: Richard Runciman Terry, 1865-1938

NEWMAN (BILLINGS)
86.86

616   I sing the mighty power of God

1 I sing the might- y power of God that made the moun- tains rise,
2 I sing the good- ness of the Lord that filled the earth with food;
3 There's not a plant or flow'r be - low but makes thy glo - ries known;

that spread the flow- ing seas a- broad, and built the loft - y skies.
he formed the crea-tures with his word, and then pro-nounced them good.
and clouds a - rise, and tem-pests blow, by or - der from thy throne;

I sing the wis- dom that or - dained the sun to rule the day;
Lord, how thy won- ders are dis- played wher- e'er I turn my eye;
while all that bor-rows life from thee is ev - er in thy care,

the moon shines full at his com- mand and all the stars o - bey.
if I sur - vey the ground I tread, or gaze up - on the sky!
and ev - 'ry - where that man can be, thou, God, art pres- ent there.

TEXT: Isaac Watts, 1674-1748
MELODY: adapted from a melody in the *Würtemburg Gesangbuch*, 1784
HARMONIZATION: William Henry Monk, 1823-1889, alt.

ELLACOMBE
76.76.D

Most ancient of all mysteries 617

1 Most an-cient of all mys-ter-ies, Be-fore your throne we lie;
2 When heaven and earth were still un-made, When time was yet un-known,
3 You were not born, there was no source From which your Be-ing flowed;
4 How won-der-ful cre-a-tion is, The work which you did bless,
5 Most an-cient of all mys-ter-ies, Be-fore your throne we lie;

Have mer-cy now, most mer-ci-ful, Most ho-ly Tri-ni-ty.
You in your ra-diant ma-jes-ty Did live and love a-lone.
There is no end which you can reach, For you are sim-ply God.
What then must you be like, dear God, E-ter-nal lov-li-ness!
Have mer-cy now and ev-er-more, Most ho-ly Tri-ni-ty. A-men.

TEXT: Frederick William Faber, 1814-1863, adapted by Geoffrey Laycock,
copyright © by Faber Music Ltd., London
MELODY: Alexander Robert Reinagle, 1799-1877
HARMONIZATION: Alexander Robert Reinagle, 1799-1877, alt.

ST. PETER
86.86.D

O radiant Light, O sun divine 618

1 O ra-diant Light, O sun di-vine Of God the Fa-ther's death-less face,
2 Lord Je-sus Christ, as day-light fades, As shine the lights of ev-en-tide,
3 O Son of God, the source of life, Praise is your due by night and day;

O im-age of the light sub-lime   That fills the heav'nly dwelling place.
We praise the Father with the Son,   The Spi-rit blest and with them one.
Un-sul-lied lips must raise the strain   Of your proclaimed and splendid name.

TEXT: *Phos Hilaron*, Greek 3rd century, translated by William G. Storey,
copyright © 1973 by Fides Publishers, Notre Dame, Indiana
MELODY: Plainchant, Mode I
HARMONIZATION: Jean-Hébert Desrocquettes, O.S.B., copyright © 1958 by Ralph Jusko Publications

JESU DULCIS MEMORIA
88.88

619

Te lucis ante terminum

1 Te lu - cis an - te tér - mi - num,   Re - rum Cre - á - tor pó - sci - mus,
2 Te cor - da nos - tra sóm - ni - ent,   te per so - pó - rem sén - ti - ant,
3 Vi - tam sal - ú - brem tri - bue   nos-trum ca - lór - em ré - fi - ce,
4 Prae-sta, Pa - ter om - ní - po-tens,   per Ie-sum Christ-um Dó - mi - num,

Ut só - li - ta cle-mén - ti - a   Sis prae-sul ad cus - tó - di - am.
tu - ám-que sem-per gló - ri - am   vi - cí - na lu - ce cón - cin-ant.
tae-tram noc-tis ca - lí - gi-nem   tu - a col - lús-tret clá - ri - tas.
qui te-cum in per-pé - tu - um   re-gnat cum San-cto Spí - ri - tu.

1 *Creator of all things, before the close of the day,*
   we earnestly beg thee to be,
   with thy customary mercy, our Protector and Preserver.

2 *May our hearts dream of thee and experience thee through sleep;*
   and, with a light near, let them always celebrate thy grace in song.

3 *Grant us health; keep us warm;*
   and let thy light illuminate the frightful darkness of the night.

4 *Grant these things, Almighty Father, through Jesus Christ our Lord,*
   who reigns throughout eternity with thee and the Holy Spirit.

TEXT: Chant, c.7th cent., translated by Richard Divozzo, b.1955. Used with permission.
MELODY: Plainchant, Mode VIII
HARMONIZATION: Charles Winfred Douglas, 1867-1944, alt., copyright © by Church Publishing, Inc.

TE LUCIS ANTE TERMINUM
88.88

We praise you, Father, for your gift 620

1 We praise you, Fa-ther, for your gift   Of dusk and night-fall ov-er earth,
2 With-in your hands we rest se-cure;   In qui-et sleep our strength re-new;
3 Your glo-ry may we ev-er seek   In rest, as in ac-ti-vi-ty,

Fore-sha-dow-ing the mys-ter-y   Of death that leads to end-less day.
Yet give your peo-ple hearts that wake   In love to you, un-sleep-ing Lord.
Un-til its full-ness is re-vealed,   O source of life, O Tri-ni-ty.

TEXT: West Malling Abbey, copyright © by West Malling Abbey   TE LUCIS ANTE TERMINUM
MELODY: Plainchant, Mode VIII   88.88
HARMONIZATION: Charles Winfred Douglas, 1867-1944, alt., copyright © by Church Publishing, Inc.

Praise God, from whom all blessings flow 621

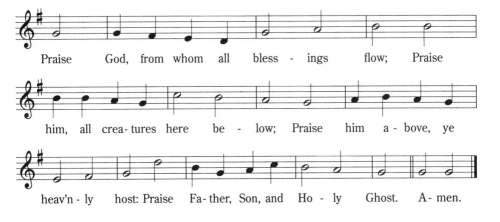

Praise God, from whom all bless - ings flow; Praise

him, all crea-tures here be - low; Praise him a - bove, ye

heav'n - ly host: Praise Fa-ther, Son, and Ho - ly Ghost. A - men.

TEXT: Thomas Ken, 1637-1711   OLD HUNDREDTH
MELODY: Louis Bourgeois, c.1510-c1561   88.88
HARMONIZATION: Louis Bourgeois, c.1510-c1561

622 All people that on earth do dwell

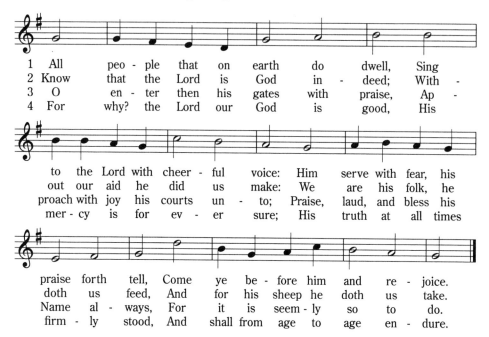

1 All peo - ple that on earth do dwell, Sing
2 Know that the Lord is God in - deed; With -
3 O en - ter then his gates with praise, Ap -
4 For why? the Lord our God is good, His

to the Lord with cheer - ful voice: Him serve with fear, his
out our aid he did us make: We are his folk, he
proach with joy his courts un - to; Praise, laud, and bless his
mer - cy is for ev - er sure; His truth at all times

praise forth tell, Come ye be - fore him and re - joice.
doth us feed, And for his sheep he doth us take.
Name al - ways, For it is seem - ly so to do.
firm - ly stood, And shall from age to age en - dure.

TEXT: Based on Psalm 100, William Kethe, d.1608?
MELODY: Louis Bourgeois, c.1510-c1561
HARMONIZATION: Louis Bourgeois, c.1510-c1561

OLD HUNDREDTH
88.88

Be thou my vision

1 Be thou my vi - sion, O Lord of my heart;
2 Be thou my wis - dom, and thou my true word;
3 High King of heav - en, when vic - tory is won,

All else be nought to me, save that thou art.
I ev - er with thee and thou with me, Lord;
May I reach heav - en's joys, bright heav - en's Sun!

Thou my best thought, by day or by night,
Thou my great Fa - ther; thine own may I be:
Heart of my heart, what - ev - er be - fall,

Wak - ing or sleep - ing, thy pres - ence my light.
Thou in me dwell - ing, and I one with thee.
Still be my vi - sion, O Rul - er of all.

TEXT: Irish, c.700, versified by Mary Elizabeth Byrne, 1880-1931, translated by Eleanor H. Hull, 1860-1935
MELODY: Irish, adapted from *The Church Hymnary,* 1927
HARMONIZATION: David Evans, 1874-1948, copyright © 1927 by Oxford University Press,
  from *The Revised Church Hymnary,* 1927, by permission of Oxford University Press.

SLANE
10.10.9.10

624 O God, our help in ages past

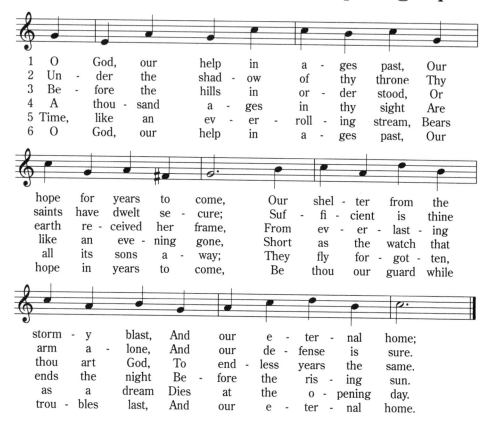

```
1  O     God,    our    help    in     a  -  ges    past,    Our
2  Un - der     the    shad - ow     of     thy    throne.  Thy
3  Be - fore    the    hills   in     or - der     stood,   Or
4  A    thou - sand   a  -  ges   in     thy    sight    Are
5  Time, like   an     ev  -  er  - roll - ing    stream,  Bears
6  O     God,    our    help    in     a  -  ges    past,    Our

hope    for    years   to     come,   Our    shel - ter   from   the
saints  have   dwelt   se  -  cure;   Suf  - fi - cient  is     thine
earth   re - ceived   her    frame,   From   ev  - er  - last - ing
like    an     eve - ning   gone,    Short  as     the    watch  that
all     its    sons    a  -  way;    They   fly    for - got - ten,
hope    in     years   to     come,   Be     thou   our    guard  while

storm - y      blast,  And    our     e  -  ter - nal    home;
arm     a  -   lone,   And    our     de - fense    is     sure.
thou    art    God,    To     end - less  years    the    same.
ends    the    night   Be  -  fore    the    ris - ing    sun.
as      a      dream   Dies   at      the    o - pening    day.
trou - bles    last,   And    our     e  -  ter - nal    home.
```

TEXT: Based on Psalm 90, Isaac Watts, 1674-1748
MELODY: William Croft, 1678-1727
HARMONIZATION: William Croft, 1678-1727

ST. ANNE
88.88

God of our fathers, whose almighty hand 625

1 God of our fa - thers, whose al - migh - ty hand
2 Thy love di - vine hath led us in the past,
3 From war's al - arms, from dead - ly pest - i - lence,
4 Re - fresh thy peo - ple on their toil - some way,

Leads forth in beau - ty all the star - ry band
In this free land by thee our lot is cast;
Be thy strong arm our ev - er sure de - fense;
Lead us from night to nev - er - end - ing day;

Of shin - ing worlds in splen - dor through the skies,
Be thou our rul - er, guar - dian, guide, and stay,
Thy true re - li - gion in our hearts in - crease,
Fill all our lives with love and grace di - vine,

Our grate - ful songs be - fore thy throne a - rise.
Thy word our law, thy paths our cho - sen way.
Thy boun - teous good - ness nour - ish us in peace.
And glo - ry, laud, and praise be ev - er thine.

TEXT: Daniel Crane Roberts, 1841-1907
MELODY: George William Warren, 1828-1902
HARMONIZATION: George William Warren, 1828-1902

NATIONAL HYMN
10.10.10.10

626   Come with us, O blessed Jesus

Come with us, O bless-ed Je-sus, With us ev-er-more to be; And in leav-ing now thine al-tar, Let us nev-er-more leave thee! O let thine an-gel cho-rus Cease not the heav'n-ly strain, But in us, thy lov-ing chil-dren, Bring peace, good will to men.

TEXT: John Henry Hopkins, Jr., 1861-1945
MELODY: Johann Schop, d.1642?, arranged by Johann Sebastian Bach, 1685-1750
HARMONIZATION: Johann Sebastian Bach, 1685-1750

JESU JOY OF MAN'S DESIRING
87.87.76.86

BENEDICTION

700 Eucharistic Exposition and Benediction

EXPOSITION—After the people have assembled, the following (for music see hymn #519, 520) or another suitable song may be sung while the celebrant comes to the altar with the Eucharist.

O salutáris Hóstia,
Quae caeli pandis óstium,
Bella premunt hostília,
Da robur, fer auxílium.

O saving Victim, opening wide
The gate of heav'n to man below!
Our foes press on from ev'ry side:
Thine aid supply, thy strength bestow.

Uni trinóque Dómino
Sit sempitérna glória:
Qui vitam sine término
Nobis donet in pátria. Amen.

To thy great name be endless praise,
Immortal Godhead, One in Three:
Oh, grant us endless length of days
When our true native land we see. Amen.

After Exposition, the celebrant incenses the Sacrament. If the adoration is to be lengthy, he may then withdraw.

ADORATION—During the exposition there should be prayers, songs, readings from Scripture, and a brief homily to direct the attention of the faithful to the worship of the Lord.

BENEDICTION—Toward the end of the exposition the priest goes to the altar, genuflects, and kneels. Then the following (for music see hymn #393) or another suitable eucharistic song is sung.

Tantum ergo Sacraméntum
  Venerémur cérnui:
Et antíquum documéntum
  Novo cedat rítui:
Praestet fides suppleméntum
  Sénsuum deféctui.

Down in adoration falling,
  Lo! The sacred Host we hail;
Lo! o'er ancient forms departing,
  Newer rites of grace prevail;
Faith for all defects supplying
Where the feeble senses fail.

Genitóri, Genitóque
  Laus et jubilátio,
Salus, honor, virtus quoque
  Sit et benedíctio:
Procedénti ab utróque
  Compar sit laudátio. Amen.

To the everlasting Father,
  And the Son who reigns on high,
With the Spirit Blest proceeding
  Forth from each eternally,
Be salvation, honor, blessing,
  Might and endless majesty. Amen.

V. Panem de caelo praestitísti eis
(T.P. Alleluia).

Priest: You have given them Bread from
heaven (P.T. Alleluia).

R. Omne delectaméntum in se habentem
(T.P. Alleluia).

All: Having all sweetness within it (P.T.
Alleluia).

Sacerdos: Orémus. Deus, qui nobis
sub Sacraménto mirábili, passiónis
tuæ memóriam reliquísti: tríbue,
quæsumus, ita nos Córporis et
Sánguinis tui sacra mystéria
venerari, ut redemptiónis tuæ
fructum in nobis júgiter sentiámus.
Qui vivis et regnas in sǽcula
sæculorum.

R. Amen.

Priest: Let us pray. Lord Jesus Christ,
you gave us the Eucharist
as the memorial of your suffering
and death.
May our worship of this sacrament
of your body and blood,
help us to experience the salvation
you won for us
and the peace of the kingdom
where you live with the Father and
the Holy Spirit,
one God, for ever and ever.

All: Amen.

The celebrant then blesses the people with the Eucharist.

*After the blessing the priest replaces the Blessed Sacrament in the tabernacle and
genuflects. The following acclamation may be said at this time.*

Blessed be God.
Blessed be his Holy Name.
Blessed be Jesus Christ, true God and true Man.
Blessed be the Name of Jesus.
Blessed be his most Sacred Heart.
Blessed be his most Precious Blood.
Blessed be Jesus in the most Holy Sacrament of the Altar.
Blessed be the Holy Spirit, the Paraclete.
Blessed be the great Mother of God, Mary most holy.
Blessed be her holy and Immaculate Conception.
Blessed be her glorious Assumption.
Blessed be the name of Mary, Virgin and Mother.
Blessed be St. Joseph, her most chaste spouse.
Blessed be God in his angels and in his saints.

*As the celebrant leaves, the following (for music see hymn #461) or another suitable
hymn may be sung.*

Holy God, we praise thy name;
Lord of all, we bow before thee;
All on earth thy scepter claim,
All in heaven above adore thee.
Infinite thy vast domain,
Everlasting is thy reign!

Hark, the loud celestial hymn;
Angel choirs above are raising;
Cherubim and Seraphim,
In unceasing chorus praising,
Fill the heavens with sweet accord:
Holy, holy, holy Lord!

INDICES

INDEX OF ORDINARIES

INDEX OF FIRST LINES

INDEX BY LITURGICAL SEASON OR OCCASION